Reflexive Research in Music Therapy

Andeline dos Santos

Reflexive Research in Music Therapy

Six Approaches in Practice

palgrave
macmillan

Andeline dos Santos
University of Pretoria
Pretoria, South Africa

ISBN 978-3-032-02032-1 ISBN 978-3-032-02033-8 (eBook)
https://doi.org/10.1007/978-3-032-02033-8

This Palgrave Macmillan imprint is published by the registered company Springer Nature Switzerland AG.
The registered company address is: Gewerbestrasse 11, 6330 Cham, Switzerland

For you, Dad.

"Authors never can choose to vanish completely from their texts;
they can only pick the disguise in which they will appear."
(Golden-Biddle K, Locke K. Composing qualitative
research. Thousand Oaks, CA: Sage; 1997. p. 72)

Acknowledgements

I am very grateful to those who shared their wisdom about reflexivity with me for this book: Claire Ghetti, Efrat Roginsky, Gro Trondalen, Kerry Devlin, Luke Annesley, Moshe Bensimon, Michael Viega, Martina Bingham, Natasha Thomas, Nicky Haire, Noah Potvin, Simon Gilbertson, Anthony Meadows, Tríona McCaffrey, and Viggo Krüger. Thank you, my family—Miguel, Emilio, Judah and Khaya—for listening to me speak continuously about reflexivity for a few years! Your good humour and patience make this possible.

Competing Interests The author has no competing interests to declare that are relevant to the content of this manuscript.

Contents

CHAPTER 1

The Value of Reflexivity

Here's a quick reflexivity check-in to get us started:

1. What are you most aware of in this moment inside yourself or in relation to your body?
2. What are you most aware of outside yourself in your immediate environment that you can perceive with your senses right now?
3. What is at the top of your awareness at the moment about the world at large (your relationships, current affairs, items on your to-do list…)?
4. How do you imagine that those aspects will inform how you embark on and read this book?

As researchers, we actively invite, create, and shape meaning in our studies. This can happen in subtle or profound ways. Often, we're also shaped in return. We may choose to welcome and critically examine the productive impact of our influence, or we may elect to reduce and manage it. What we can't do is ignore it. We can never stand outside our writing. The research we put out into the world reveals as much about who we are as people as it does about what we have studied [1].

Broadly speaking, the process of deliberately exploring our impact on the research we conduct is called reflexivity. By engaging in reflexivity with

A. dos Santos, *Reflexive Research in Music Therapy*,
https://doi.org/10.1007/978-3-032-02033-8_1

care and intentionality, we enhance the integrity and quality of our studies. Within the field of music therapy, I was curious about how researchers define reflexivity, how we do it, and what reflexivity accomplishes. While music therapy research has unique features, our approaches also overlap significantly with researchers in other humanities and social science fields. We're all learning from each other.

To write this book, I critically reviewed music therapy literature from the past 20 years and interviewed many of the authors of those papers. Music therapists draw on a wide range of specific perspectives on reflexivity. Through this book, I present a framework for understanding these perspectives, show the foundations they're built upon, and clarify the strategies researchers use in practice. As I constructed meaning from and with these texts and interviews, *I* needed to be reflexive. This book is not the definitive position. It is a voice in the conversation.

Thinking about our thinking (and about our feeling, moving and relating) allows us to critically examine how we are in the world with others and the impact of our actions. If we can recognise and scrutinise how we're making meaning, then we can also better imagine a world that could be different. Enhancing our desire and ability to be reflexive is profoundly important for our work as researchers, therapists, colleagues, teachers, citizens, family members, friends, and strangers. I'd like to think that my perspectives on the world are quite accurate, that my values are good, my beliefs are sensible, and my approaches are helpful. Living reflexively means that I'm willing to fold back on those positions with humility, ask tough questions, and be willing to adjust. This is neither comfortable nor easy work to do. This book focuses on research, but my journey to become a more reflexive researcher has been inextricably linked to my ongoing journey of becoming a more reflexive human being. I welcome you to this conversation as a whole human, not only a researcher.

It's Good to Meet You...

Let me introduce myself. I'm a music therapist, researcher, and lecturer in South Africa. I'm also a mom to three delightful teenagers, a wife, and a friend. I grew up in a home with my mother, father, and older sister. During his working career, my father was a university dean and an exceptional teacher. He would respond to my questions with other questions, prompting me to think critically through problems from the ground up.

Learning was always tantalising and these are the roots that grew into my lifelong research enthusiasm. I learned that I could trust my curiosity.

I identify as female and adhere to the feminist notion that the personal is political. In this book, I cover a spectrum of approaches from objective reasoning to experiential, empathic, relational ways of thinking and feeling one's way through analysing the implications of one's presence in a research study. However, I don't see these as gendered approaches [2]; in fact, I resist these stereotypes. As a white South African, I was 16 years old when our first post-Apartheid elections were held in 1994. Learning and teaching in this country in the years since have imprinted a deep commitment to social justice upon me. My music therapy practice has included work with autistic children, children who have hearing challenges, teenagers engaging in violent behaviour, young people emerging from gangs and substance use disorders, and university students struggling with mental health difficulties. As a researcher, I've always been drawn to the richness of qualitative research. I appreciate how it can hold the complexity of the human experience well. However, I greatly value every research approach because our multifaceted field depends for its growth and advocacy on many layers of insights (and the links between them).

I found my way to the study of reflexivity via my work on empathy [3]. I've always been interested in examining the congruence (and sometimes incongruence) between what we study and how we study it. As I researched empathy in music therapy practice, I needed to examine how I drew on empathy as a researcher to design studies, engage with participants, interpret data, and interact with readers. In other words, I wanted to empathically study empathy, and thinking about how best to do this required reflexivity. Some approaches to reflexivity that we'll explore in this book are also enriched by an understanding of what it means to be an empathic researcher, and I'll draw on links to these insights as we go along.

Sometimes, reflexivity is presented in research only as a positionality statement: This is who I am as a researcher; these are the elements of my background that are most relevant to this topic; and these are the lenses I'm using to seek and interpret information. As a researcher and writer, I'm in a relationship with you, the reader, who is also positioned in multiple ways. The heading of this section states that it is good to meet *you.* I am aware of, acknowledge, and respect your presence "here" and wish to communicate with you in a generative way. I have written this book for a broad audience, from new researchers to those with years of experience under your belts. While seasoned researchers may have a solid grip on facets of reflexivity, my review of the literature and interviews with authors demonstrated that the desire and need to deepen and clarify understanding and use of reflexivity in research is relevant across the spectrum of experience. I invite you to lean into the sections that feel most useful for you.

Reflexivity for New Researchers

The term reflexivity was introduced by Talcott Parsons within sociology to refer to people's capacity to give an account of their actions consciously [4]. Etymologically, reflexivity refers to bending back on oneself [5]. However, as with many terms in research methodology, different authors define the concept in different ways [6]. A definition that elegantly captures the essence of reflexivity is that "reflexive practice is about recognising who we are and how we are part of the worlds we study" [7, p. 57]. Reflexivity has been described as a kind of awareness, a form of comprehension, and a realisation [8]. It's been referred to as a marker of humanness because humans innately think about their thinking [9]. Reflexivity can be seen as a defining human feature because "we are aware of being aware" [5, p. 1]. It's also an act of interpreting one's interpretation [10]. For Kenneth Bruscia [11], it's a process of focusing on one's consciousness. Reflexivity has been described as a concept, but also as a skill or ability [12], a personal or methodological choice, a practice [8], and a strategy [13]. It's been understood as a way of being, a virtue [12], a principle [8], and a value [11].

The "reflexive turn," as described by Norman Denzin and Yvonna Lincoln [14], permitted researchers to write themselves into their studies. We're allowed to be present in our own research, instead of only using third-person writing and an "objective" stance that claims that we're neutral, distanced observers of what we find before us. Reflexivity is an interpersonal sensitivity [8], and it's been referred to as an assessment of the relationship between knowledge and ways of doing knowledge. Through reflexivity, we don't simply replicate or highlight existing knowledge; we also create new knowledge [15].

Linda Finlay [16] offered what has become quite a well-used typology of five reflexivity variants: (1) introspection (critically examining one's own experiences and perceptions); (2) intersubjective reflection (examining how meaning emerges through situated research relationships); (3) mutual collaboration (where participants as co-researchers are also part of cycles of reflection); (4) social critique (experiential accounts are situated within critiques of power and authority); and (5) discursive deconstruction (critically observing how researchers and participants are presenting themselves and how meaning is represented). As we see in this typology, the realm of reflexivity covers the personal and the social. We can engage in a micro-examination of our innermost thoughts and feelings, and we can critique social structures. In *Doing reflexivity*, Jon Dean [17] argued that reflexive work can never only be about the person doing the research. It always requires critically examining the personal and structural conditions that help us make sense of the knowledge we create.

Several authors have offered ways of thinking about the similarities and differences between reflexivity and reflection. For example, Finlay and Gough [5, p. ix] explained that reflection entails thinking about something after it's occurred, while reflexivity involves "immediate, dynamic and continuing self-awareness." Tim May and Beth Perry [18, p. 3] contrasted the terms as follows: "reflexivity is not just about the ability to think about our actions—that is called reflection—but an examination of the foundations of frameworks of thought themselves." Reflexivity and reflection have also been described as occurring along a continuum: reflection happens afterwards as we look back on our study, while reflexivity occurs before, during, and after [19]. According to Elyssa Smith and Melissa Luke [20], reflection entails introspection. Reflexivity includes reflection, but it's essentially an intersubjective act in which self, other, and self-in-relation-to-others are recognised and explored. Guy Enosh and Adital Ben-Ari [15] depicted reflexivity as happening in a liminal space between inside and outside perspectives, as we constantly move between being in a phenomenon and standing outside of it.

There's an enormous amount to consider when beginning a research study. If you're an early postgraduate student who is a "becoming-researcher," you may be finding the process of gaining a working understanding of the spectrum of available research methodologies, selecting a topic and finding worthwhile research questions, familiarising yourself with the literature that's already available about your topic, designing a plan for your study and writing the proposal, obtaining ethical clearance, executing your plan, and writing up the findings to be a gargantuan task. Realising that it's essential during all these phases to also be thinking about your thinking, critically examining all your decisions, who you are as a researcher, how you're relating to other role-players, why you're studying what you're studying, the implications of your meaning-making processes, and carefully conveying all this in a transparent way to your readers may feel too overwhelming. You might understandably feel that you don't yet have the skills or gymnastic flexibility to "bend back on yourself." You may also certainly feel that you simply don't have the time.

There is no destination marked "fully-reflexive-researcher." Every researcher, no matter how inexperienced or masterful, can grow in their reflexive journey. Self-awareness, for example, is one aspect of reflexivity, and this is an ongoing life quest. Examining our motivations, assumptions, and blind spots has no finish line. Exploring our relationships with others is always a dynamic endeavour as they're constantly shifting. Reflecting on how our engagement with data shapes our findings is like zooming in on a fractal: the closer you look, the more there is to see. No matter where we are in our journey as researchers, we can learn more about reflexivity and work on applying reflexive strategies within our studies in manageable ways that also stretch our growth.

Relationships with the World and How We Can Know It

Different approaches to reflexivity are grounded in ontology and epistemology understandings of the world and how we can get to know it. Ontologically (as we think about the nature of reality and existence), do we see the world and objects in it as separate and independent from the human beings who try to get to know them? Or do we see humans as interconnected with the phenomenon they're experiencing and seeking to understand? Epistemologically (as we think about how we can know this reality), do we engage in objectivity, an exploration of "givenness", subjectivity, intersubjectivity, and/or interobjectivity? If we acknowledge that we, as researchers, are playing a role in developing our findings, then we need to make these choices purposefully and with a clear understanding of what they entail.

Objectivity

When we're being objective, we're standing back from our beliefs, perceptions, and opinions to reflect on and scrutinise them. Importantly, "it requires a degree of indifference in judging that may conflict with our needs and desires" [21, p. 1]. There are different modes of objectivity

[22]. Firstly, objectivity can involve processes where humans aim to access objects directly or reliably through interacting with them or through scientific experiments. Secondly, objectivity can entail refraining from using values in the place of evidence. Personal values shouldn't blind us to the reality of unpleasant or inconvenient evidence, and just because we want something to be true doesn't make it so. However, values are always in play to some degree. Our sense organs and brain don't simply record the world around us. Our minds fundamentally structure our experiences and thoughts. Proposing that this undermines objectivity is like imagining thinking without brains or seeing without eyes. Unmediated perception is not objective perception; it is not perception *at all* and, therefore, this can't serve as a model of objectivity. A better approach is to work to ensure our values aren't overshadowing evidence and to openly acknowledge the value judgements that are in play (e.g., how objectivity may be functioning as a value) [21].

Thirdly, we can consider objectivity in relation to the social processes through which we develop knowledge and reach agreement. An outcome is considered objective when it's produced regardless of who conducts the process. People may also use different procedures and then check whether their findings concur. Alternatively, people might debate as they present their findings to one another, highlighting sources of disagreement, discussing theories and challenging each other's conclusions to reach the best one [21].

Givenness: A Bridge Between Objectivity and Subjectivity

Some phenomenological perspectives can be difficult to organise under either "objectivity" or "subjectivity". While Edmund Husserl is considered the founder of phenomenology, post-Husserlian phenomenologists (like Scheler, Heidegger, Satre, and Merleau-Ponty) developed phenomenology in diverse ways, making classifications even more tricky. Husserl [23] sought to establish the rich everyday human experience as the foundation of science. The phenomenologist suspends (they don't obliterate) their belief in the existence of objects in the external world, focusing instead on how these objects are "given" to human consciousness. Husserl [24] defined phenomenology as the study of the essence of conscious experience. He argued that we should examine "the things themselves" [24, p. 35] by setting aside prior knowledge and biases to see phenomena as they are experienced. Husserl emphasised that consciousness is always directed towards something. He was interested in examining both acts of consciousness (noesis) and the objects of consciousness (noema) as they are experienced [25, 26]. In this way, "givenness" bridges objectivity and subjectivity.

Subjectivity

We each have a personalised viewpoint through which we interpret our experiences, expectations, and immediate perceptions [27]. This is subjectivity. Our perspective is inherently tied to our sense of self—the "I" that perceives and interacts with the external world. However, subjectivity extends beyond personal viewpoints. It also involves how we're recognised and categorised by others, we become an "Other" in the eyes of those around us [28]. Subjectivity spans different dimensions of self-knowledge. Bruscia [11] categorised self-knowledge into individual self-knowledge, co-constituted knowledge of others in relation to the self, collective self-knowledge within group dynamics, and self-knowledge of the object world.

A criterion for identifying subjectivity is "faultless disagreement" [29]. If two people hold opposing viewpoints that can coexist without meaning that one of them is logically wrong, then their disagreement probably involves subjective elements. For example, if two individuals disagree on whether a piece of music is beautiful, both perspectives can exist without invalidating the other—a faultless disagreement. In contrast, disagreements over factual details, such as whether the piece of music is played by a viola or a cello, indicate an objective assessment where one viewpoint aligns with reality while the other doesn't.

From an epistemology standpoint, subjectivity implies that all knowledge production is inherently influenced by the knower—the subjective agent engaged in the process. Any piece of knowledge reflects not only the facts it claims to represent but also the knowing subject's interpretive framework and contextual biases. Knowledge is constructed through a dialogue between the knower and the known. In other words, subjectivity is an interactive process where the actions of the knowing person shape and are shaped by the object/person/event they're observing [30].

Both Objective and Subjective

We could argue whether knowledge reflects absolute Truth about reality or if it's always inherently relative, shaped by the observer's state of mind, environmental conditions, and interactions with the observed object. However, there's a case to be made that both subjective perceptions and objectivity measurements can coexist harmoniously [21, 31]. A person might feel that a room is too warm or too cold based on their subjective comfort level, and an objective thermometer measurement provides a fixed numerical value. People may perceive colours differently based on lighting conditions, individual eyesight, or even cultural associations, however, the wavelength of light can also be measured objectively. In music therapy, we may blend subjective and objective assessment methods. For example, a service user might report their subjective perception of how their social relating is shifting and the music therapist tracks evidence of behavioural changes in group sessions as the person interacts with other group members frequently or in more varied ways. Instead of fighting over whether researchers should be objective or embrace subjectivity, it's arguably more interesting to explore the interrelationship between the two.

Intersubjectivity

The term intersubjectivity has been used in various ways. From its phenomenological roots, individuals can be understood to share a common definition of an object despite viewing it from different perspectives. You look at the back of a guitar and I look at the front, but we both know it's a guitar because we have a shared sense of reality, which is crucial for meaningful interactions [24]. In this phenomenological framing of the idea, objectivity is intersubjective because others' perspectives are necessary in addition to my own to establish the validity of the world. ("Yes, indeed, we are both seeing the same thing.") We can't simultaneously be in precisely the same position, but we can agree that if we were, we would see the same thing.

We can also consider intersubjectivity as what occurs between minds [32]. A positivist researcher studying an object "out there in the world" claims to be able to detect this object's characteristics objectively. However, when we study people by interacting with them, we get to know them subjectively while they get to know us. We're all "knowers" who are co-creating knowledge together as we're influenced by this interaction. When people interact with each other, they don't simply bring their pre-existing individual feelings, perceptions, thoughts, and meanings into the encounter. These are formed in the encounter itself. Participatory sense-making unfolds [33, 34] and there's real-time reciprocal adjustment and alignment of mental states [35]. As we collaboratively create our shared encounter, we simultaneously define our identities and our situation together [36]. Through communicating, we co-construct worlds with others [37].

Drawing from developmental psychologists' views (such as Stern [38], Papoušek and Papoušek [39], and Trevarthen and Malloch [40]), especially their work on parent-infant interaction, we can understand that "the mind begins as a shared mind…Experience begins as dyadic and dialogic" [32, p. 807]. As infants and caregivers mirror each other, they sense, "You are like me" and "I am like you," forming preverbal intersubjectivity [41]. The therapeutic alliance is also intersubjective as therapist and client form their relationship and are formed by it [42, 43]. Similarly, in research processes, we can explore how researchers and participants create meaning together.

Interobjectivity

Although intersubjectivity speaks to relationships, it focuses solely on humans. Postmodern, poststructural, and posthuman perspectives have questioned Western Enlightenment humanism's portrayal of the unitary, rational individual [44]. Living beings can rather be viewed as part of ongoing, dynamic relationships with their environment, including the objects within it. This is interobjectivity. Objects are as much implicated in social reality as people are. We witness this in music therapy every day. Our intentions develop during sessions not only through our interactions with people, but with the instruments we play, the spaces we inhabit, and the paper and crayons we draw with… [3] Both subjects and objects function as "comrades, colleagues, partners, accomplices, or associates in the weaving of social life" [45, p. 235]. Indigenous knowledge systems have also held these more inclusive relational views for centuries [46]. We now also need to explore how artificial intelligence plays a role in these processes too [47] and we'll discuss this further in a moment.

The Relationships Between Clinical and Research Reflexivity

Mercedes Pavlicevic and Charlotte Cripps [48, p. 5] used the term reflexivity to refer to "the emergence of a critical awareness of the self as part of the event, the environment, and social field, while concurrently being the self who is observing, participating, and documenting." We see how this definition is compatible with both research and clinical practice. Kenneth Bruscia [11] argued that reflexivity is essential for all endeavours in music therapy. He first discussed reflexivity within clinical practice, exploring processes such as countertransference and modes of consciousness. Music therapists examine and work with their awareness of who they are in relation to their client, their awareness of their client, and the therapeutic relationship. Reflexivity entails critically exploring the appropriateness of goals and methods, the use of music and whether and how the client benefits from the process. Crucially, reflexivity also refers to the careful shifts in attention between all these facets. Clinically, Bruscia [11, p. 42] defined reflexivity as "the therapist's efforts to continually bring into awareness, evaluate, and when necessary, modify one's work with a client—before, during, and after each session, as well as at various stages of the therapy process." He suggested that this is accomplished through self-inquiry, self-observation, collaboration with clients, and consultation with supervisors. When Bruscia turned his attention to reflexivity in research, he highlighted the personal role of the researcher in qualitative research, requiring self-inquiry as we seek to become more aware of and understand our own experiences, needs, concerns, reactions, feelings, thoughts, beliefs, and values.

When interviewing the authors of the papers I analysed for this book, I asked for their perspectives on the differences and similarities between reflexivity in research and clinical practice. Some saw these as very similar, particularly in relation to the need for self-awareness and flexibly adjusting one's responses in relation to the unfolding process. Others saw them as notably distinct due to the differences in the nature and requirements of the therapeutic relationship compared to the research relationship and the role of the therapist versus the role of the researcher. However, many affirmed that their reflexive research skills enhance their clinical skills, and their reflexive clinical skills beneficially inform their research practices. We'll discuss these matters further as the book proceeds.

The Value of Reflexivity in All Research

Reflexivity has become a trademark of qualitative research [49]. Bruscia [11, p. 42] emphasised how qualitative research is always "an intensely personal experience for the researcher" because every step in the process is decided and implemented by the researcher as a unique individual. This personal influence isn't hidden. The researcher embraces it, is transparent about it, and takes responsibility for it.

Even though reflexivity is strongly emphasised within qualitative research, arguments can be found for considering the importance of reflexivity in quantitative and mixed methods studies as well. Whether employing qualitative or quantitative methods, social research "requires us to account for our humanness" [14, p. 8]. As Moshe Bensimon said in our interview, "I think that reflexivity is good for all researchers." Every study always has some kind of intervention, even in the most objective scientific fields. We can't research something we have no contact with. So, representation and intervention are always deeply interconnected and it's essential in every study to consider both the object of knowledge and how we engage with it [50].

This view that reflexivity can (and even should) be a feature of all research is not new. In fact, selecting whether to use quantitative, qualitative, or mixed methods within one's study can be seen as a reflexive process in itself [51]. In 1998, Finlay [52] wrote an article entitled *Reflexivity: An essential component for all research?*, in which she argued that it's impossible to conform to the role of objective, rational, distant researcher. She recognised how her behaviour affected her participants and influenced the direction of her findings. A different researcher would have a different relationship with the participants and an alternative story would unfold. Also, the research process itself has the potential to transform the phenomenon being studied. Therefore, "to deny the relevance of both subjectivity and intersubjectivity must undermine the validity of research…this applies equally to qualitative and quantitative research" [52, p. 4].

Many scholars have written about the subjectivity and interpretation processes that occur within quantitative studies [49, 53]. Quantitative research is just as likely as qualitative research to involve implicit assumptions, conflicts of interest, opinions held as facts, and emotional and political investments [19]. All scientific knowledge is positioned, provisional, and incomplete. Claims of objectivity can be a mask that researchers hide behind as they assert their authority [17]. It's been suggested that placing subjectivity at the heart of research may paradoxically bring us closer to objectivity than approaches that merely centre objectivity, because subjectivity leads us to a more complete, but still realistically inconclusive, account of the complexity of reality [54].

In music therapy, the term reflexivity is certainly mentioned predominantly—but not only—in studies using qualitative methods. In Natasha Thomas' [55, p. 112] mixed methods study on community-based referential music making with limited-resource adolescents, she engaged in "the reflexive challenging of traditional power differentials in the design, implementation, interpretation, and dissemination of research." We also see reflexive journals used within mixed methods studies (by researchers such as Barry et al. [56] and Roberts and McFerran [57]).

We need to pause here for a moment to note that simply because a research paper doesn't include the term "reflexivity", this does not mean that the researchers didn't engage in reflexive processes. For example, motivations for conducting research into particular topics have been reflexively explored by authors such as Joke Bradt et al. [58] in their mixed methods study on Vocal music therapy (VMT) for chronic pain management in inner-city African Americans. Shelly Zeiser [59] took care to explain how she used particular theoretical frameworks to underpin her study and what these brought to the forefront. In their longitudinal quantitative micro-analysis study on group music therapy for people living with mental health conditions, Alona Schneidman [60] and colleagues were explicit about the definition of music therapy they used to guide their project. Maija Salokivi et al. [61] took care to explain their use of terminology and the implications of that choice. Katelyn Beebe [62] reflected on their choice of methods within their paper on perceptions of self-determination in music therapy for individuals diagnosed with intellectual disabilities. Beebe wrote that "In research, it is often impossible to claim true objectivity because results are produced from implicit underlying assumptions presented by the researchers" [62, p. 97]. She then explained her choice to conduct her study using the social model of disability. Despite these examples, there's still much more room in our field for quantitative and mixed methods studies to explicitly engage with reflexivity in their research process.

In a world in which the use of artificial intelligence (AI) is skyrocketing in research [63], is a book about the importance of reflecting on the role of human meaning-making still relevant? Or could it be more relevant than ever? Researchers are increasingly using AI tools like Natural

Language Processing, not only for quantitative meta-inferences but in qualitative research too. Themes in interview transcripts can be identified much quicker with AI [64]. However, qualitative researchers are, by definition, seen as the main instrument for data collection, analysis, and interpretation, and the strength of qualitative studies lies in their nuanced, contextual, and human-centred approach. In qualitative studies, phenomena often have multiple interpretations rather than a single true meaning, and when different researchers reach varying conclusions, this can be embraced as a strength [65].

Large language models still face significant challenges, including their lack of true reasoning capabilities and emotional understanding. Important questions about data ownership, consent, and protection are being debated. For example, what happens to participants' data when AI processes it? What are the implications when participants withdraw from studies? [65]

Integrating AI into research requires more, not less reflexivity, as well as new dimensions of reflexivity. We need to continue to critically explore our own role in meaning-making, as well as the "subjectivities" built into algorithms, and how meanings emerge through our relationships with AI [65]. AI systems learn from internet data that contains societal biases [66]. Historical records used for AI training often underrepresent marginalised groups, potentially perpetuating existing power imbalances. Biases and shortcomings of AI in research can be acknowledged and then mitigated in reflexive ways. We can consider AI as a tool that can enhance human expertise rather than replace it entirely [67]. When employing AI in research, it's essential to incorporate reflexivity at every stage, including design, data collection, development, deployment, and usage of data [68, 69].

The Value of Reflexivity in Music Therapy Research

While calls for the importance of reflexivity in music therapy research have grown louder in the last few years, early voices were already drawing our attention to it. In my interview with Gro Trondalen, she remembered the following:

> ...I went back and started to think 'When did I really start to reflect upon it?' And I think the first written text must have been in 1987. And I started to remember I was invited to write a text in 2000 for the British Society of

> Music Therapy and I found it. I talked about qualitative research and I asked if it is necessary for the researcher to take a special interest in introspection and personal growth—to *choose* such a process-oriented approach to research, as I did. And does a research methodology of this kind also require a theoretical rationale, giving room for self-assertion and development in a relational context? And then [I wrote] in the end: 'This implies constant social and ethical responsibility when analysing and contextualising during the research process'...I wrote that 23 years ago.

As we stand here now, at this moment in the development of our profession and in the context of the world at large, why is it more important than ever for music therapy researchers to grapple with reflexivity? There are many reasons. We must continue to reflect critically on the values our research supports. This matters for service users, music therapists, training programmes, funders, and interdisciplinary relationships. We are growing in our awareness of epistemic justice, and reflexivity is a core component of research that speaks to this agenda. In many contexts, our profession is still required to advocate for its value, and our skills as science communicators are essential, including our ability to argue for how and why we conduct the research we do as well as how we position ourselves. Reflexivity is also essential for thinking about and engaging in ethical relationships with research participants, which is always an essential endeavour. Reflexivity contributes towards our continued scientific and academic rigour. It calls us to honestly reflect on our studies' contribution, meaningfulness, usefulness, and limitations.

In my experience, researchers are being required to engage in reflexivity more and more by supervisors, examiners, and academic article reviewers. However, we don't have a clear enough map of how to approach reflexivity and how to engage in it practically. If it matters this much, we need to have more purposeful conversations about *how* to be reflexive. Instead of attempting to offer my personal, unique take on the subject for the sake of it, or impose an existing framework onto music therapy literature, my guiding objective was to explore what music therapy researchers are already actually doing in practice. I wondered: As music therapists, when we use the word "reflexivity" in our papers, how do *we* understand this term? How deeply and authentically are we diving into reflexivity? How does our use of reflexivity in the real world of our studies resonate with and/or deviate from the literature on reflexivity? How are we using, discarding, integrating, and re-shaping the textbook knowledge? What are we engaging in reflexivity for?

Once we have a map of what is already going on in our studies, we can understand our choices better, have a clearer view of our options, critique our approaches, and make better-informed decisions moving forward as we seek to conduct research that we hope will do good in the world. Reflexivity has been described as a "meta-methodology" [70, p. 533]. This book is yet an additional "meta" view on top of this meta-methodology, but we will not keep taking additional steps backwards as we think about our thinking (and then think about that thinking until we fall off the ledge and float off into clouds of abstract theory). We'll hold tightly onto implications for practice in research that intends to make a difference in the lives of real people in the real world. In the words of Jon Dean [17, p. 12],

> To not recognise subjectivities or deny subjective influences, or to not think about the choices made in research and the reasons behind these choices and the unmistakable consequences of them, will inevitably lead to substantially less scientifically useful insights…It's not just that in research honesty is the best policy: it's that a lack of clarity and exposition ends up invalidating your work, and potentially the work of others who wish to make use of it.

Reflexivity asks us to be brave. We can build psychological safety in our research processes, teams and interactions, but, as Natasha Thomas explained in our interview, "safety doesn't mean we don't ask very difficult questions…And some of the questions can lead to difficult discussions and real stretching and changing and humility…[Y]our skill doesn't come across as safe, it's not trying to be safe, it's trying to be a little provocative, but in a relational way".

References

1. Nash R. Liberating scholarly writing: the power of personal narrative. IAP; 2019.
2. Grant J. I feel therefore, I am: a critique of female experience as the basis for a feminist epistemology. Women Polit. 1987;7(3):99–114.
3. Dos Santos A. Empathy pathways: a view from music therapy. London: Palgrave Macmillan; 2022.
4. Howitt D. Introduction to qualitative methods in psychology. 4th ed. London: Pearson; 2019.

5. Finlay L, Gough B. Prologue. In: Finlay L, Gough B, editors. Reflexivity: a practical guide for researchers in health and social sciences. Oxford: Blackwell; 2003. p. ix–xi.
6. Etherington K. Becoming a reflexive researcher: using our selves in research. London: Jessica Kingsley; 2004.
7. Arber A. Managing the dual identity: practitioner and researcher. In: Allan H, Arber A, editors. Emotions and reflexivity in health and social care field research. Palgrave Macmillan; 2018. p. 57–74.
8. Leigh J. What would a rhythmanalysis of a qualitative researcher's life look like? In: Clift BC, Gore J, Gustafsson S, Bekker S, Batlle IC, Hatchard J, editors. Temporality in qualitative inquiry: theories, methods and practices. London: Routledge; 2021. p. 72–92.
9. Evens T, Handelman D, Roberts C. Preface. In: Evens T, Handelman D, Roberts C, editors. Reflecting on reflexivity: the human condition as an ontological surprise. New York: Berghahn Books; 2016. p. vii–xiv.
10. Alvesson M, Sköldberg K. Reflexive methodology: new vistas for qualitative research. 3rd ed. Los Angeles: Sage; 2018.
11. Bruscia K. Forms of reflexivity in music therapy: an anthology. Phoenixville, PA: Barcelona Publishers; 2015.
12. Ahern KJ. Ten tips for reflexive bracketing. Qual Health Res. 1999;9(3):407–11.
13. Kuenher A, Ploder A, Langer P. Introduction to the special issue: European contributions to strong reflexivity. Qual Inq. 2016;22:699–704.
14. Denzin N, Lincoln Y, editors. The landscape of qualitative research: theories and issues. Thousand Oaks, CA: Sage; 1998.
15. Enosh G, Ben-Ari A. Reflexivity: the creation of liminal spaces—researchers, participants, and research encounters. Qual Health Res. 2016;26(4):578–84.
16. Finlay L. Negotiating the swamp: the opportunity and challenge of reflexivity in research practice. Qual Res. 2002;2(2):209–30.
17. Dean J. Doing reflexivity: an introduction. Bristol: Policy Press; 2017.
18. May T, Perry B. Reflexivity: the essential guide. Los Angeles: Sage; 2017.
19. Jamieson MK, Govaart GH, Pownall M. Reflexivity in quantitative research: a rationale and beginner's guide. Soc Personal Psychol Compass. 2023;17.
20. Smith EB, Luke MM. A call for radical reflexivity in counseling qualitative research. Couns Educ Superv. 2021;60(2):164–72.
21. Gaukroger S. Objectivity: a very short introduction. Oxford University Press; 2012.
22. Douglas H. The irreducible complexity of objectivity. Synthese. 2004;138(3):453–73.
23. Husserl E. Philosophy as a rigorous science. In: Lauer Q, editor and translator. Phenomenology and the crisis of philosophy. New York, NY: Harper Torchbacks; 1965. (German original, 1911)

24. Husserl E. Ideas pertaining to a pure phenomenology and to a phenomenological philosophy, second book: Studies in the phenomenology of constitution. Rojcewicz R, Schuwer A, translators. Kluwer; 1989.
25. Finlay L. Phenomenology for therapists: researching the lived world. John Wiley & Sons; 2011.
26. Heinämaa S, Kaitaro T. Descartes' notion of the mind-body union and its phenomenological expositions. In: Zahavi D, editor. The Oxford Handbook of the history of phenomenology. Oxford University Press; 2018. p. 25–44.
27. Ladkin D. 'The enigma of subjectivity': how might phenomenology help action researchers negotiate the relationship between 'self', 'other' and 'truth'? Action Res. 2005;3(1):108–26.
28. Hall D. Subjectivity. Routledge; 2004.
29. Kölbel M. Truth without objectivity. London: Routledge; 2002.
30. Breuer F, Roth W. Subjectivity and reflexivity in the social sciences: epistemic windows and methodical consequences. Forum Qualitative Sozialforschung/Forum: Qualitative Social Research. 2003;4(2).
31. Dahlberg H, Dahlberg K. Open and reflective lifeworld research: a third way. Qual Inq. 2020;26(5):458–64.
32. Beebe B, Rustin J, Sorter D, Knoblauch S. An expanded view of intersubjectivity in infancy and its application to psychoanalysis. Psychoanalytic Dialogues. 2003;13(6):805–41.
33. Zlatev J. The co-evolution of intersubjectivity and bodily mimesis. In: The shared mind: perspectives on intersubjectivity. John Benjamins Publishing Company; 2008. p. 215–44.
34. De Jaegher H, Di Paolo E. Participatory sense-making: an enactive approach to social cognition. Phenomenol Cogn Sci. 2007;6:485–507.
35. Talbert BM. Knowing other people: a second-person framework. Ratio. 2015;28(2):190–206.
36. Dimitrakopoulou D, Theodorou P. Affective facilitation: a framework for surfacing lived experiences and harnessing creativity in focus group research. Int J Qual Methods. 2022;21:16094069221133225.
37. Lipari L. Listening, thinking, being: toward an ethics of attunement. University Park, Pennsylvania: Penn State University Press; 2015.
38. Stern D. Intersubjectivity. In: Person E, Cooper A, Gabbard G, editors. Textbook of psychoanalysis. Arlington, VA: American Psychiatric Publishing; 2005. p. 77–92.
39. Papoušek M, Papoušek H. Musical elements in the infant's vocalization: their significance for communication, cognition, and creativity. In: Lipsitt LP, Rovee-Collier CK, editors. Advances in infancy research, vol. 1. Ablex; 1981. p. 163–224.
40. Trevarthen C, Malloch S. The dance of wellbeing: defining the musical therapeutic effect. Norwegian J MusTher. 2000;9(2):3–17.

41. Meltzoff A. The roots of social and cognitive development: models of man's original nature. In: Field T, Fox N, editors. Social perception in infants. Norwood, NJ: Ablex; 1985. p. 1–30.
42. Buirski P, Haglund P. Making sense together. Jason Aronson; 2001.
43. Orange DM, Atwood GE, Stolorow RD. Working intersubjectively: contextualism in psychoanalytic practice. Analytic Press; 1997.
44. McLeod K. Orientating to assembling: qualitative inquiry for more-than-human worlds. Int J Qual Methods. 2014;13(1):377–94.
45. Latour B. On interobjectivity. Mind, Culture, and Activity: An International Journal. 1996;3:228–45.
46. Matsika C. Traditional African education: its significance to current education practices with special reference to Zimbabwe. Gweru: Mambo Press; 2012.
47. Lim A, Nicolaides A. Becoming-with-AI: rethinking professional knowledge through generative knowing. Reflective Pract. 2024;25(3):391–405.
48. Pavlicevic M, Cripps C. Muti music-in search of suspicion. Voices: A World Forum for Music Therapy [Internet]. 2015;15(3). Available from: https://voices.no/index.php/voices/article/view/2286/2041.
49. Lakew Y. Statistical tales: bringing in reflexivity to make sense of quantitative data. Present Scenarios of Media Production and Engagement. Bremen: edition Lumiere; 2017. p. 225–38.
50. Vangkilde KT, Sausdal DB. Overponderabilia: overcoming overthinking when studying "ourselves". Forum Qualitative Sozialforschung/Forum: Qualitative Social Research. 2016;17(2).
51. Weber R. The reflexive researcher. MIS Q. 2003;27:4.
52. Finlay L. Reflexivity: an essential component for all research? Br J Occup Ther. 1998;61(10):453–6.
53. Sulkunen P. Social research and social practice in post-positivist society. In: Alasuutari P, Bickman L, Brannen J, editors. The SAGE handbook of social research methods. Los Angeles, CA: Sage; 2008. p. 68–80.
54. Parker I. Qualitative data and the subjectivity of "objective" facts. In: Dorling D, Simpson S, editors. Statistics in society: the arithmetic of politics. London: Arnold; 1999.
55. Thomas N. Community-based referential music making with limited-resource adolescents: a pilot study. Music Ther Perspect. 2020;38(2):112–8.
56. Barry P, O'Callaghan C, Wheeler G, Grocke D. Music therapy CD creation for initial pediatric radiation therapy: a mixed methods analysis. J Music Ther. 2010;47(3):233–63.
57. Roberts M, McFerran K. A mixed methods analysis of songs written by bereaved preadolescents in individual music therapy. J Music Ther. 2013;50(1):25–52.

58. Bradt J, Norris M, Shim M, Gracely EJ, Gerrity P. Vocal music therapy for chronic pain management in inner-city African Americans: a mixed methods feasibility study. J Music Ther. 2016;53(2):178–206.
59. Zeiser SR. Quality improvement evaluation of a veterans' palliative care telehealth music therapy program. Music Ther Perspect. 2023;41(1):54–62.
60. Schneidman A, Elefant C, Keren R, Ben-Shachar S, Roe D. A pilot study. Nord J Music Ther. 2024;33(1):29–47.
61. Salokivi M, Salanterä S, Saarikallio S, Ala-Ruona E. Validation of item pool for early adolescents' emotional skills assessment in music therapy. Nord J Music Ther. 2023;1–14.
62. Beebe K. Perceptions of self-determination in music therapy for individuals diagnosed with intellectual disabilities: a survey of music therapists. Music Ther Perspect. 2022;40(1):94–103.
63. Cappelli O, Aliberti M, Praino R. The 'Implicit Intelligence' of artificial intelligence. Investigating the potential of large language models in social science research. Polit Res Exchange. 2024;6(1):2351794.
64. Chang T, DeJonckheere M, Vydiswaran V, et al. Accelerating mixed methods research with natural language processing of big text data. J Mixed Methods Res. 2021;15:398–412.
65. Williams RT. Paradigm shifts: exploring AI's influence on qualitative inquiry and analysis. Front Res Met Anal. 2024;9:1331589.
66. Bolukbasi T, Chang KW, Zou JY, Saligrama V, Kalai AT. Man is to computer programmer as woman is to homemaker? Debiasing word embeddings. Adv Neural Inf Proces Syst. 2016;29.
67. Anis S, French JA. Efficient, explicatory, and equitable: why qualitative researchers should embrace AI, but cautiously. Bus Soc. 2023;62(6):1139–44.
68. Aguilar N, Landau A, Mathiyazhagan S, Auyeung A, Dillard S, Patton D. Applying reflexivity to artificial intelligence for researching marginalized communities and real-world problems; 2023.
69. Khair AR. Reflections on AI in humanities: amplifying marginalized voices of women. Exchanges: Interdiscip Res J. 2023;11(1):77–84.
70. Freshwater D, Rolfe G. Critical reflexivity: a politically and ethically engaged research methodology. Nursing Times Res. 2001;6(1):526–38.
71. Golden-Biddle K, Locke K. Composing qualitative research. Thousand Oaks, CA: Sage; 1997.

CHAPTER 2

A Map of Six Approaches to Reflexivity

As I embarked on the process of exploring reflexivity in music therapy research, I formalised three research questions: (1) How is reflexivity defined? (2) How do we engage in reflexivity? and (3) What does reflexivity accomplish? I first needed some provisional sense of what reflexivity was so that I could recognise the "sort of thing" I was looking for in the texts. Some of the books and articles I consulted were by Mats Alvesson and Kaj Sköldberg [1], Kim Etherington [2], Linda Finlay [3], Finlay and Brendan Gough [4], Lisa Lazard and Jean McAvoy [5], Emilie Whitaker and Paul Atkinson [6], Guy Enosh and Adital Ben-Ari [7], Yvonne Sliep and Andrew Gilbert [8] and Michael Ebe Kalu [9], either because they appeared prominently in the literature or because their descriptions were especially clear or particularly intriguing to me. Those that related more closely to music therapy included articles by Kenneth Bruscia [10] and Brynjulf Stige et al. [11] By drawing on this literature, I crafted the following statement as an initial broad guide: *Reflexivity involves the researcher(s) deliberately acknowledging and exploring how they are active participants in the creation/shaping of knowledge in their study and responding to these insights.*

A. dos Santos, *Reflexive Research in Music Therapy*,
https://doi.org/10.1007/978-3-032-02033-8_2

Phase One

To begin my quest to explore how music therapists explain and use reflexivity, I searched through all the published journal articles and doctoral theses from 2000 to January 2024 via EBSCOhost, Google Scholar, Humanities Index, JStor, Medline, Proquest, PsycINFO, PubMed, and Scopus. The selection of the year 2000 as a starting point was relatively arbitrary and reflected a need for some starting boundary simply for feasibility purposes while still including a substantial number of years' worth of research to mine for rich insights. I used the keywords "music therapy" + "reflexiv*" (to capture "reflexivity" and "reflexive"). After seeing how many texts were being identified and that most of the studies conducted for doctoral theses were also presented in the form of a journal article, I elected to focus only on journal articles. I identified a total of 4842 texts that met this criterion. After removing duplicates and screening for overtly irrelevant articles, I was left with 571. I then conducted another closer screening and removed articles that weren't relevant because, for example, the paper mentioned music therapy in passing but wasn't a study related to music therapy, reflexivity was mentioned only in relation to clinical practice, not research, the paper was entirely theoretical, or the word "reflexivity" appeared in the reference list but not the paper itself. I was then left with 170 articles.

It's important to note that this search criteria meant that I examined papers that mentioned the word "reflexivity". This was a decision based on feasibility, as I couldn't analyse every article written in the field of music therapy. This is an important limitation though, because, as mentioned in the previous chapter, a researcher could be reflexive in their research, but they may not overtly use the term "reflexivity."

Initially, I imagined that I'd simply extract and analyse sections from the articles where reflexivity was explicitly discussed. I very quickly realised that this was woefully inadequate. Reflexivity is everywhere. The choice of literature to review, the wording of research questions, how participants are described, how methodological decisions are justified, whether critique of preconceptions is mentioned in the description of data analysis or the discussion of findings, and how a study's limitations are articulated are all elements of reflexivity. I needed to analyse each article as a whole.

I developed a template table that I could use when examining the many facets of each article (e.g., the abstract, literature review, descriptions of participants, the context, paradigm, methodology, and limitations), including any definitions of reflexivity that were stated, any reflexive strategies that were explicitly named, and descriptions of how authors "folded back on themselves." I placed text from each article into its own template document.

What started to take shape in my thinking early in the process was the anchoring function of the authors' ontology and epistemology perspectives. Practical reflexive steps often appeared to grow out of how a researcher understood the phenomenon they were studying and how it was possible to get to know aspects of this phenomenon. I've also been primed to look for this "rootedness" from my earliest formative experiences with my dad (who often invited me to ask questions such as, "Why does this work the way it works?" "How can we understand why this is happening?"; "What beliefs underpin my thinking here?") and throughout my training as a music therapist and researcher.

As I filled in the template tables for all the articles, I was also struck by the diverse descriptions of reflexivity in the papers: from bias management in the service of objectivity, to fully embracing subjectivity. It appeared to me that different authors seemed to be taking quite distinct reflexive journeys, so I started to highlight these approaches in different colours on the completed template documents. I then created a separate Word document for each "colour" and pulled text in from the articles that related to these colours. (The colours eventually evolved into the names of the six reflexivity approaches in this book.)

I selected the order of articles to analyse completely randomly. After I'd analysed 50 articles, I felt that I was starting to develop a helpful framework and knew that if I began reading through the articles from the beginning again, with this framework now in mind, I could analyse the initial articles with more clarity in relation to how my sense-making was taking shape. Therefore, I began again with article 1, completing a new blank template document and proceeding onwards through each article, using the colour-coding system I'd developed. Once I finished article 100, more reflexivity approaches had taken shape in my mind (and I was using additional highlighting colours for these), and so I made the decision to start from the beginning once more. The process had a grounded theory flavour as I kept testing out the framework by revisiting the articles. This time, I progressed through all 170 articles and felt that the notion of six reflexivity approaches was operating solidly. The frame appeared to me to offer a robust thinking tool.

Phase Two

As I developed this framework, I was vividly aware that I was making interpretation judgements about what authors meant by statements in their studies and how different statements may be connecting. I didn't want to simply presume that I had full insight into their decisions, especially given the limited word count that we have to describe complex processes in journal articles. I needed to ask the authors some questions. So, I decided to select a range of articles and invite the authors to have a conversation with me so I could dive deeper into their thinking processes, particularly in relation to studies that seemed to me to include multiple reflexive approaches. I acknowledge that this still did not give me unfettered access into their perspectives. My interpretations were still an active part of this meaning-making layer.

In addition to filling in the template individually for each article, I'd created a spreadsheet that listed the 170 articles, with the colours of the reflexivity approaches I perceived to be at play within them. I selected authors to invite to participate in interviews such that each of the distinct colours and colour combinations would be represented. I also included each article with colour combinations that puzzled me in terms of how these reflexive approaches were being used in relation to each other. Finally, I included individual authors with multiple papers so that I could gather as much information as possible from a single interview.

I created a list of 20 authors to invite. Of these, 15 replied and agreed to my invitation. These authors generously engaged in conversations with me, and I am extremely grateful. While the conversations affirmed the framework I was developing, they certainly highlighted how a neat and tidy list of approaches may look good on paper, but real life is significantly more complex. I chose to lean into the ambiguities, grey areas and uncertainties that the researchers drew my attention to. Quotes from the authors I interviewed feature in the upcoming chapters (and have already popped up a few times in this book so far). I sought their consent to include their names as I wish to honour their insights and their presence in this conversation. Even though I couldn't interview every author of a music therapy paper that mentioned reflexivity, their views are all included in the chapters that lie ahead and, as such, I hope to present a thorough and fair representation of the spectrum of authors who engage with this topic in their music therapy research.

Paradigms

As I mentioned a moment ago, many authors' reflexive processes seemed linked to their ontology and epistemology alignments. Because reflexivity can be baked into the entirety of a research process, one way of beginning the conversation about specific reflexive approaches is to talk about research paradigms. It could make sense to say that a researcher needs to be very clear about which paradigm they're situating their study within, as all their decisions flow from this.

If you randomly choose three textbooks on research methodology from the library, you'll undoubtedly find three different accounts of which paradigms are available to researchers and what these entail. The books will contain some overlaps, but there will also be some major and confusing differences. As researchers, it can be tempting to feel that we must find the right "-ism" to hold our study, and yet few people seem to agree exactly on what these "-isms" mean. (They also change over time.)

Even the notion of "paradigm" comes from a particular paradigm; it doesn't somehow stand outside our thinking and practice. The idea of a paradigm (a worldview, context, a conceptual scheme, a philosophical framework) reinforces a relativist perspective on the world [12]. To push back against the idea that there are universal Truths and standards—a notion that has oppressed and subjugated many—the case can be made that a conclusion (e.g., only women should become music therapists as they're better suited to be in caring professions) would be reached in a very particular social, cultural, historical, and political context within a certain time and place. Take a different context, use the thinking processes within *that* context, and different conclusions can be reached (men make excellent music therapists). We can't understand the nature of the conclusion, why it's reached and how it operates without understanding the beliefs and processes that generate it. We can also assess it according to the context within which it operates. As we try to deal with legacies of epistemic injustice, and as we celebrate the value of multiple ways of knowing and being in the world, embracing the idea of paradigms seems like a very good idea. Who is this person in front of me? How are they situated? How do they see the world? What questions matter to them? How can I journey with them as they seek to thrive in ways that are meaningful for them and their community?

In research terms, we tend to ground our study in particular paradigm, which involves a combination of commitments to ontology (what is reality?), axiology (what do I value?), epistemology (how can I know this reality?), methodology (what plan of action can I use to study this reality?), and methods (what practical tools will I use to do so?). The selected paradigm then sets the scene for certain paths to become possible to travel and other paths to be blocked off. For example, if we choose a paradigm that affirms that reality is subjectively perceived and interpreted, then we might interview participants and reflect on how our findings are interpretations of their interpretations. Alternatively, if we believe that reality exists independently of our perceptions, and our goal is to measure a particular aspect of that reality most accurately, then this informs our task of collecting and analysing data as objectively as possible.

A framework for thinking about paradigms that I've taught my students and used in my own research comes from Michael Crotty [13], as published in his book *The foundations of social research*. Bill Matney [14] subsequently offered a revised version of Crotty's knowledge framework within the context of music therapy. Many other authors have drawn from and built upon Crotty's ideas too. One of these is Merry-Jo Levers [15]. Levers wrote an article specifically related to grounded theory, but her explanation of paradigms is particularly clear. She explained two *ontologies*. Firstly, a critical realist ontology is one in which the world is seen to exist independently of the human mind. Reality is observable, but humans can only observe it in imperfect fragments. We engage in research to collect information and get closer and closer to the truth. Secondly, a relativist ontology holds that reality is a subjectivity experience. Human experience *is* reality. Therefore, there are as many realities as there are people.

Levers [15] then articulated two *epistemological* approaches. An objectivist epistemology is one in which objects are understood to have essences beyond human influence. The essence of an object doesn't change based on who's studying it, and knowledge is seen as being universally applicable. The goal is to explain, control, and predict. Alternatively, a subjectivist epistemology contends that knowledge is shaped by our values and is always filtered through language, culture, class, gender, ethnicity, race, and so on. Observations are impacted by the observer and the observer is impacted by what they observe. You can have two (or more) different, right answers.

We combine an ontology and an epistemology to make a paradigm. Crotty [13], Matney [14], and Levers [15] discuss three paradigms: post-positivism (critical realist ontology + objectivist epistemology = there is a real world out there and I can get to know it objectively); constructionism (critical realist ontology + subjectivist epistemology = there is a real world out there but I can only get to know it subjectively through my experience of it) and interpretivism (relativist ontology + subjectivist epistemology = there isn't a real world out there; my subjective experience is reality).

In post-positivist research, methods are often quantitative but qualitative ones could also be used (e.g., to try to ask people what is "really" going on). In constructionism we explore how meaning is created through the interaction between the interpreter and the interpreted. We are crafting meaning. When guided by interpretivism, we're interested in how we perceive subjective reality. Knowledge is always relative to circumstances and viewpoints, and therefore exists in multiple representations. We focus on narrating human experiences and actions and their meanings for those concerned.

As I examined the articles I'd gathered that included reference to reflexivity, completing the template for each one, I tried to fill in "post-positivist", "constructionist", or "interpretivist" in the row for "paradigm" in my template. I quickly encountered some problems. The first I'll call the "basement problem." A study may be interested in a certain client group's views of music therapy (i.e., their subjective perceptions). The researcher seems to acknowledge that different people can perceive the therapeutic process differently and that this should be valued. This is a relativist ontology. This researcher then interviews participants who fall into this group, transcribes the data, and seeks to analyse it. Here, they wish to know what these participants were "really saying", what they "really thought", and how they "really felt". They send the transcripts back to the participants for member-checking. They use multiple people in the research team to analyse the data, they seek to validate their findings and present their conclusions in a way that is as faithful as possible to what the participants "really meant." So, as soon as these researchers "captured" the phenomenon in the form of data, that data were treated as artefacts that existed independently of observers. Whilst they saw the *phenomenon* through the lens of a relativist ontology, within the *study* itself, their focus was based on a critical realist ontology and an objectivist epistemology. One could suggest that this is critical realism with a relativist ontology in the basement, so to speak. (There are also studies that function within a constructionist ontology and have a relativist ontology at the basement level.)

Another problem I encountered links to the textbook debate I mentioned earlier. According to the criteria offered by Crotty [13], Matney

[14], and Levers [15]—which formed the lens I was using—a certain study could be categorised as constructionist, and yet the authors themselves may have labelled it as interpretivist. How should I classify this then? Should I override the author's statement, claiming to know better and to have a preferred classification system, or do I hold space for this difference of opinion? Additionally, some authors included statements that drew from multiple paradigms within one paper. A final problem I encountered was that fully relational approaches (as reflected in, for example, some Indigenous research methodologies [16] and posthuman approaches) are not sufficiently captured in a three-paradigm framework of post-positivism, constructionism, and interpretivism.

As I discussed these matters with learned colleagues [17] and read more widely about paradigms, I saw how complex and resistant to simple classification these matters are. I also became aware of extensive debates about relativist ontology in particular. While some thinkers may choose to adhere to aspects of relativism, particularly in relation to valuing multiple forms of knowledge, ways of knowing (and the knowers themselves), we also do live our daily lives with a degree of agreement that we are seeing certain things, places and spaces in the same way, otherwise it would be very difficult to navigate social life ("Please pass the salt." "What's that?").

As Michael Hart [18], an Indigenous researcher working among the Cree peoples, noted, many conversations emphasise cognitive processes as the key determinants of worldviews. This focus often overlooks the dynamics of others' experiences in the world, which include feelings and intuition [19]. We come to reflexivity as whole beings (always in relationships with others and the environment) and we need understandings of reflexivity and ways of being reflexive that can embrace this. In addition, the new era we live in appears to be birthing a computational paradigm, through the rise of artificial intelligence [20] and we need the tools to reflexively explore the human-technology assemblage and how meaning emerges through this.

As a result of these processes and conundrums, I decided that instead of presenting an argument for a neat framework of paradigms in this book, building an understanding of different approaches to reflexivity upon this, and instead of getting too hung up on the "-isms", I would choose the route of emphasising the importance of a research study's scholarly coherence and internal congruence. Thus, as we think about our research through this book, we'll consider four broad questions: What kind of self am I? What area do I wish to study? What quest am I on? And what tools should I use? Yes, themes related to components of paradigms are intertwined within this discussion, but they will not be our main scaffolding.

What Kind of Self Am I?

Who am I as a researcher and how am I able to know things? Reflexivity is a relational process between the world of the study and the researcher doing the studying. We can't just ask about the world we're studying, our views of it, and the tools that could help us to explore it; we need to be aware of and critically reflect on how we see ourselves, the theories we're using to explain what a self is, and our practices of "selfing."

There are endless debates about how we can understand what it means to be a self [21]. Am I essentially a cerebral subject or do I experience myself as fully and vitally embodied? Do I see myself as a unitary, distinct, bounded, autonomous self (clearly separating "I" and "Others")? Alternatively, am I an ensemble of social relations and an intersection of social relatedness? Am I ceaselessly interdependent? [22] Do I view myself as a system? Am I *of* nature, decentralised, intertwined with others, the environment, objects, ideas? A union of mind-body-world? [23] Am I fully knowable to myself? Am I knowable to others, who are also knowable to me? Or am I opaque and not fully knowable, just as I don't presume to be able to fully know others? Am I grounded, stable and coherent, or am I a multi-being who is ever shifting and fluidly (re)creating as I am continuously becoming? Am I a self who is made up of narratives? Can I define myself in a-political ways or are persons always political? [24]

The approaches to reflexivity that we'll explore in this book differ in terms of how the researcher understands the world they're studying and how they understand who they are. If we don't have a clear idea of how we're conceptualising our "self" then it's hard to build a coherent formulation of the reflexivity approach we should use.

What Area Do I Wish to Study?

When I'm seeking to settle on a topic to investigate, I'm exploring a wide range of questions. Here are some of them:

- What topics are inviting my attention?
- Out of all the possible topics to examine, why this one?
- How do I feel about this topic?

- How does my body respond as I lean into exploring this area?
- How am I describing the phenomenon as I think about whether I want to study it, and what are the implications of doing so?
- Why am I the person to explore this?
- How am I positioned in relation to what I want to explore? How is what I want to explore positioned in relation to me?
- What is my current understanding of this topic? Where does that understanding come from?
- Whose voices have I been listening to about this topic?
- What literature is informing my current understanding of this phenomenon? How am I reading the literature through the lenses of my own experiences, beliefs, values, hopes, and assumptions? What literature have I ignored? What literature do I disagree with? Why?
- Why am I drawn to this particular knowledge gap?
- As I narrow down my focus, what am I excluding from my gaze and what are the implications of that?
- What language have I used to answer these questions? What is that language doing?

What Quest Am I On?

As I decide what I wish to investigate, I need to make some decisions about the kind of quest I'm embarking on. In the music therapy literature I reviewed, I perceived six quests:

1. Do I want to accurately know and reveal something about this topic or how participants perceive it?
2. Do I wish to discover and share facets of what I'm studying, knowing that this is filtered through my perceptions or represented through my constructions, at least in part?
3. Do I want to explore and share my own experiences of and/or responses to this topic?
4. Is my goal to share an understanding of this topic that I've gained through closeness with participants?
5. Do I want to explore and argue for a better, more socially just view of what I'm studying?
6. Or will I be exploring and sharing unfolding meaning about this topic, knowing that this meaning emerges relationally?

We need to know what our quest is so that we can make a congruent decision about our approach to reflexivity. The strategy we're using is also closely associated with how we see ourselves in relation to what we are studying. The motivation for these decisions tends to link to our values. Axiology is the study of values and value judgements. Research could be driven by values such as rigour, creating solutions to real-world problems, aesthetics, social justice, empathic understanding, environmental responsibility, career advancement, and so on. Often, it's a combination.

What Tools Should I Use?

As we decide what area we wish to study and the quest we'll be embarking on, we can make choices about appropriate tools to use. There are a range of questions we need to think through here as well, for example:

- What theory/theoretical frame should I use? Why am I drawn to that?
- Where does this theory come from? What values is it grounded in?
- What does this theory do? What does it enable me to see? What does this theory blind me from seeing?
- What methodology is most appropriate? Why?
- How should I design the study? What does this enable me to do? What does this design restrain from happening?
- What methods will I use? Why have I chosen these?
- What will the data be? What are the implications of that choice?
- Am I thinking of collecting data? Gathering data? Making data?
- Am I really open to being surprised, or am I just looking for what I want/expect to find?
- Who should be involved in this study, and what kinds of relationships should be developed?
- How will I be (re)presenting my findings? What are the implications of this?

Six Approaches to Reflexivity

It's within the connections between our understanding of self, the area we're exploring, our quest and the tools we're using that we make decisions about our approach to reflexivity. After conducting the process of critically examining the literature and interviewing authors, I slightly refined my initial broad definition of research reflexivity to now read as follows: *Reflexivity entails researchers deliberately acknowledging and exploring how they are (or have the potential to be) active role players in creating and shaping knowledge in their studies (and beyond) and how they might respond or be transformed in return.* Under this umbrella definition, I contend that there are six specific approaches to reflexivity: (1) Sentinel Reflexivity; (2) Lens Reflexivity; (3) Authorial Reflexivity; (4) Empathic Reflexivity; (5) Restorative Reflexivity; and (6) Relational Reflexivity.

As Brynjulf Stige [11, p. 69] wrote, "For researchers and for referees evaluating submitted research articles, one question remains: how should reflexivity be demonstrated and documented?...I think there is no general answer to this question. Solutions must be found in relation to each research project." In our interview, I asked Gro Trondalen how she invites her students to grow their reflexivity. She replied that she wants them "foremost to be aware that there is diversity in ways that people approach understanding research and the role of the researcher and their influence..." Working with students is about "empowering them; making a space where they feel empowered to investigate and come to their own conclusions...then they explore in a way that make sense to them". My goal is not to argue that one approach to reflexivity is better than another. It's to advocate for research that is coherent and congruent in terms of its stated purpose and its processes of accomplishing that purpose.

In the interviews I conducted, the authors discussed a particular paper they had published and we investigated their reflexive processes within that study. However, the conversations invariably extended to where their ideas on reflexivity had come from, how the strategies they used had unfolded through previous experiences and learnings, how their reflexivity in a study was contextualised in relation to who they are as researchers, music therapists and humans in the world, and where their ideas on reflexivity were going. Therefore, I added the words "and beyond" to my formulation. Yes, our reflexivity becomes concentrated in certain ways within a particular project, but it's inseparable from who we are as people, what we care most deeply about, and how our life stories are unfolding.

In Table 2.1 we see how the six approaches to reflexivity link to particular quests. In this table, I've also included simplified statements to capture the spirit of each approach, and an image to capture the "movement" involved.

We could consider some of these approaches along continua. For example, Sentinel Reflexivity and Lens Reflexivity differ in terms of the degree to which subjectivity inevitably influences what we can know about a

Table 2.1 Six reflexivity approaches

	Quest	*Approach to reflexivity*	*Simple language*	
1	Accurately knowing and revealing what we're investigating or how participants perceive it	SENTINEL REFLEXIVITY Deliberately acknowledging and exploring our potential participation in creating and shaping knowledge in our study *through preconceived ideas and biases* and responding *by setting these aside as much as possible.*	"I'm getting out of the way so that I and you can see this phenomenon clearly" "I'm open to receive what this phenomenon is revealing to me" "I'm getting out of the way so that I and you can see the participants' experiences clearly" "I'm open to receive what the participants are revealing to me."	
2	Discovering and sharing facets of what we're studying, knowing that this is filtered through our perceptions or represented through our constructions, at least in part	LENS REFLEXIVITY Deliberately acknowledging and exploring our active participation in creating and shaping knowledge in our study through *employing our subjective perspectives with awareness* and responding to these insights *by being transparent, as well as challenging these perspectives and related actions when necessary.*	"I'm aware that you see this through my perceptions and constructions of it." "I know that I cast a shadow on this topic throughout my process of exploring it."	

(*continued*)

Table 2.1 (continued)

	Quest	*Approach to reflexivity*	*Simple language*	
3	Exploring and sharing our own experiences of and/or response to what we're studying	AUTHORIAL REFLEXIVITY Deliberately acknowledging and exploring our active participation in creating and shaping knowledge in our study *because we can only see the world from our own vantage point* and responding to these insights *by recognising that this is one of many possible stories.*	"I'm experiencing and perceiving aspects of this and will explain that experience to you. This is one possible story."	
4	Sharing an understanding of what we're studying that we have gained through closeness with participants	EMPATHIC REFLEXIVITY Deliberately acknowledging and exploring our active participation in creating and shaping knowledge in our study *as we work to insightfully attune to our participants* and responding to these insights *by making interactional adjustments.*	"I'm getting close to this phenomenon and those who experience it so I can understand it better."	

5	Exploring and arguing for a better, more just view of what we're studying	RESTORATIVE REFLEXIVITY Deliberately acknowledging and exploring our active participation in creating and shaping knowledge in our study *as we seek to promote greater social justice* and responding *by continuously critiquing power relations and acting in the best service of others' flourishing*.	"I'm holding up a better interpretation of what I am studying and seeking to participate in working towards a better world."	
6	Exploring and sharing unfolding meaning about what is being studied, knowing that this meaning emerges relationally	RELATIONAL REFLEXIVITY Deliberately acknowledging and exploring our active participation in creating and shaping knowledge in our study *as interconnected, mutually affecting threads within dynamic assemblages* and being affected by these insights *as part of emergent processes*.	"Meaning is created through all the relational interconnections (between people, things, objects, spaces etc.) in this research study."	

reality outside ourselves. Sentinel Reflexivity and Restorative Reflexivity differ in terms of the degree to which a researcher is trying to present truth "as it is" or "as it should be". Lens Reflexivity and Authorial Reflexivity move along a continuum related to how far one is able to step outside one's own perspectives. Authorial Reflexivity and Empathic Reflexivity also lie along a continuum because Authorial Reflexivity entails the stance that my vantage point is the only place I can stand as I turn to you to listen to your perspectives, and in Empathic Reflexivity I am seeking to deeply empathise with you and I believe it is possible to gain some access to your internal experiences, but I acknowledge that my process is still informed by my perspectives. Empathic Reflexivity and Relational Reflexivity can be considered along a continuum regarding the degree to which meaning develops through interactions. In Empathic Reflexivity, individuals each bring their pre-existing personal "backpack" of ideas into their developing relationship with each other, but in Relational Reflexivity there are no backpacks to be seen: we become who we are within the dynamic process of the research relationship.

Having said this, all forms of reflexivity are always ongoing, evolving *processes.* Reflexivity is about who we are as humans and particularly as humans-in-relationship. This is always in motion. Even if we write a statement in an article to present our preconceived ideas, to let the reader know about our experience with a topic and our positioning in relation to it, aspects of this and aspects of our views on these matters may change even through the process of the study itself and certainly after it's published as we continue to grow and develop.

I contend that the goal is good-enough reflexivity. We'll never see all the ways that we are influencing or have the potential to influence our studies. As Michael Viega highlighted in our interview, "the spiral just keeps expanding and expanding as you allow more…[I]f you see yourself as 'this reflexive researcher', sometimes that can blind you to some of that hard work that still needs to happen." The process is always ongoing.

I also believe that it's difficult (maybe even impossible) to engage in thorough reflexivity completely alone. We need others to help us see ourselves. So, by "reflexivity," I mean "the process of good-enough reflexivity in community." That community could be a research team, peers, a supervisor, or even one's family or friends who are available to bounce ideas off (as I've certainly done in the process of writing this book!). All the images in Table 2.1 also imply an audience. I'm showing someone something. I'm getting out of the way so that someone else can see something. I'm sharing my experience with someone. I'm holding up a version of meaning for someone. I'm intertwined relationally with people in the study, including the readers/audience.

My Own Reflexive Approaches

My desire in this book was to engage with all the studies in music therapy over the last 20 years that mention reflexivity and to take their insights seriously. Within each chapter of this book, I sought to respectfully honour each research quest and offer strategies that a researcher working in that manner might find helpful. In this process, I had to acknowledge and explore how *I* was (or had the potential to be) an active role player in the creation/shaping of knowledge in this book and how I am shaped in return.

As a researcher (and a human being in the world), I'm personally drawn to four quests: to discover and share some facets of what I am studying, knowing that this is filtered through my perceptions or represented through my constructions at least in part (because I hold a view that there is an independent reality but I perceive it subjectively); to share an understanding of what I'm studying that I've gained through closeness with participants (because, as a music therapist, I am drawn to empathic, humble encounters that do not presume knowledge but require deep listening as a fellow human being); to explore and argue for a better, more just view of what I am studying (because injustice and oppression are profoundly harmful, ongoing, and require a response); and to explore and share an unfolding meaning about what I am studying, created relationally (because I'm fascinated by relational ontologies, especially growing up in a South African context). These four approaches excite me and are aligned with my sense of professional and personal purpose, not because they are superior to others.

In addition to our personal overarching commitments and preferences, the nature of each specific research project may necessitate a unique approach. As Martyn Hammersley and Roger Gomm [25] explained, concepts are part of networks, and their sense relies on their relationships with other concepts in those networks. Our quest may be driven by our values and convictions and what makes the most sense to us theoretically and methodologically. However, the decision to embark on a certain quest can also be driven by the needs and requirements of a particular study we're working on, the training we've received and the skills we possess to do the work well, the funding we've been granted or are in the process of applying for, the needs of the organisation we work for if they have commissioned the research, the nature, skills and priorities of the research team we may be working with, or the affordances and limitations of researching alone [26].

Therefore, as researchers, we might draw on different approaches to reflexivity in different studies we conduct. In my conversation with Tríona McCaffrey, she explained that

> The ideas might be similar, the person driving the study might be the same person, but actually the cards that you have in each study can be very, very different and you've got to play those differently depending on where you are and who's involved. That's what makes the research exciting, that you do have to tailor and change as you go, and I think it just gives you more of an appreciation for the context that you're in. Once we're open to that learning along the way about the process, well, then I think it just makes us better researchers. If we were to have the exact same approach all the time, it will be quite worrisome because you think, 'Gosh, if there's any reflexivity going on here, what's being reflected on it? How can it all be the same?'

Therefore, while I'm drawn to certain approaches in general terms, my goal in this particular research project, as expressed through this book, was to explore what was currently happening in music therapy research regarding reflexivity, while critically examining my own interpretive processes as I did so. As mentioned, I did this through examining the literature and interviewing some of the authors. In balancing my personal preferences and values, and responding to the needs of this specific study, I elected to draw on Lens Reflexivity, Restorative Reflexivity, and Empathic Reflexivity.

My Personal Engagement with Lens Reflexivity

As I proceeded through the critical interpretive synthesis, I sought to balance openness to reading what the authors were presenting (to see what was "in" the texts) with recognising that I'm unable to extricate myself from my own brain, life experiences, and library of learning. I am a "situated interpreter of meaning" [27, p. 21]. I worked on articulating my thinking process, not just the conclusions I reached, through conversations with peers, in classes and supervision with postgraduate research students, as well as in continuing professional development courses with other local music therapists. The process of organising the information into six approaches was a highly active one. I kept a reflexive journal where I engaged in free writing about my motivations for conducting this study. I explored what I felt were key insights that began to stand out for me as I proceeded through the data collection and analysis, and included my emotional responses too (such as when I decided to return to article 1 in the analysis process after completing the first 50!). I've detailed the methodological steps I proceeded through with transparency in this book. The constructs I drew on and crafted *shaped* the findings; they did not *reveal* the findings. I did not *make* the findings out of nothing, though, such that they would reflect only my personal thoughts. I grounded my interpretations in the data—through detailed, methodical reflexive thematic analysis [27] of the systematically identified texts and the interview transcripts and by drawing on quotes to substantiate points raised.

As I draw on content from articles and interviews with the researchers in the chapters that follow, I urge you to bear in mind that these are snapshots. The researchers whose work I'm drawing on are dynamic, complex and evolving, as are all of us. I've tried to engage in multiple hermeneutic circles, interpreting sentences in relation to whole articles and interview transcripts and whole articles and transcripts in relation to the sentences that make them up. When I offer a quote from an article or interview within the context of one particular approach to reflexivity, this means that this is how I perceive this content to fit best (and I will present my arguments for this). Most articles held multiple viewpoints though, and different components of an article, or different strategies that authors used at different points in their process, relate to more than one approach. As a result, you'll see some authors being referenced in more than one chapter. (We all hold multitudes [28].) Therefore, as I draw on an article or interview in a particular chapter, I am not arguing that this is *the* box that this article fits into (and I'm definitely not saying that this is *the* box that this *author* fits into). In some interviews, I spoke to researchers about an article they'd written a number of years ago and the conversation included how their views on reflexivity had changed over time. In my interview with Kerry Devlin, for example, she explained looking back on some previous reflections and positions she held and thinking, "I can't believe that was me but also I honour the fact that that was me." She described how that is one of the reasons why "reflexivity is really messy and maybe why it makes some folks uncomfortable because I think when you really go there you dig up a lot of skeletons in your own closet, you know? Things that are uncomfortable to confront. But for me the process of confronting them is essential—like I can't imagine doing research or clinical practice without doing those things." In our conversation, Gro Trondalen said,

> Our theoretical thinking affects how we live. I met Daniel Stern at the right point in my life. And he said something that really meant something to me. I remember I asked him a question that was important for me. And then he said, that's interesting, but you know something? I'm not concerned with this anymore. And I *loved*, I *loved* that sentence. I really didn't feel offended at all. It was kind of opening up something new. I can mean something in a paper a long time ago and maybe I don't mean that anymore. I can *change* and I can change my whole life. It was so liberating.

In addition to grounding this book in my analysis of the published music therapy literature that mentions reflexivity, I've also supplemented each chapter with insights from other authors who have written about these matters. I speak in my own voice too, suggesting ways of thinking and engaging that I argue could support each reflexivity approach, as well as carrying us forward as we continue to grow reflexivity within our field.

My Personal Engagement with Restorative Reflexivity

Arguing for more socially just perspectives is one of the six approaches described in this book. However, the overarching argument that relates to all six approaches is that we need to continue to develop our abilities to think about our thinking. Methodology is political. Reflexivity is an invaluable tool as we continue to critique power relations in the music therapy field, to work towards greater epistemic justice, and to examine how our stated values do and/or do not play out in research practice. It's potentially the core tool. This has certainly been one of my key motivating factors for writing this book.

Almost all the articles that met the inclusion criteria for the critical interpretive synthesis I conducted were written within Western contexts. As my research questions related to what was currently happening in our field, this is then reflected in the findings. However, Restorative Reflexivity enables me to critically reflect on this, which I've endeavoured to do. I've tried to be very careful when using the pronoun "we" in this book. There are many instances where "we" serves an appropriately expansive purpose, referring to all of us as researchers in this field. However, in my early draft edits I noticed how I'd sometimes use this word in a sentence to refer to a group of researchers who are positioned within my in-group of privilege. I can only write from my position; I can't pretend to be able to transcend this, and I don't wish to appropriate others' perspectives, but I need to recognise the limits of my "we". I also don't want to gloss over how this word "we" has served to exclude and make others invisible. Therefore, when I refer to groups with different experiences with respect to the topic I'm discussing at that point, I have avoided this word to acknowledge the limitations of my lived experience.

As I examine my own power and privilege, I'm aware that by being one of the early cohorts of registered music therapists in South Africa, I've had opportunities to teach and mentor others in my context. I was able to access university education and was well-prepared to do so. I had family support from well-educated parents who could guide me. As I progressed in my career, I could take hold of service and leadership opportunities that came my way because of the need to include voices from more diverse spaces. In my teaching and research, I value collaborative approaches and collective meaning-making, as well as intellectual humility, but I can never ignore the fact that I have grown in and speak from a place of privilege. In this book, I offer options, not directives. I hope we sit at a round table together while we explore this topic. I included interviews with many of the authors of the texts I identified rather than merely "decoding" the meaning of the articles so that I could present my interpretations to them and welcome their responses, including feedback that my interpretations may be wrong. As I mentioned in the previous chapter, my desire is for this book to be part of an ongoing conversation, not a declaration.

My Personal Engagement with Empathic Reflexivity

As I read the journal articles that met the inclusion criteria, I began to get to know a little about the authors. I could learn about the central aspects of their research process and encounter their findings. Given the limited wordcount of journal articles, readers may frequently be left with additional questions, and this was the case for me. I wanted to delve deeper into the authors' experiences and decisions. Ideally, I would have liked to interview every author, but this was not feasible within the timeframe of this project.

In the interviews, I sought to create a relaxed, conversational space where we could get to know each other and where the authors could share their views more expansively. Before the interview with each author, I read through their paper again, reviewed the template I'd completed for this article, notated any additional interpretations and responses, and then purposefully assumed a stance of openness and curiosity, delighting in the fact that my assumptions and sense-making may be completely wrong. I only had a few planned, open questions ("What is your understanding of reflexivity in research?; Please talk to me about your article and how you engaged in reflexivity during this research study; These are my interpretations of your approach to reflexivity in this study....What are your thoughts?"). I attempted to use active listening and focussed on flexibly being "in the moment" with each participant rather than planning what question to ask next, so that I could respond closely to what they were saying and where they were leading the conversation. Therefore, each interview unfolded in unique ways. As the authors were spread across the globe, I needed to conduct the interviews online, which was limiting in terms of the human-to-human encounter. However, having an hour of open discussion with each participant (all of whom were very familiar with online interaction) still afforded rich conversations. I drew on my understanding of empathic "stepping stones" as I sought to attune to their experiences. As I analysed the transcripts and drew on quotes from them within this book, I have vivid memories of being in conversation with these authors, rather than reviewing their work at a distance. I was changed by my interactions with them.

As we embark on our exploration of the map of six approaches, we can bear in mind that reflexivity is serious and playful. It requires looking inwards as well as having refined relational sensitivities. It needs focussed precision and critical thinking as well as explorative, open flexibility. Reflexivity is interested in the micro and the macro, it looks behind, ahead, and is mindfully present in the moment.

References

1. Alvesson M, Sköldberg K. Reflexive methodology: new vistas for qualitative research. 3rd ed. London: Sage; 2018.
2. Etherington K. Becoming a reflexive researcher: using our selves in research. London: Jessica Kingsley Publishers; 2004.

3. Finlay L. Negotiating the swamp: the opportunity and challenge of reflexivity in research practice. Qual Res. 2002;2(2):209–30.
4. Finlay L, Gough B, editors. Reflexivity: a practical guide for researchers in health and social sciences. Chichester: John Wiley & Sons; 2008.
5. Lazard L, McAvoy J. Doing reflexivity in psychological research: what's the point? What's the practice? Qual Res Psychol. 2020;17(2):159–77.
6. Whitaker EM, Atkinson P. Reflexivity in social research. London: Palgrave Macmillan; 2021.
7. Enosh G, Ben-Ari A. Reflexivity: the creation of liminal spaces—researchers, participants, and research encounters. Qual Health Res. 2016;26(4):578–84.
8. Sliep Y, Gilbert A. Promoting inter-relational reflexivity with psychosocial workers in community work: a case study from Burundi. J Psychol Afr. 2006;16(2):293–302.
9. Kalu ME. How does "subjective I" influence a qualitative research question, theoretical approach and methodologies? Global J Pure Appl Sci. 2019;25(1):97–101.
10. Bruscia K. Forms of reflexivity in music therapy: an anthology. Phoenixville, PA: Barcelona Publishers; 2015.
11. Stige B. Do we need general criteria for the evaluation of qualitative research articles, and if we do, how could such criteria be formulated? Nord J Music Ther. 2002;11(1):65–71.
12. O'Grady P. Relativism. London: Acumen; 2002.
13. Crotty MJ. The foundations of social research: meaning and perspective in the research process. London: Sage; 1998.
14. Matney B. A knowledge framework for the philosophical underpinnings of research: implications for music therapy. J Music Ther. 2019;56(1):1–29.
15. Levers MJD. Philosophical paradigms, grounded theory, and perspectives on emergence. SAGE Open. 2013;3(4):2158244013517243.
16. Chilisa B, Mertens DM. Indigenous made in Africa evaluation frameworks: addressing epistemic violence and contributing to social transformation. Am J Eval. 2021;42(2):241–53.
17. Van Staden W. Personal communication. 2024 Jan.
18. Hart MA. Indigenous worldviews, knowledge, and research: the development of an Indigenous research paradigm. J Indigen Voices Soc Work. 2010;1(1):1–16.
19. Kuokkanen R. Reshaping the university: responsibility, indigenous epistemes, and the logic of the gift. Vancouver, BC: UBC Press; 2007.
20. Williams RT. Paradigm shifts: exploring AI's influence on qualitative inquiry and analysis. Frontiers in Research Metrics and Analytics. 2024;9:1331589.
21. Kockelman P. Agent, person, subject, self: a theory of ontology, interaction and infrastructure. Oxford: Oxford University Press; 2013.

22. Marková I. Constitution of the self: intersubjectivity and dialogicality. Cult Psychol. 2003;9(3):249–59.
23. Facco E, Al Khafaji BE, Tressoldi P. In search of the true self. J Theor Philos Psychol. 2019;39(3):157–80.
24. Hanisch C. The personal is political: the women's liberation movement classic with a new explanatory introduction. In: Hanisch C, editor. Women of the world, unite! Writings by Carol Hanisch [Internet]. 2006 [cited 2024 Jul 18]. Available from: http://www.carolhanisch.org/CHwritings/PIP.html.
25. Hammersley M, Gomm R. Bias in social research. Sociological Research Online [Internet]. 1997;2(1). Available from: http://www.socresonline.org.uk/2/1/2.htm.
26. May T, Perry B. Reflexivity: the essential guide. London: Sage; 2017.
27. Braun V, Clarke V. Thematic analysis: a practical guide. London: Sage; 2021.
28. Whitman W. Song of myself. 1855.

CHAPTER 3

Sentinel Reflexivity

If our quest is to understand and represent an object, event or process as accurately as possible, we attempt to restrain our influence on the research process and findings. We try to stand back and not get in the way so that what we're studying can be seen for what it is. We want to know what's really happening, or how participants really perceive what's happening. We may also seek to allow a phenomenon to reveal itself, or to show how our findings are grounded in the data. As Martina Bingham said in our interview, "I needed to make sure that I left room for the data to do the talking."

The notion of seeking truth has been intensely debated. Positivism—also called foundationalism—aims at its extreme, to produce conclusions that are valid because they follow directly from the data. Data are seen as having an independent existence and the researcher collects and analyses this data objectively by avoiding bias and error. This approach has guided, and in many ways continues to guide, research using quantitative methods. However, forms of foundationalism have also influenced qualitative research [1].

Deliberately acknowledging and exploring our potential participation in creating and shaping knowledge in our study *through preconceived ideas and biases* and responding *by setting these aside as much as possible.*

A. dos Santos, *Reflexive Research in Music Therapy*,
https://doi.org/10.1007/978-3-032-02033-8_3

Post-positivism softened this pursuit. Within a critical realist ontology (as we discussed in the previous chapter), real objects are still presumed to exist independently of our experience of them. However, we concede that our knowledge of these real objects can't be obtained directly but is mediated by our concepts, language, and interests [2]. Only approximations or segments of truth can be accessed. We're fallible as researchers, even as we may be trying to be as objective as possible [3]. A critical realist would acknowledge their role in terms of having imperfect access to the full truth and would reflect on the implications of this for the findings they present.

In this chapter, we'll draw some insights from phenomenological studies as well. Phenomenological research includes a vast array of perspectives (some are relatively at home in this chapter and others are much more comfortable in subsequent chapters). For example, in their paper on gender aware music therapy, Cassidy Besse [4, p. 154] wrote that phenomenological research requires reflexivity through recognising and setting aside assumptions to delve into the experiences and understandings of participants, which is accomplished through bracketing, involving open dialogue, journaling, "and reporting potential biases." According to my reading, whether a phenomenological researcher's approach falls within our current quest relates largely to how they understand and work with the concepts of "essence" (what kinds of claims we make about how we can and have identified the core structure of a phenomenon), "bracketing" (to what extent we believe we can set aside our preconceived ideas—our natural attitude—to access the essence of the phenomenon), and the difference between description and interpretation (or whether they are always intertwined). I'd argue that what ties all the approaches in this current chapter together is a movement by the researcher to try to step out of the way as much as possible, even though the theoretical intricacies of what we mean by that can vary.

Bias

According to the Oxford Dictionary [5], bias is "an inclination or prejudice for or against one person or group, especially in a way considered to be unfair"; "a concentration on an interest in one particular area or subject"; or "a systematic distortion of statistical results due to a factor not allowed for in their derivation". Humans often face time and cognitive limitations when tasked with processing complex stimuli and information, so we've developed shortcuts [6]. The problem is that these hasty assessments are often less accurate because we use our biases to reach quick answers.

From the perspective of evolutionary psychology and with specific reference to cognitive bias, Martie Haselton et al. [6, p. 968] described bias as "cases in which human cognition reliably produces representations that are systematically distorted compared to some aspect of objective reality." In other words, my perception and interpretations can produce a representation that is not completely in line with how things "really are" or generate findings that are not reliable. In music therapy literature, researchers appear to be referring more to this notion of bias as opposed to being on the lookout only for prejudice and unfair representations. We might even present an event or outcome in more glowing terms than is warranted (e.g., we could claim that music therapy was effective when it wasn't). In my interview with Luke Annesley, he explained how he embraces a range of feedback from participants, being aware that if all of them simply say how "wonderful" music therapy is then the research process is probably flawed.

Overt biases involve open expressions of personal preferences and prejudices. Implicit biases operate below conscious awareness. If we're using a psychodynamic orientation, we could also think of a researcher's Shadow as a source of bias [7]. Implicit biases can be expressed in instant assumptions and subtle behaviours, but they can also manifest in overtly blundering behaviour and can feed systems of oppression [8]. It's possible that our explicit beliefs can diverge from our implicit biases [9]. A music therapist might explicitly believe that they appreciate all musical genres equally and can work effectively with any client's musical preferences. However, they find themselves spending more time preparing for sessions with clients who prefer jazz, or show more enthusiasm and engagement when clients choose this genre to explore in sessions.

We are biased against seeing our bias [10]. However, we need to become both aware of our biases and concerned about the consequences before we become motivated to eliminate them. Some researchers have argued that when people who are motivated to reduce implicit bias become aware of their biases, they tend to work to adjust them [11]. This process may not be easy, though. Implicit biases are like deeply entrenched habits [12]. To break the habit, we need to learn about the contexts that activate the bias and how to replace it with an alternate response that better aligns with our nonprejudiced goals.

There are some techniques that have been shown to be effective in reducing bias, such as exposure to counterstereotypical examples [13, 14], mindfulness training [15], affect regulation [13, 16], educational techniques [17], structured intergroup contact [17], counter-prejudicial training [18]. Encouraging individuals to consider multi-layered criteria for social categorisation can also reduce intergroup bias (seeing another person as having many characteristics, not just within a dominant identity "box") [19]. Patricia Devine et al. [12] developed an intervention that significantly reduced implicit race bias. Their participants used stereotype replacement: recognising that a response was based on a stereotype, labelling the response as stereotypical, reflecting on why the response occurred, considering how the biased response could be avoided in the future and replacing it with an unbiased response. They also took part in counterstereotypic imaging (by envisioning alternatives to their stereotypes and highlighting positive examples); individuation (obtaining specific information about others instead of relying on stereotypes); and perspective-taking (attempting to take the perspective of a member of a stereotyped group).

Psychologists Joseph Vitriol and Gordon Mokkowitz [20] argued that when people learn that their actions are biased, they may not necessarily work to fix this because it can feel threatening to be confronted with this realisation and the desire to self-protect rises up. They found that interventions work better when people's sense of blame decreases combined with an increase in their perceived ability to control their bias. (This is important for research supervisors to bear in mind.) Another group of psychologists, Jason Okonofua et al. [21], challenged the common assumption that biased behaviour stems from deeply embedded internal qualities, focusing rather on the interplay between a person and their situation. Their approach conceptualised people as inherently complex, with multiple, often contradictory selves and goals. While all individuals have the potential for bias, this is not all they are or want to be. Situations can evoke biased or nonbiased potentials in individuals and these situations can be altered to bring out people's better selves. A biased or nonbiased self can become active based on goals relevant to specific situations. The responsibility then shifts from changing "bad individuals" to changing "bad contexts," and people who shape contexts can explore how to create environments that elicit better selves and behaviours.

Research Bias

Research bias has been defined as "a predisposition or partiality" [22, p. 60] that compromises the accuracy of sampling, data collection, analysis, and reporting. We may tend to gather, interpret, and present data in a way that favours false results that align with our preconceived ideas, or practical or political affiliations. We may also exclude true conclusions that don't align with these. When we've settled on a certain interpretation, we may struggle to let go of it [1]. Bias has the potential to enter the research process from the point that we select one topic instead of another, one or more research questions over other potential options, and frame our study using a certain theory rather than another.

In music therapy literature where researchers are on a quest to know and reveal something about a topic accurately, some argue that they intentionally come to their study with an open mind and that assumptions are not in play or can be set side. For example, Michael Silverman [23, p. 95] wrote, "I had no preconceived ideas concerning participants' experiences and was interested in the realities associated with developing therapeutic alliance with adult mental health service users."

Others recognise that their preconceived ideas *will* impact the study and this is an undesirable limitation that can weaken their findings. For example, Stephen Venkatarangam [24] explained how his involvement in a study on live-receptive raga intervention as a performer and researcher who took part in all aspects of data collection meant that bias was possible even though he tried not to lead participants. In Silverman and Bibb's [25] study, they explained how they created epochés before embarking on data analysis to recognise their preconceptions or expectations, however, the study was still contextually based on the authors' perspectives and experiences, which inevitably influenced the interpretation of the data.

A third set acknowledge that their preconceived ideas may impact the study and so they need to manage this well to *avoid* such impact. Jennifer Bibb et al. [26] explained how they used reflexive strategies to ensure that they examined their own pre-assumptions carefully and didn't merely project their own experiences. Besse [4] also described how she attempted to counteract bias. In my interview with Moshe Bensimon, he referred to trying to approach findings "clean," without unfinished business that generates emotional blind spots.

This third approach is the most common. We see many examples in the literature where researchers whose quest was to reveal an aspect of truth about a phenomenon wished to identify their biases, personal experiences, assumptions, preunderstandings and beliefs that could potentially shape their interpretation of the phenomenon they were exploring, document and account for these, and then try to move them aside as far as possible to see past them most clearly. They sought to do this to be more objective, honour the phenomenon "for what it is," and present an accurate understanding that can be helpful to others.

You may hold the view that the term "bias" belongs in quantitative studies, where the researcher is seeking to be objective, and the term "reflexivity" belongs in qualitative studies, where the researcher values subjectivity and seeks to work carefully with it. However, in many qualitative music therapy studies—especially where researchers are on a quest to present a phenomenon "for what it is"—the term "bias" does appear, especially in relation to reflexivity. Moshe Bensimon explained how he tries to remain alert to potential bias:

> [I need to] be aware of potential bias due to my personal history, stances, and life perspective concerning the specific issue. By being aware and observing [and] reporting it, we can minimise bias. Of course, in qualitative research, the researcher is a key instrument. Interpretation goes through our body, through our senses, through our thoughts…But also within this concept there are borders. And the borders have to do with things that you are not aware of, which can impact your interpretation. By being aware, we can minimise this. I don't think that we can totally avoid any bias, any influence, but we can dramatically minimise it. There can't be 100% success, so this keeps me alert all the time during all the stages of research about potential bias.

Trying to see a phenomenon for what it is versus perceiving, interpreting, and representing it through subjective experience are ends of a continuum. In the next chapter, we'll be on the quest to discover and share some facets of a phenomenon, embracing the idea that this *will always* be filtered through one's perceptions and experiences. Even here in this chapter, though, as we attempt to step out of the way, we need to acknowledge that it may not be entirely achievable. The researcher's task when using Sentinel Reflexivity is to show they've made the best attempt possible.

Trustworthiness in a Study Employing Sentinel Reflexivity

As we think of reflexivity as restraining our influence in the pursuit of an accurate understanding of a phenomenon, we are doing so to bolster the trustworthiness of our study. In some music therapy literature, reflexivity is stated as explicitly contributing towards trustworthiness [27–30]. As explained by Yvonna Lincoln and Egon Guba [31], trustworthiness was an attempt to develop parallel qualitative concepts alongside the tools for establishing research quality in quantitative studies. The quality criteria they proposed were credibility, transferability, dependability, and confirmability. Guba and Lincoln [32] added a fifth criterion in 1994: authenticity. These criteria are well discussed elsewhere, so I won't unpack them too much here. To produce a trustworthy study, a researcher needs to be transparent about the theoretical frame or orientation they've used to ground their design and strategies, as well as meeting standards to show that their study has been conducted competently and ethically [33]. In a study employing Sentinel Reflexivity, the researcher works to gain the reader's trust in the findings' close representation of the phenomenon. In the remainder of this chapter, we'll explore how we can reflexively enhance this kind of trustworthiness by examining and minimising our bias, and by using methods that best enable a phenomenon to reveal itself.

Examining and Restraining Assumptions and Feelings

Let's first discuss how we could explore what preconceived ideas, experiences, values, and beliefs could be influencing the research we're conducting. We'll then look at how we could work to examine whether they're getting in the way of a fair assessment of the evidence and, if so, how we can work to set them aside as much as possible.

Identifying What Could Be Getting in the Way

Tasha Eurich [34, p. 6] defined self-awareness as "the ability to see ourselves clearly—to understand who we are, how others see us, and how we fit into the world around us." This has two dimensions. Internal self-awareness refers to whether we're seeing ourselves clearly. External self-awareness refers to having an understanding of how other people perceive us. The two dimensions don't necessarily correlate. A person may have an accurate external self-awareness but weak internal self-awareness. Reflexive researchers need to be working on enhancing both their internal and external self-awareness. For example, our values may shape the focus of our research question, and others' perceptions of us in an interview may be shaping their responses.

Music therapy researchers show their self-awareness of what could be producing distorted representations through numerous factors. Authors have noted how their interpretations could be influenced by their past experiences [4, 35], identity and privilege [28, 36], worldview [37], professional or academic background and interests [28, 29, 38], beliefs [29, 30], preconceived assumptions and understandings [4, 28, 30, 35, 39], expectations [26], and their dual role as researcher and therapist [24, 40–43]. In our interview, Moshe Bensimon explained,

> [Reflexivity] should begin from the first question. The first question should be, why am I a music therapist? Why am I interested in doing research about a certain topic? What attracts me? To do research, maybe it's part of my healing process. Or to do good in the world? What are the incentives for doing research under a specific topic? And this is equal for all the researchers, also quantitative research. If you do your research on cancer, because a relative of yourself suffered from cancer, it may impact, for example, in quantitative research, your motivation to find a significant result.

Identifying Biases

There are many bias typologies. Some focus on specific research biases, while others list cognitive biases that play out in general life. Statements about bias in general seem to be the trend in music therapy literature, with specific types of biases hardly mentioned at all. In the body of literature I examined, only selection bias was alluded to by Alexa Economos [44, p. 316] "remaining mindful of potential bias in the results due to my selection of "participants" and "researcher bias" was mentioned by Claire Hogan-Gibbons et al. [45]

I suggest that it may be valuable to include more specific references to the kinds of biases that could be at play in our studies and how we tailor our strategies to address these. In Appendix A, I include forms of bias that one could consider within the different stages of the research journey. This is not a complete account of every possible bias; it's merely an invitation to get us thinking. We can reflect on this list as we seek to identify our biases, exploring these through journalling, supervision, peer review, group discussions within a research team (comprised of people who don't all have the same perspectives), and even through therapy.

Bracketing

One of the processes we use as researchers to engage in and be more open to a phenomenon "as it is" or even "as it is presenting itself to us" by mindfully restraining our own influence is bracketing. If we used bracketing in a mathematical equation, we'd be placing certain components in brackets to focus on them, while suspending our focus on what was outside the brackets [46]. Some music therapy researchers explain that bracketing is a way of attempting to minimise bias (i.e., bracketing out one's bias) [26, 29, 30, 47–49]. Phenomenologist Edmund Husserl introduced the idea of bracketing to refer to detaching ourselves from our natural, everyday attitude (our assumptions, constructions, theories, and preconceptions). We step aside from these so we can attend to a phenomenon openly as it presents itself to us, not in terms of how we think about it. We're attempting to look beyond our preconceptions, constructions, and assumptions to the essence of what we're studying [46]. As Amedeo Giorgi [50, p. 240] noted, "past interpretations can predetermine present experience," so we need to find ways to experience a phenomenon freshly so we can focus on what's essential about it. One can alternatively use the terms "phenomenological reduction" or "epoché." (There are some slight philosophical differences between these concepts, but they're usually considered to be interchangeable [51].) Husserl used the term bracketing quite freely, without providing a uniform definition [46].

In Felicity Baker and Phoebe Stretton-Smith's [39, p. 51] paper on group therapeutic songwriting with people with dementia, they included an epoché to show their process of "actively identifying and consciously bracketing off their preconceived ideas and notions" regarding the phenomenon in question. They described how Baker had many years' experience working as a music therapist and researcher with people with dementia as well as healthy ageing adults, and was invested in the potential of songwriting for therapeutic change. Stretton-Smith was a newly trained music therapist. The authors transparently described how they came to the study speculating that people with dementia may focus on the enjoyable aspects of the group and may experience the process positively, however they may also find therapeutic songwriting challenging.

Once we've acknowledged our preconceived ideas, we can more consciously loosen ourselves from them. We humbly acknowledge that we don't understand a phenomenon completely. Bracketing begins when we become curious and open-minded, exercising intellectual bravery and humility [52, 53]. As Clark Moustakas [54, p. 74] argued, bracketing gives us

> an original vantage point, a clearing of mind, space, and time, a holding in abeyance of whatever colours the experience or directs us, anything what-

ever that has been put into our minds by science or society, or government, or other people, especially one's parents, teachers, and authorities, but also one's friends and enemies. Epoché includes entering a pure internal place, as an open self, ready to embrace life in what it truly offers.

Bracketing isn't a one-time event; it's a process that needs to unfold throughout the entire research study [51]. Importantly, we need to explain how and where bracketing took place [55]. Robin Gearing [46] offered a typology of bracketing. In ideal (philosophical) bracketing, prior knowledge is suspended and set aside. The phenomenon is experienced freshly and its true, universal meaning is made explicit. In descriptive (eidetic) bracketing, there's a bit more flexibility. The goal is still to set aside preconceived ideas so the essence of the phenomenon can be revealed, but one is only seeking to know the immediate, local, specific phenomena rather than attaining universal truths. When engaging in existential bracketing, we're aware of our presuppositions when investigating the phenomenon, but we don't claim to be able to detach ourselves from them.

There are always certain aspects that we purposefully don't bracket. We sustain the belief that our research participant is a competent person whose lifeworld is open to understanding due to a foundation of shared humanity and a shared world [56]. In my interview with Luke Annesley, he presented an interesting question that he asks himself: "There's something here about having a position of healthy scepticism about the participants. Then [I think], 'Should I be sceptical about what the participants say, or should I just accept what they say?'" In response, we can bear in mind that the last phase in the bracketing process is reintegration. We begin with openness to the phenomenon as it presents itself, but we can engage in critique as we discuss our findings. At the latter stages of the process, we fold our interpretations back into our findings as we examine them contextually and critically, and propose how they may be useful within our field. This process of reintegration also needs to be carefully and transparently articulated [46].

Practical Bracketing Techniques

As we're identifying aspects that may be problematically driving or subtly nudging our research decisions, how do we set them aside? In the music therapy literature, we don't often get a detailed description of what bracketing looks like in practice. In some studies, only a general comment is included about the importance of bracketing preconceptions [30, 57].

Other authors do briefly mention specific approaches they used to engage in bracketing, such as explicitly identifying and stating their backgrounds and expectations [39], writing in a journal [4, 47, 48, 58], peer debriefing [48], and visual artmaking and writing memos [49]. In our interview, Moshe Bensimon also referred to the value of personal therapy in this regard.

The argument could be made that conscious insight is already a helpful step in the right direction. However, this might not be enough. For example, in a descriptive phenomenological study I conducted on music therapy for groups of teenagers referred for violent behaviour [59] where I was seeking the essence of their experiences, I wrote in my journal about my perceptions of "aggressive teens" and my fears for my personal safety living in a violent country. However, as I worked with the participants in my role as music therapist and then analysed the data as the researcher, I knew that acknowledging this was insufficient. I needed to *work* on challenging my assumptions, asking many questions, actively staying open-minded, being committed to ongoing learning, holding my views humbly and being freshly and playfully present with these participants because they were unique beings in front of me who may or certainly may not behave in ways I expected. I could engage in some of these processes alone but I also benefitted greatly from critical conversations with my research supervisors. In addition, I needed to use specific methods (in this case, the strategies of descriptive phenomenology) that afforded opportunities for the phenomenon to show itself.

Let's look at two hypothetical examples of a researcher becoming aware of their thoughts and feelings and working to set these aside. A postgraduate student is passionately committed to his views about deconstructing pathologising diagnostic labels of mental illnesses because he believes that this perspective is too limiting and has the potential to be stigmatising. He feels frustrated and sometimes cross when others challenge this view. This is becoming difficult because he's conducting his study on the role of music therapy in an in-patient mental health facility, which operates rigidly according to a diagnostic model. His supervisor has invited him to do some thinking around this, saying, "Your energy and enthusiastic perspectives may helpfully inform this study in certain ways, but might also limit your study and make relationships with gatekeepers difficult. Your position could also result in processes and findings that are problematically biased. How could you be faithful to your values while also embracing flexibility and open-mindedness to increase the quality and objectivity of your research?" While the student initially feels frustrated and resistant, he trusts his supervisor and decides to give it a try. At home, he begins journalling about his perspectives, the roots of his feelings and thinking. He then leaves what he's written for a few days, returning to read it with fresh eyes. He also decides to read papers that present multiple perspectives on the role of diagnostic categories. Taking what he's written and read back to his supervisor, they discuss how, instead of seeing the facility's diagnostic approach as only problematic, he could also view it as an interesting contextual factor that shapes how music therapy is offered and received here. The student realises that he could expand his research questions to also explore how diagnostic frameworks influence treatment decisions and therapeutic relationships here and how patients themselves relate to their diagnoses, because he realises that some may potentially find them helpful while others may find them limiting. In this process he finds that his feelings of frustration start to lift and curiosity moves to the foreground.

Another researcher is studying the role of music therapy for young children who've lost a parent. She's serving in a dual role in this study, both as the researcher and as the music therapist. She notices that participants in her study don't seem to want to use the music therapy space to explore their loss, which is puzzling her as this is not what she expected her data to show. The researcher is also a mother to a young child. When she watches the recordings of the sessions with her participants, she notices that each time one of them ventures towards expressing their grief, she intervenes by adjusting the music they are improvising together so that it's lighter, brighter, in a major key, and using ascending melody lines. A lightbulb turns on for her. She realises that she didn't spend the necessary time when conceptualising the study reflecting on her own experiences and position as a mother and how hard it is to think about a scenario where her own child could experience losing her. This has resulted in her resisting being present with expressions of grief in sessions with her participants. Through conversations with trusted peers, by journalling, and through giving herself extra time before and after sessions she becomes more mindful of her own difficult feelings, better at setting these aside in sessions, and allows room for her participants to explore their full range of emotions. They have more meaningful therapeutic processes and she is able to generate rich data that more closely represents her participants' experiences.

Supervision

The music therapy studies that embraced reflexivity as a form of minimising bias discussed supervision regularly. Supervision was seen to help manage personal reactions [60]. It assisted researchers in organising data well [24], preserving data integrity [60] and in not becoming overwhelmed by large amounts of data [61]. It also enabled researchers to disentangle dual roles [28, 62]. If a researcher is acting as a sentinel (a sentry, guardian, watcher, lookout) regarding ways that bias can distort findings, then the role of the academic supervisor or peer supervisor is also to be a sentinel—to spot things that the researcher may not yet have seen, to point these out carefully and constructively, and to assist the researcher in minimising their influence.

Using Research Methods that Invite a Phenomenon to Reveal Itself

In the first half of this chapter, we've discussed the personal work we can do to identify and restrain our preconceived notions from skewing our findings. We can also build methods and strategies into our studies that assist us in accomplishing this goal. In the music therapy literature that mentions reflexivity, most of the articles are qualitative and this is reflected in the sections that follow. However, when a researcher uses quantitative methods, there's a lot of information available on how to reduce bias through the design of the study itself. We can build a structure—a well-designed research protocol—that assists in holding back our bias [63]. We can preregister our research plans and hypotheses and submit a pre-analysis plan to reduce the likelihood of engaging in "p-hacking" (manipulating data to reach statistically significant results) [64, 65]. We can also use randomisation to reduce selection bias [66, 67]; include a control group, random assignment and blinding [68, 69]; use standardised data collection procedures and protocols [70, 71]; and address confounding variables [70, 71]. We can ensure research transparency where data and analysis procedures are made publicly available for scrutiny; conduct replication studies to validate findings and identify potential biases; and include publication of negative results to address the issue of publication bias [64]. As we discussed in Chap. 1, however, using these strategies still doesn't mean that the study is fully objective. Reflexivity is always still required to see how we have carefully managed our potential influence.

Reflexively Exploring One's Engagement with and Use of Literature and Theory

Our biases, interpretive frames, emotions and preferences can play a role as we search for, read, summarise, critique, and write about the literature that contextualises our studies. We purposefully use published literature to build our argument—an argument that we may be particularly invested in. If we want to contextualise our study within literature in a manner that is thorough, fair, and balanced, we need to overtly employ specific strategies (and it would be preferable to transparently report on these).

Here are some questions to consider:

- Am I conducting a truly comprehensive search across various platforms and databases, or am I settling for easily accessible literature?
- How actively am I seeking out diverse viewpoints and perspectives on my research topic?
- Can I clearly explain *how* I am identifying common themes, trends, and debates emerging across different sources?
- Have I provided sufficient historical and contextual background to help readers understand the broader socio-cultural, political, and intellectual context of the studies I'm reviewing?
- How rigorously am I evaluating the quality, relevance, and credibility of my sources?
- Am I considering each author's expertise, methodology, research design, and context when evaluating the reliability of evidence?
- Does my critique effectively highlight gaps, inconsistencies, and unresolved questions in the literature?
- Have I justified the need for my study beyond personal interest, establishing its significance within broader scholarly discourse?
- To what extent am I engaging in discussions with colleagues, mentors, and peers about the literature? How is collaborative dialogue helping me identify blind spots, challenge assumptions, and refine my critical thinking skills?

Considering these kinds of questions isn't merely a strategy for writing a "good" literature review. When we're on a quest to present accurate findings and make sense of them in ways that are faithful to the phenomenon itself, these are the techniques we need to use to write a reflexive literature review.

Getting to Know Participants

As we select and engage with participants, we can use methods that invite their voices to be heard clearly instead of being throttled by our own perspectives. Let's look at how researchers using Sentinel Reflexivity can think through selecting participants and managing dual relationships.

Selecting Participants Well

To capture perspectives on a phenomenon as accurately and thoroughly as possible, music therapy researchers raise certain considerations related to selecting participants. When selecting participants purposefully, they acknowledge that this can skew their findings [44]. Including too few participants can limit findings [36], however, smaller sample sizes can also be considered as amplifying participants' voices [72]. On the one hand, researchers acknowledge that a lack of diversity in samples limits the findings and the extent to which they can be generalised [73]. Recruiting participants with a range of experiences can generate a fuller picture of the phenomenon [74]. On the other hand, some researchers acknowledge that more homogenous samples can be advantageous because findings can then be applied within specifically defined contexts [62]. Some researchers use categorical saturation [75], or theoretical sampling [76].

Managing Dual Relationships When the Goal Is to Restrain One's Own Influence

Assuming a dual role in a research study is relatively common in our field. There's a spectrum of types of dual relationships that could be in play. Silverman [23] for example, interviewed some colleagues whom he had previously established professional relationships with. Often, researchers are also the music therapists who facilitate the sessions that are examined in the study. While this kind of dual relationship appears frequently in music therapy studies, it requires very careful consideration [42]. Blurring boundaries is risky [77]. One's reflexive expertise needs to be of a high level to do this well if one's quest is ultimately to allow a phenomenon to speak for itself as much as possible and one is also playing such a close role in the unfolding of this phenomenon.

A therapist's agenda and a researcher's agenda could compete with or complement each other. In Cherry Hense's [78] study on young people's journeys from mental health services to everyday social musicking, she described how being the music therapist required a commitment to supporting participants' outcomes, while being the researcher necessitated a slightly more detached perspective on what the participants gained through the project.

Both in therapy and in research, there's an unequal distribution of power, no matter how hard the therapist or researcher seeks to ameliorate this. For example, Riabzev and Bensimon [28] wrote about how their participants may have felt a need to please the researcher/therapist during interviews. In their study on music-oriented parent counselling with parents of autistic children, Tali Gottfried et al. [41] also reflected on how the ongoing relationship between the researcher/music therapist and the parents may have skewed the parents' answers according to perceived expectations.

While attempting to reduce the potential impacts of dual relationships, some researchers acknowledge that this is never fully possible and that bias can be inevitable [41, 79] Sometimes, the choice is then specifically made not to have a dual role with research participants because of the problems it can present. In my interview with Luke Annesley, he explained that he was taught to "separate [the roles]...partly because it might unduly influence the research in some way but also because it might have a detrimental effect on the therapy." In Selle and Silverman's [80] study, they acknowledged that employing another person to conduct the interviews may be preferable.

When researchers do engage in dual relationships, they employ a range of strategies to manage potentially problematic aspects of this as they try to generate findings that can reveal the phenomenon itself as far as possible in a trustworthy manner. These can include recruiting participants via a third party [77]. Researchers encourage participants to be honest and try to emphasise their freedom to do so [23, 41], and they check their interpretations with participants [42, 77, 79]. Some select lengthy excerpts in their data to avoid conscious or unconscious selection of excerpts that promote one view of the participants or the process [59]. Researchers work to bring their assumptions into consciousness [77], sometimes by writing personal and theoretical notes to reflect on their possible biases and to separate out their roles [28]. They distinguish between interpretation and description [42], consult with a research supervisors [41, 77, 78], and use peer supervision [78].

While the potentially problematic aspects of dual relationships are frequently acknowledged, they're also viewed at times as beneficial. If managed well, they can enhance deep, nuanced, multifaceted, and contextual understanding of what's happening and how participants are experiencing the process [79]. For Bronte Arns and Grace Thompson [77], the benefits of being an insider within the research included easier access to participants, greater buy-in owing to previously established relationships, already-developing knowledge of the context, and the potential to understand the reactions of their participants in more nuanced ways. When one is the therapist and the researcher, rapport can be enhanced [57]. Riabzev and Bensimon [28] explained that participants may feel more comfortable in interviews when the interviewer is also the music therapist. In their study, they felt that their participants could draw on shared moments from the sessions within in-depth discussions during focus groups afterwards.

Collecting Data

Observing Accurately

When music therapy researchers discuss using observation as part of their quest to reveal some truth about a phenomenon and as they reflexively seek to minimise the influence of their own preconceived ideas, they use a few different strategies. Some engage in prolonged observation, taking their time to get to know participants as well as they can [27, 79]. They may specifically seek not to interfere in the environment they're observing [81]. In my interview with Martina Bingham, for example, she explained how the goal in her study on how music therapists use their singing voice was not to interfere. However, being in the room and being able to perceive people in person added to the richness of her understanding:

> I didn't want to affect the process at all. So, I really was there just to observe. And sometimes there's another human body in the room, right? So sometimes you're included in a clinical exercise or they acknowledge that you're there, or sometimes it's children or older adults, and they want to play with you. If I could have been invisible, it would have been better, you know? But to contradict myself immediately, yeah, it would be nice to be invisible, but having a presence in the room actually does make a difference because

> you feel people's energy, you're able to see more facial expression, how close they are to each other and the immediate reactions of a client to a therapist. It's like the difference between going to a live performance and watching something on the television.

In their study on healthcare workers' views on the challenges and possibilities of music therapy within medication-free services, Christine Oedegaard et al. [82] found that participant observation afforded a deeper knowledge of how music therapy unfolds within the context they were examining. When observation takes place through video recording, some researchers [59] choose to include many excerpts to give a fuller picture of the processes and reduce the likelihood of "cherry picking". When watching video excerpts within her study on musical gestures, Danielle Jakubiak [83] explained how she sought to separate objective and subjective observations to help analyse her own perceptions versus what was perceived by the music therapists and clients in the study.

Gathering Accurate Data Through Surveys

Surveys are mentioned infrequently in music therapy research that is on a quest to illuminate the reality of a particular phenomenon and in which the authors explicitly refer to reflexivity. One example can be found in the work of Belinda Densley and Katrina Andrews [60, p. 6] on participation in group singing. They explained that "reflexivity was built into the study design and into each phase of the data analysis." These authors used anonymous online surveys to capture participants' experiences in their own words without interacting with them personally. When designing surveys we need to carefully think through how our assumptions, biases, and theoretical perspectives are shaping the questions we include and how we phrase them. Whose voices will be included and excluded through our sampling methods? As a tool to access what people "really think or feel" or how people "really are," surveys can still be limited inherently both by the need participants may feel to express what they think the researcher wants to hear or to express themselves as the people they wish to be [84–86]. Descriptive survey research also only offers a snapshot rather than capturing any kind of process of change. Response rates are also typically low [87]. So, whilst they may help a researcher to personally "step out the way" as opposed to using a data collection method such as an interview, researchers are still faced with the task of interpreting complex and partial findings.

Interviewing Thoroughly

Designing Interviews Well

Music therapy researchers (who mention reflexivity in their papers) often use semi-structured interviews, as these are seen to allow for reflexivity, sensitivity, and flexibility so that participants have space to think, speak, and be heard [39]. They may prefer open-ended questions [23, 61]. Some do acknowledge, however, that the lack of standardisation in qualitative interviews can evoke concerns about bias and reliability [61]. Researchers take care when inviting a phenomenon to reveal itself by piloting the questions to ensure they are understood well [48], and asking peers to review the questions and offer feedback before diving into the data collection phase [23, 43]. They remove leading interview questions and terminology that emphasises their own orientation [38].

Conducting Interviews Well

While some authors highlight the importance of flexible semi-structured interviews to tap into participants' experiences [39, p. 6], others emphasise the "careful execution" of interviews "in order to maintain consistency and objectivity" [61, p. 6]. Participants are invited to be as honest and transparent as possible, including sharing about what they didn't enjoy or benefit from and what they disagree with [24]. Researchers ask additional probing questions to elicit more detailed responses [72]. They use active listening [61] and carefully attend to what the participants share, honouring their experiences and giving them a space to be heard [43]. Meanings can be verified by the participants in the interviews themselves [61].

Some researchers show awareness of potential power imbalances [77] although there is not enough yet in our literature on how this is specifically addressed. When there is a dual relationship, researchers may choose to ask a different person to conduct the interviews to reduce bias [35]. There are also studies where two interviewers are used [75]. Researchers may seek to bracket their views through journalling before and after each interview they conduct [48] to remain grounded in the participants' data.

Checking the Transcriptions

After verbatim transcriptions have been written for interviews or focus groups, these can be checked in a few ways. Students may ask faculty advisors to check them [88]. Most frequently, participants are asked to engage in member checking by reading through the transcriptions to verify that they are accurate, congruent with their experiences, and to correct any errors [89]. The point of member checking is to enhance trustworthiness, to avoid misrepresentation of participants' views and to empower participants as active role players [90].

Member checking is conducted at different stages in the research process. Some researchers send transcripts out to participants for them to review, which is what we're exploring here in this section. (In the next section on data analysis, we'll discuss sending research findings, such as themes, to participants for their feedback as this is the second main form of member checking). The third involves sending a draft copy of the research report, which is uncommon in music therapy literature mentioning reflexivity, although this is what I did for this book so the interviewees could check how I'd integrated their statements into my argument. (Only one asked for a quote to be slightly adjusted as their thinking had slightly changed since the interview and I made this change.) The choice about when to engage in member checking should be made flexibly in light of the duration of the project, cycles of data collection, and challenges in analysis.

In Bingham's [88] study, she gave participants the opportunity to check the content of the transcripts and to comment on them. Two of her four participants provided minor edits to their interview transcripts. In our interview, Bingham also explained how she returned to participants with some follow-up questions to ensure that she was crystal clear about the meaning of their answers: "I just didn't want to misrepresent them in any way or misquote them". Lincoln and Guba [31] claimed that member checking is the most important technique for establishing credibility and authenticity. Much of our research as music therapists is conducted with people who may not find reading transcripts accessible, though, which means that in our field, it can't be *the* pillar of credibility, even while we may value it when appropriate.

Details about how member checking is done are quite rare in music therapy literature (perhaps due to the limitations on manuscript length in academic journals) and descriptions of how member checks actually resulted in any changes being made are also hard to find. While the goal is to check that the interview transcripts are accurate, the time that has lapsed since the participant gave the interview, the accuracy of their recall, a desire to please the researcher, or even their mood during the interview compared to while reviewing the transcript all call into question the idea of assessing the accuracy of the words on the page of the transcript [91].

Even though a researcher may have good intentions in sending the transcriptions back to participants for them to read and check, participants' responses might include indifference and even embarrassment or shame. They may feel more vulnerable than they did in the initial interview, seeing their words presented back to them on the page. While reading through a transcription can be therapeutic for a participant, it can also be distressing [91]. Silverman [72] carefully noted how, as a researcher, he needed to balance honouring participants and their mental health with verifying his results through member checking.

Participants may notice poor grammar, pauses or fillers in speech and feel that they were inarticulate [92]. (As a researcher, I also have moments of wishing I had asked a question differently or articulated myself better when reviewing transcripts). Participants might not feel confident to give feedback because of the perceived expertise of the researcher or they may feel uncomfortable giving negative feedback. In a situation where experts are being interviewed, they could feel pressured to come across in a polished, informed, and insightful way. Participants might simply feel disinterested in continuing their engagement with the research project and response rates may be low (in which case it would be problematic to state that member checking contributed to credibility). It could also be difficult to locate participants. Member checking can be inconveniently time-consuming for participants [93]. Some groups are already overburdened.

Sometimes participants' perspectives change over time. If our quest is to stand back and let participants' voices be heard as far as possible, we need to acknowledge that an interview is merely a snapshot in time and people are dynamic and evolving [90]. These challenges need to be dealt with transparently. When participants do give feedback, researchers then need to find ways to include, work with and represent the changes that the participants added to the transcriptions as their views changed. This is certainly not an easy task.

Triangulation

To gain a broader, fuller or more secure [94] understanding of a phenomenon, reducing the risk of bias and overcoming the limitations of a singular method, triangulation can be helpful. This concept refers in a general way to the use of multiple methods. It's been employed in a narrower sense to refer to using a second method to check the findings generated by an initial method. Triangulation can also include interviewing multiple witnesses of an event who played different roles in it, using a number of theoretical perspectives, investigators, or analysis techniques. Some researchers now consider that when multiple methods are used, these can include qualitative and quantitative approaches. Originally, in Norman Denzin's [95] view, triangulation only involved multiple qualitative methods.

In music therapy literature, authors have combined methods such as semi-structured interviews and participant observation of music therapy sessions [96], interviews and song-writing activities [45], and focus groups and interviews [58]. In their study on music therapy and agitation in dementia, Kristiansen et al. [76] used recordings of conversations from fortnightly group meetings, semi-structured interviews with the music therapist and the nurse and patient record notes. Gro Trondalen and Finn Skårderud [97] identified significant moments from session recordings through triangulating different people's perspectives. A researcher, a music therapist (who was not the therapist in the sessions) and the music therapist who facilitated the sessions listened to the music. Each indicated when something meaningful was happening and the moments when all three indicated this were identified as significant. Gitta Strehlow and Reinhard Lindner [62] used triangulation by integrating experts' reflections on the researcher's interpretations. In research with children specifically, Guro Klyve and Randi Rolvsjord [96] argued that it's important to combine methods to strengthen one's understanding.

Analysing Rigorously

During data analysis, tensions can arise between bracketing ideas and using them as insight, as well as between openness and critical thinking. In my interview with Moshe Bensimon, he explained:

> ...sometimes when I analyse the data, some theory is in my head, I might get stuck with it and continue analysing the data so the glove fits the hand at the end. I'm thinking about the next stage: I want the theory and the discussion to be good and strong and convince the readers and the editor about the results...I have to be very aware and keep myself from fixating on a certain theory and continuing analysing the data in order to fit the theory. And it might not fit. And this may be the innovation.

Some general techniques that music therapy researchers use when seeking to be reflexive in their data analysis procedures include repeated reading of textual data [98] and repeated viewing of video excerpts to get to know the data as well as they can. Collaborative analysis with participants can take place as the researcher openly discusses what they interpreted from data gathered in the previous week's session [78]. Researchers focus on the explicit content of the data [25, 43]; and some separate transcriptions into subjective and objective observations [83]. Specific forms of analysis that appear within this quest (bearing in mind that most were qualitative studies) include phenomenological methods [30]; systematic text condensation [82]; and thematic analysis [25, 43, 48, 60, 74, 99]. A combination of constant comparison and narrative description was also used [99].

Team discussions can take place among the researchers to establish consensus [45]. (We'll discuss the value of working in research teams further in a moment). Analysis can be conducted independently and then corroborated between researchers to verify the findings [48]. Audit trails are also used [100].

Asking Participants to Check the Researcher's Interpretations

Earlier, we discussed member checking in the form of sending transcriptions to participants and asking for their feedback. Another variant of member checking involves asking for participants' feedback on the accuracy of the analysis. They are asked to read through the interpretation to see whether any researcher bias or misinterpretation is visible and whether their experiences have been presented authentically, whether the findings "ring true", and if anything is missing [30, 90]. The participants' alternative viewpoints can help the researcher detect their own bias [61]. (Some studies use member checking at multiple points, both in relation to the interview transcripts and then in relation to the analysis [43].)

In Silverman's [101] study on change mechanisms in patient-preferred live music, he completed the analysis and then asked participants to review and verify his findings. They reported being able to relate to each subtheme and felt that their experiences and opinions were accurately reflected. While some authors (such as Creswell [102]) argued that member checking is best done with polished findings rather than transcripts, others highlight the challenges that researchers face when asking participants to give feedback on findings. Interpreted findings may be complex and difficult to understand [91]. While participants in Silverman's [101] study mentioned above didn't encounter this as a problem, participants in other studies may struggle with checking findings as they are no longer validating their own words; they're reviewing interpretations synthesised from data gathered from multiple participants. Participants may no longer clearly see their experiences in the finalised results. From a phenomenological perspective, participants could be seen to describe their experiences from the perspective of the "natural attitude" whilst researchers are trying to employ the phenomenological attitude (by bracketing). As a result, participants and researchers may be seeing the phenomenon differently [56].

The iterative process of interpretation in qualitative analysis results in second- and third-order meaning constructs that are decontextualised, abstracted, and are at a greater distance from the original data. This could also be particularly problematic when the topic of study relates to unconscious processes or cultural dynamics. Interestingly, in a study with women with breast cancer on their experiences of music therapy by Stephanie Thompson et al. [30], participants initially verified the distilled essence of their own individual experiences rather than the essence of the experience that was identified across all the participants' data.

Participants may reject findings that disagree with their personal positions (e.g., that highlight the limitations of an intervention that they were highly invested in). However, due to power differences between researchers and participants, they might defer to the researcher's expertise, even if their own perspectives differ. The researcher is placed in a position of epistemic power as one who has spoken to many people about this topic. While researchers may view the use of member checking as giving the participants more power to assert the accuracy of views, some participants experience having greater power in interviews as they express their opinions and less power when they read through how the researcher controlled the interpretation of the data [92].

The researcher's interpretations may feel intrusive, demeaning, or even insulting to participants [103]. If they experience discomfort with the researcher's interpretations of them, could it be that the researcher's interpretation is wrong, or is the participant resistant to the researcher's correct interpretation and articulation…and how is that decision made?

Challenges can also emerge as the researcher attempts to integrate the participants' feedback from member checking into the findings [89]. How should these comments be weighed? How should divergent perspectives from participants be incorporated? Should one delete comments that the participants wish to be removed even if valuable data is lost? Who "owns" the data? If the researcher merely mentions that not all participants agreed with all aspects of the findings then the purpose of member checking becomes unclear [92]. There are no definitive answers to these questions and, as researchers, we need to be careful and transparent about how we deal with these matters. These complexities may also justifiably serve as reasons not to use member checking.

An option is to conduct an additional interview or focus group (or multiple ones if participants are able and willing) to discuss the findings and glean feedback. Courtney McKim [93, p. 46] proposed brief (10–15 minute) interviews with participants. Questions here can include the following:

1. After reading through the findings, what are your general thoughts?
2. How accurately do you feel the findings captured your thoughts/experiences?
3. What could be added to the findings to capture your experiences better?
4. If there is anything you would like removed, what would that be and why?

While this additional interview process can be seen as an ideal, in reality participants may not have the time to engage in this way. In music therapy studies, member checking may not be appropriate or helpful if participants do not communicate with words. This again leaves us with more questions than answers regarding how to accomplish the goal of presenting findings that most authentically convey participants' experiences. Careful and transparent consideration and ethics decision making is essential.

The Value of Working with a Research Team

As a strategy to enhance reflexivity, it can be immensely valuable to work in a team. When we engage in a solo project to attempt to ensure that we're stepping aside to allow a phenomenon to present itself most clearly, we may miss many of our own blind spots. Others can assist us greatly as they hold up a mirror for us, ask challenging questions, critique our findings, and add their insights. Engaging in bracketing interviews with a colleague, supervisor, or research associate can serve as an interface between the researcher and the data, to help bring awareness to biases and preconceptions. Agreements about the confidentiality of the information shared in these interviews are made in advance [46]. Edmund Husserl [104, p. 163] wrote, "in living with one another each one can take part in the life of the others. In this communalisation there constantly occurs an alteration of validity through reciprocal correction." Through such corrections, we can move towards greater accuracy and fullness in our layers of meaning.

Many music therapy researchers use peer debriefing to elicit critique regarding the accuracy of their findings and generate consensus. In a study by Shulamit Epstein et al. [40], music therapy colleagues who had experience working in the study setting reviewed the same interview transcripts and memos. They met with the researcher to share their thoughts about what the participants were communicating. The researcher then offered their own findings so the colleagues could give further feedback. When there are multiple authors, the first sometimes engages in peer debriefing with the others [43, 48]. Experts can be called on (who are specialists in analysis [35, 75], methodology [101], and the techniques being studied [79]). In my interview with Moshe Bensimon, he highlighted that one may need funding to engage with peer debriefing to show appropriate value and remuneration for colleagues' time. However, this can be a limitation for researchers working in resource-scare contexts.

Results can be presented to the music therapist who conducted the sessions that were facilitated as part of the study to gain further perspectives and clarify the themes [72]. When research is conducted by a postgraduate student, other students can be consulted for constructive feedback regarding the trustworthiness of the findings [27]. Peer debriefing can take place during postgraduate research seminars [30].

Writing Up the Manuscript

In the final stage, we seek to reveal a phenomenon on the page as we write up our findings. The process of bracketing is still in play as we remain aware of how our preconceptions can influence how we present these findings and, in fact, how we write up the entire manuscript. What do we foreground and what do we place in the background or leave out altogether? In qualitative research, what voices do we highlight, how do we highlight them, and how do these voices relate to our own? How do we organise our themes, and select quotations to substantiate our findings? What context do we include, which theories do we use to frame the paper, and how do we use them? In quantitative research, what do we highlight from the data as being most important and how do we discuss what the findings mean?

What writing style do we choose to use? How formulaic or innovative do we want to be, or feel we are allowed to be? Do we write in the first or third person? For example, we may elect to use the third person to convey a sense of objectivity (particularly in the quest we are covering in this chapter). We may wish to present ourselves clearly in the text. For example, in my interview with Martina Bingham, a voice specialist examining therapeutic singing in music therapy, she explained,

> It was always very important to me to be transparent about who I am. You know, I wasn't trying to sort of sneakily pretend that I knew more about music therapy than I did. I came in very green about the discipline. And I think, I actually think that that sort of fresh perspective gave something slightly different to the data analysis too, because I was learning as I went and I noticed things that are commonplace for music therapists, right? So, I think that that's helpful when I'm trying to talk to other voice teachers and other people in our parallel disciplines about what music therapy students are experiencing and what music therapists are doing in practice. So, mostly I wanted to be honest and transparent. That was very important because I felt like I wanted to make sure that I had a firm place in the research but that I wasn't overstepping. So that I can be very clear about why I'm here, why I'm in the room. And then I can speak confidently about what I actually do know.

A key component of writing up in our current quest is to show how the findings really are grounded in the data, not our own personal subjective opinion. This is, in essence, what Sentinel Reflexivity is all about. Researchers display the rigour of their methodological process, substantiate the logic of their analysis, and argue for trustworthiness. After doing so, qualitative researchers in particular tend to use phrases such as data analysis "yielded" themes; themes "emerged"; themes were "identified"; "found"; "extracted"; "analysis revealed that…"; and authors describe how they represented the "essence" of the "phenomenon". The use of this kind of language is earned through engaging in the reflexive steps outlined in this chapter.

An Accessible Summary

Sentinel Reflexivity involves consciously recognising and examining how our biases, assumptions, and preconceived notions can shape our research. Our task is to recognise these influences and try to set them aside as much as possible so that we can allow the research phenomenon to reveal itself for what it truly is. Think of yourself as a "sentinel" or watchful guard, continuously looking out for ways your own perspective could interfere with understanding your research topic objectively. This approach is particularly important when you aim to present accurate, unbiased findings about a phenomenon.

To notice what may be getting in the way of clearly seeing what you're studying, you need self-awareness. In music therapy research, factors that can influence our interpretations include past experiences and professional background, identity, privilege, worldview, beliefs, preconceived assumptions, and dual roles such as being both researcher and therapist. We can identify these potential influences through careful self-reflection in the form of journaling, engaging in supervision, and peer discussions.

Bias refers to inclinations or prejudices that systematically distort our perceptions and interpretations. Humans naturally develop mental shortcuts to process complex information quickly, but these can lead to less accurate assessments. We struggle to recognise our own blind spots. However, when we're motivated to reduce bias and are made aware of it, we can learn to adjust our responses.

Bracketing is a technique that involves consciously setting aside our natural, everyday assumptions to attend to a phenomenon freshly. This isn't a one-time event but an ongoing process throughout the research. It takes intellectual bravery and humility to acknowledge that we don't understand a phenomenon completely. As researchers, we need to explain how and where bracketing took place and demonstrate our consistent commitment to this process.

Research methods that help us minimise our own influence include prolonged observation to truly get to know participants, semi-structured interviews with open-ended questions, member checking where participants verify transcripts and interpretations, triangulation using multiple methods or perspectives, and working in research teams for

(*continued*)

(continued)

collaborative analysis. During data collection and analysis, we can use methods that allow participants' voices to be heard clearly, read or view data repeatedly, use lengthy data excerpts to avoid selective presentation, focus on explicit content rather than over-interpreting, collaborate with participants in analysis where appropriate, distinguish clearly between interpretation and description, and maintain audit trails of our decision-making processes. We need to take great care when we function as both the researcher and music therapist in the same study. Strategies for managing this dual relationship include recruiting participants through third parties, encouraging honesty and emphasising participants' freedom to speak openly, and checking interpretations with participants. When we present findings, we need to remain aware of how our preconceptions might influence what we place in the foreground or background.

Sentinel Reflexivity ultimately aims to enhance trustworthiness by demonstrating that researchers have made their best attempt to step aside and let the phenomenon speak for itself. Complete objectivity may be impossible, however, in this approach, researchers use rigorous effort to minimise personal influence and present findings that accurately represent the research phenomenon.

References

1. Hammersley M, Gomm R. Bias in social research. Sociological Research Online [Internet]. 1997;2(1). Available from: http://www.socresonline.org.uk/2/1/2.html.
2. Erickson F. A history of qualitative inquiry in social and educational research. In: Denzin N, Lincoln Y, editors. The SAGE handbook of qualitative research. 5th ed. Thousand Oaks, CA: Sage; 2018. p. 87–141.
3. Levers M. Philosophical paradigms, grounded theory, and perspectives on emergence. SAGE Open. 2013;3(4):2158244013517243.
4. Besse C. Gender aware music therapy: an interpretative phenomenological analysis. Music Ther Perspect. 2021;39(2):152–61.
5. Oxford English Dictionary [Internet]. Oxford: Oxford University Press; [cited 2024 Apr 10]. Available from: http://www.oxforddictionaries.com.

6. Haselton M, Nettle D, Murray D. The evolution of cognitive bias. In: Buss D, editor. The handbook of evolutionary psychology. 2nd ed. Hoboken, NJ: Wiley; 2016. p. 968–1006.
7. Macaskie J, Lees J, Freshwater D. Talking about talking: interpersonal process recall as an intersubjective approach to research. Psychodyn Pract. 2015;21(3):226–40.
8. Brown C. Unravelling bias. Dallas, TX: BenBella Books; 2021.
9. Johnson G. The psychology of bias: from data to theory. In: Beeghly E, Madva A, editors. An introduction to implicit bias. New York: Routledge; 2020. p. 20–40.
10. Myers D, Twenge J. Exploring social psychology. 8th ed. New York: McGraw Hill Education; 2018.
11. Perry SP, Murphy MC, Dovidio JF. Modern prejudice: subtle, but unconscious? The role of bias awareness in Whites' perceptions of personal and others' biases. J Exp Soc Psychol. 2015;61:64–78.
12. Devine P, Forscher PS, Austin AJ, Cox WT. Long-term reduction in implicit race bias: a prejudice habit-breaking intervention. J Exp Soc Psychol. 2012;48(6):1267–78.
13. Calanchini J, Gonsalkorale K, Sherman JW, Klauer KC. Counter-prejudicial training reduces activation of biased associations and enhances response monitoring. Eur J Soc Psychol. 2013;43(5):321–5.
14. Fitzgerald C, Martin A, Berner D, Hurst S. Interventions designed to reduce implicit prejudices and implicit stereotypes in real-world contexts: a systematic review. BMC Psychol. 2019;7:29. Available from: https://doi.org/10.1186/s40359-019-0299-7
15. Hopthrow T, Hooper N, Mahmood L, Meier BP, Weger U. Mindfulness reduces the correspondence bias. Q J Exp Psychol. 2017;70(3):351–60.
16. Huntsinger JR, Sinclair S, Clore GL. Affective regulation of implicitly measured stereotypes and attitudes: automatic and controlled processes. J Exp Soc Psychol. 2009;45(3):560–6.
17. Dovidio JF, Gaertner SL. Reducing prejudice: combating intergroup biases. Curr Dir Psychol Sci. 1999;8(4):101–5.
18. Zhu B. What steps can be taken to reduce unconscious bias in the workplace. Academic Journal of Management and Social Sciences. 2023;5(1):200–2.
19. Hall NR, Crisp RJ, Suen M. Reducing implicit prejudice by blurring intergroup boundaries. Basic Appl Soc Psychol. 2009;31(3):244–54.
20. Vitriol JA, Moskowitz GB. Reducing defensive responding to implicit bias feedback: on the role of perceived moral threat and efficacy to change. J Exp Soc Psychol. 2021;96:104165.
21. Okonofua JA, Harris LT, Walton GM. Sidelining bias: a situationist approach to reduce the consequences of bias in real-world contexts. Curr Dir Psychol Sci. 2022;31(5):395–404.

22. Ogden R. Bias. In: Given L, editor. The SAGE encyclopedia of qualitative research methods. Thousand Oaks, CA: Sage; 2008. p. 60–1.
23. Silverman MJ. Music therapy and therapeutic alliance in adult mental health: a qualitative investigation. J Music Ther. 2019;56(1):90–116.
24. Venkatarangam S. Participants' experiences of a receptive music therapy intervention that incorporates raga: an interpretative phenomenological analysis. Arts Psychother. 2021;73:101762.
25. Silverman MJ, Bibb J. Acute care mental health workers' assumptions and expectations of music therapy: a qualitative investigation. Arts Psychother. 2018;59:94–100.
26. Bibb J, Howden A, McFerran KS. Exploring the experiences of professional practice for Australian-based registered music therapists. Aust J Music Ther. 2021;32(2):79–98.
27. Roberts M, McFerran K. A mixed methods analysis of songs written by bereaved preadolescents in individual music therapy. J Music Ther. 2013;50(1):25–52.
28. Riabzev A, Bensimon M. A qualitative investigation of self-compassion in music therapy group voicework with women coping with incest. J Music Ther. 2023;60(4):463–92.
29. Reid A, Nicolla SK. Exploring music therapists' experiences with and perceptions about copyrighted music: a thematic analysis. J Music Ther. 2022;59(3):269–306.
30. Thompson S, Grocke D, Dileo C. The use of group descriptive phenomenology within a mixed methods study to understand the experience of music therapy for women with breast cancer. Nord J Music Ther. 2017;26(4):320–37.
31. Lincoln YS, Guba EG. Naturalistic inquiry. 1st ed. Newbury Park, CA: Sage Publications; 1985.
32. Lincoln YS, Guba EG. RSVP: we are pleased to accept your invitation. Eval Pract. 1994;15(2):179–92.
33. Rallis SF, Rossman GB. Ethics and trustworthiness. In: Heigham J, Croker RA, editors. Qualitative research in applied linguistics: a practical introduction. London: Palgrave Macmillan; 2009. p. 263–87.
34. Eurich T. Insight. New York: Crown Business; 2017.
35. Bensimon M. Integration of trauma in music therapy: a qualitative study. Psychol Trauma Theory Res Pract Policy. 2022;14(3):367–74.
36. Campbell KS. A qualitative exploration of music therapist beliefs, education, and uses of hip hop in clinical practice. Music Ther Perspect 2023;41(1).
37. Muralidharan A, Silverman MJ. An exploratory thematic analysis of factors that influence sleep in music therapy undergraduate students. Music Ther Perspect. 2023;41(1).

38. Letulė N, Ala-Ruona E, Erkkilä J. Professional freedom: a grounded theory on the use of music analysis in psychodynamic music therapy. Nord J Music Ther. 2018;27(5):448–66.
39. Baker FA, Stretton-Smith PA. Group therapeutic songwriting and dementia: exploring the perspectives of participants through interpretative phenomenological analysis. Music Ther Perspect. 2018;36(1):50–66.
40. Epstein S, Elefant C, Ghetti C. Israeli parents' lived experiences of music therapy with their preterm infants post-hospitalization. J Music Ther. 2022;59(3):239–68.
41. Gottfried T, Elefant C, Gold C. Music-oriented parent counseling to promote improvement in level of parental stress, quality of life and the use of music in everyday life among parents of children with autism: a mixed-methods randomized controlled study. Nord J Music Ther. 2023;32(5):397–422.
42. Lindblad K. "No, I guess it's kind of sensitive"- Communication patterns in a music listening group with older men. Nord J Music Ther. 2021;30(5):424–39.
43. West R, Furman A, Silverman MJ. Individualized education program team members' perceptions of music therapy: an interpretivist investigation. J Music Ther. 2021;58(4):437–62.
44. Economos AD. Music therapy when death is imminent: a phenomenological inquiry. J Music Ther. 2018;55(3):309–39.
45. Hogan-Gibbons C, Short AE, Isobel S. Mental health inpatient experiences of songwriting: a qualitative study. Aust J Music Ther. 2020;31:29–44.
46. Gearing RE. Bracketing in research: a typology. Qual Health Res. 2004;14(10):1429–52.
47. Lauw E. When home feels familiar but yet so foreign—the professional readjustment experiences of returning internationally-trained Singaporean music therapists. Music Ther Perspect. 2017;35(2):239–46.
48. Lee S, O'Neill D, Moss H. Dementia-inclusive group-singing online during COVID-19: a qualitative exploration. Nord J Music Ther. 2021;30(5):440–58.
49. Biedka S. Music therapists' experiences of therapeutic relationships with clients with marginalized gender identities and sexual orientations. Music Ther Perspect. 2022;40(2):152–63.
50. Giorgi A. The theory, practice, and evaluation of the phenomenological method as a qualitative research. J Phenomenol Psychol. 1997;28(2):235–60.
51. Tufford L, Newman P. Bracketing in qualitative research. Qual Soc Work. 2012;11(1):80–96.
52. Hare W. Helping open-mindedness flourish. J Though. 2011;46(1–2):9–20.
53. Taylor RM. Open-mindedness: an epistemic virtue motivated by love of truth and understanding. Philosophy of Education. 2013;197–205.

54. Moustakas C. Phenomenological research methods. Thousand Oaks, CA: Sage; 1994.
55. Holloway I, Wheeler S. Qualitative research in nursing and healthcare. 3rd ed. Oxford: Wiley-Blackwell; 2010.
56. Finlay L. Phenomenology for therapists: researching the lived world. Chichester: John Wiley & Sons; 2011.
57. Annesley L, Curtis-Tyler K, McKeown E. Parents' perspectives on their child's music therapy: a qualitative study. J Music Ther. 2020;57(1):91–119.
58. McCaffrey T, Higgins P, Monahan C, Moloney S, Nelligan S, Clancy A, et al. Exploring the role and impact of group songwriting with multiple stakeholders in recovery-oriented mental health services. Nord J Music Ther. 2021;30(1):41–60.
59. Dos Santos A. Empathy and aggression in group music therapy with teenagers: a descriptive phenomenological study. Music Ther Perspect. 2019;37(1):14–27.
60. Densley B, Andrews K. How participation in group singing in the community impacts on emotional wellbeing: a qualitative study on the perspectives of group singing participants. Aust J Music Ther. 2021;32:1–18.
61. Short H. Say what you say (Eminem): managing verbal boundaries when using rap in music therapy, a qualitative study. Voices: A World Forum for Music Therapy [Internet]. 2013 Jan;13(1). Available from: https://voices.no/index.php/voices/article/view/668.
62. Strehlow G, Lindner R. Music therapy interaction patterns in relation to borderline personality disorder (BPD) patients. Nord J Music Ther. 2016;25(2):134–58.
63. Smith J, Noble H. Bias in research. Evidence-Based Nursing. 2014;17(4):100–1.
64. Nelson LD, Simmons JP, Simonsohn U. Psychology's renaissance. Annu Rev Psychol. 2018;69:511–34.
65. Reis D, Friese M. The myriad forms of p-hacking. In: Avoiding questionable research practices in applied psychology. Cham: Springer International Publishing; 2022. p. 101–21.
66. Armijo-Olivo S, Oliveira-Souza A, Mohamad N, Carletti E, Fuentes J, Ballenberger N. Selection, confounding, and attrition biases in randomized controlled trials of rehabilitation interventions. Am J Phys Med Rehabil. 2022;101(11):1042–55.
67. Markham JL, Richardson T, Stephens JR, Gay JC, Hall M. Essential concepts for reducing bias in observational studies. Hospital Pediatric. 2023;13(8).
68. Hartman JM, Forsen JW, Wallace MS, Neely JG. Tutorials in clinical research: part IV: recognizing and controlling bias. Laryngoscope. 2002;112(1):23–31.

69. Burghardt G, Bartmess-Levasseur J, Browning S, Morrison K, Stec C, Zachau C, et al. Perspectives—Minimizing observer bias in behavioral studies: a review and recommendations. Ethology. 2012;118(6):511–7.
70. Malone H, Nicholl H, Tracey C. Awareness and minimisation of systematic bias in research. Br J Nurs. 2014;23(5):279–82.
71. Ramírez-Santana M. Limitations and biases in cohort studies. In: Cohort studies in health sciences [Internet]. IntechOpen; 2018 [cited 2024 Jul 18]. Available from: https://doi.org/10.5772/INTECHOPEN.74324.
72. Silverman MJ. Songwriting, professional studio recording, and a CD release party: interviews with two adults with mental health conditions. Arts Psychother. 2022;80:101915.
73. McMahon K, Baker FA, Stretton-Smith P, Clark IN. Using group therapeutic songwriting to support the dyadic relationship between people living with dementia and their family caregivers: perspectives from music therapists. Aust J Music Ther. 2021;32(2):57–78.
74. Reid A, Kresovich A. Copyright as a barrier to music therapy telehealth interventions: qualitative interview study. JMIR Format Resear. 2022;6(3).
75. Bensimon M. Perceptions of music therapists regarding their work with children living under continuous war threat: experiential reframing of trauma through songs. Nord J Music Ther. 2020;29(4):300–16.
76. Kristiansen FA, Stige B, Helle-Valle A. Characteristics of music therapy with beneficial impacts on agitation in dementia. Voices: A World Forum for Music Therapy [Internet]. 2023 Jul;23(2). Available from: https://voices.no/index.php/voices/article/view/3463.
77. Arns B, Thompson GA. Music therapy teaming and learning: how transdisciplinary experience shapes practice in a specialist school for students with autism. Aust J Music Ther. 2019;30:31–52.
78. Hense C. Scaffolding young people's journey from mental health services into everyday social music making. Voices: A World Forum for Music Therapy [Internet]. 2019 Feb;19(1). Available from: https://voices.no/index.php/voices/article/view/2732.
79. Wlodarczyk N. "It's my time": older adults' experiences and perceived benefits of participation in an intergenerational rock band. Music Ther Perspect. 2020;38(2):187–94.
80. Selle EW, Silverman MJ. Cardiovascular patients' perceptions of music therapy in the form of patient-preferred live music: exploring service user experiences. Nord J Music Ther. 2020;29(1):57–74.
81. Enge KEA, Stige B. Musical pathways to the peer community: a collective case study of refugee children's use of music therapy. Nord J Music Ther. 2022;31(1):7–24.
82. Oedegaard CH, Engebretsen IMS, Veseth M, Blindheim A, Stige B. Health care workers' perspectives on the challenges and possibilities of music therapy

within medication-free treatment services. Nord J Music Ther. 2023;32(3):241–59.
83. Jakubiak D. Hermeneutic inquiry on musical gestures in a music therapy context/Recherche herméneutique sur le geste musical dans un contexte musicothérapeutique. Canadian Journal of Music Therapy. 2014;20(2):134–59.
84. Gnambs T, Kaspar K. Disclosure of sensitive behaviors across self-administered survey modes: a meta-analysis. Behav Res Methods. 2015;47(4):1237–59.
85. Tourangeau R, Yan T. Sensitive questions in surveys. Psychol Bull. 2007;133(5):859–83.
86. Van de Mortel TF. Faking it: social desirability response bias in self-report research. Aust J Adv Nurs. 2008;25(4):40–8.
87. Podsakoff PM, MacKenzie SB, Lee JY, Podsakoff NP. Common method biases in behavioral research: a critical review of the literature and recommended remedies. J Appl Psychol. 2003;88(5):879–903.
88. Bingham MC. Defining the therapeutic singing voice: an analysis of four music therapists' clinical work. Music Ther Perspect. 2019;37(2):176–86.
89. Kornbluh M. Combatting challenges to establishing trustworthiness in qualitative research. Qual Res Psychol. 2015;12(4):397–414.
90. Goldblatt H, Karnieli-Miller O, Neumann M. Sharing qualitative research findings with participants: study experiences of methodological and ethical dilemmas. Patient Educ Couns. 2011;82(3):389–95.
91. Birt L, Scott S, Cavers D, Campbell C, Walter F. Member checking: a tool to enhance trustworthiness or merely a nod to validation? Qual Health Res. 2016;26(13):1802–11.
92. Motulsky SL. Is member checking the gold standard of quality in qualitative research? Qual Psychol. 2021;8(3):389–406.
93. McKim C. Meaningful member-checking: a structured approach to member-checking. American Journal of Qualitative Research. 2023;7(2):41–52.
94. Maxwell JA. Collecting qualitative data: a realist approach. In: Flick U, editor. The SAGE handbook of qualitative data collection. Thousand Oaks, CA: Sage; 2018. p. 19–32.
95. Denzin NK. The research act. Chicago, IL: Aldine; 1970.
96. Klyve GP, Rolvsjord R. Moments of fun: narratives of children's experiences of music therapy in mental health care. Nord J Music Ther. 2022;31(4):361–81.
97. Trondalen G, Skårderud F. Playing with affects: ... and the importance of "affect attunement". Nord J Music Ther. 2007;16(2):100–11.
98. Beer LE. From embedded to embodied: including music in arts-based music therapy research. Music Ther Perspect. 2016;34(1):33–40.
99. Ghetti CM, Vederhus BJ, Gaden TS, Brenner AK, Bieleninik Ł, Kvestad I, et al. Longitudinal study of music therapy's effectiveness for premature

infants and their caregivers (LongSTEP): feasibility study with a Norwegian cohort. J Music Ther. 2021;58(2):201–40.
100. O'Callaghan C, Barry P. Music therapists' practice-based research in cancer and palliative care: creative methods and situated findings. Voices: A World Forum for Music Therapy [Internet]. 2009;9(3). Available from: https://voices.no/index.php/voices/article/view/257.
101. Silverman MJ. Change mechanisms in patient-preferred live music: an exploratory interpretivist study. J Music Ther. 2021;58(3):310–44.
102. Creswell JW. Research design: qualitative, quantitative, and mixed methods approaches. Thousand Oaks, CA: Sage; 2009.
103. Josselson R. The hermeneutics of faith and the hermeneutics of suspicion. Narrat Inq. 2004;14(1):1–28.
104. Husserl E. The crisis of European sciences and transcendental phenomenology. Evanston, IL: Northwestern University Press; 1970. Cited in: Moustakas C. Phenomenological research methods. Thousand Oaks, CA: Sage; 2010.

CHAPTER 4

Lens Reflexivity

In Carolyn Kenny's [1, p. 132] words, "We each view the world through a different set of glasses, fashioned uniquely by who we are." As we step into Lens Reflexivity, we maintain the belief in an independent reality while contending that we always see through clouded lenses. Our task here is to actively and critically explore, monitor, report on, and make informed decisions *about* how these lenses influence us and our research. Our participants have lenses too. In my interview with Claire Ghetti, she explained reflexivity as

> the researcher's awareness that they come to the research with various experiences, background and views that inform what they're seeing and how they're seeing what they're choosing to look at. And those that they are either researching with or researching upon have similar frames as well that are influencing them. And so the process of the research then becomes this interaction between the one (or several people) who are creating the knowledge and the concepts, interactions, events or things that are being studied. I think there are different layers that one can think about. But maybe the most important thing is to realise that it's happening.

Deliberately acknowledging and exploring our active participation in creating and shaping knowledge in our study *through employing our subjective perspectives with awareness* and responding to these insights *by being transparent, as well as challenging these perspectives and related actions when necessary.*

A. dos Santos, *Reflexive Research in Music Therapy*,
https://doi.org/10.1007/978-3-032-02033-8_4

In a research study, simply mentioning our perspectives and background in passing before moving along with our argument can be a hollow gesture that avoids accountability. As a result, our research can fail to challenge and transform us or others [2]. It's also insufficient to state *that* our experiences, perspectives, ideological commitments, relationships, and motivations impact our study, even if we do so in detail. In Lens Reflexivity we're tasked with examining and exploring *what* may be influential, *why* it may be influential and *how* this influence is taking place. We seek to make the meaning-making process explicit. "Vulnerable reflexivity" [3, p. 3] involves critically and genuinely considering how our cultural frameworks, assumptions, beliefs, values, and perspectives affect our experience and influence our storytelling. In my interview with Anthony Meadows, he described reflexivity as involving a dialogue between a phenomenon and what you think it means. We need to start by getting comfortable with not knowing what something is, instead of quickly jumping into categorising too fast. He used the phrase "deepening into the phenomenon" and acknowledged that the process is complex and multi-layered.

In our interview where we discussed his co-authored study [4] on core themes in music therapy clinical improvisation, Meadows explained that he is

> …reluctant to make generalisations about what something is. The phenomenon teaches me and so I have to really be open to that. There's this kind of paradox where you go in with a concept of something and then the phenomenon reveals itself to you and to some degree, you have to let go of what you brought in, in order to learn from what the phenomenon is. That's all reflexivity to me; that's all reflexive practice as a researcher. You sit with it, you grapple with it, you try to make sense of it, and in the process of doing that something comes from that. And for me it's becoming increasingly something that I never expected. If it's fait complete before you even start, that's problematic for me. That's not a discovery process.

You might be wondering whether this is a description of Sentinel Reflexivity as we discussed in the previous chapter, but Meadows emphasised how findings are constructions. He reflected on a study about musicianship that he and colleagues worked on:

> We gathered all this data and we wondered: How do we make sense of this? And so what that does for me is that it blows the space…it blows all of my ideas about what I think it is. Once it's deconstructed, *then* you can really

> begin to put it together as it is, or as you think it is. It's not the truth, it's just my construction of it. And these are just different ways of representing phenomena. The way I can make sense of a phenomenon is to construct it. I think to me constructing is a way of communicating its meaning to somebody else. It's like building Legos, but you don't have the little pages where you follow the directions. You've got a bunch of Legos and then you put them together: "Professional artistry", "performing self"—they're constructs. So that's a choice I think you have to make as a researcher: how do you construct the data? You always have a set of constructs that you're operating on a phenomenon. You can't not. Or else you don't have a perspective. But, I always have to really check my perspective in relation to the phenomenon and to make sure that I'm not limiting the phenomenon because of the limitations of my perspective. And to me that's being reflexive.

Music therapy researchers who explore the implications of their perspectives and constructions recognise that their experience is filtered through their own lenses during many, if not all, phases of the research process [5–11]. Gro Trondalen described reflexivity in our interview as rethinking, re-examining, and reliving phenomena while reflecting on personal and professional assumptions, interpretations, biases, and philosophical bases. In our conversation, Tríona McCaffrey described reflexivity as holding a mirror up to our reactions, engagement, and responses to the research. It involves reflecting on the inquiry, what has happened on the research journey, and how it sits with you as the researcher. Tríona emphasised the importance of sharing this reflection with readers as a way of striving for transparency in the research process, while acknowledging that complete transparency may be unattainable.

Balancing (Rather Than Fully Bracketing)

We discussed the concept of bracketing in the previous chapter. While acknowledging that completely setting aside all our preconceived ideas, past experiences, motivations and perspectives is unachievable, we still sought to bracket these as much as possible to be as freshly present with what and who we're studying. Early notions of bracketing suggested setting aside preconceptions entirely. However, contemporary scholars concur that this is neither possible nor desirable [12–14]. Heidegger [13] contended that preunderstandings can't be set aside, as humans are inextricably situated within historical and cultural contexts [15]. Maurice Merleau-Ponty [16, p., xiii] claimed that breaking contact with the world isn't necessary; rather, we should step back enough to "slacken the intentional threads that attach us to the world." In relation to qualitative research, Sarah Tracy [17, p. 15] argued that good researchers "think carefully about how they, personally, will experience research in a certain context, both *despite of* and *because of* who they are."

A researcher using Lens Reflexivity might say: "I'm trying to understand this phenomenon for what it is while acknowledging I can't fully step out of my own meaning-making system. I'll reflect carefully and take responsibility for my choices and their consequences." This represents an intricate balancing act in practice, involving being restrained yet responsive, rooted in personal values while exploring participants' values, and presenting a convincing argument while acknowledging that it's one of many possible perspectives. Researchers balance distinguishing between their own voice and those of participants [18]. They seek to be authentic when writing up their research, while not overemphasising self-disclosure, avoiding excessive introspection, and challenging their assumptions. Linda Finlay [19, p. 3] recommended "a dialectic movement between bracketing preunderstandings and exploiting them reflexively as a source of insight."

Anyone who's tried to balance on one leg for any length of time knows that balance involves movement. There's a constant interaction between the self as the creator of perception and the other as the independent focus of that perception [20]. Luke Annesley spoke of this in our interview: "Yeah, it's that sort of balancing act, isn't it? And I suppose at the same time having a kind of scepticism about my capacity to do that, to set things to one side…So I'm sort of thinking, I need to put this to one side, but it doesn't matter how hard I try to do that, I'm not going to be fully successful. And it is a kind of ongoing process, isn't it, understanding reflexivity?"

Noah Potvin also discussed these matters in our interview about his co-authored grounded theory paper on resource-oriented music therapy with informal hospice caregivers during pre-bereavement: [21]

> When I look at that work or any of my other papers, I'm not consciously aware of how it's essentially a projection of me onto it. I recognise that it is on some level, like there's no way of escaping it. I try to be as reflexive as possible to try to account for those projections as much as I can, but with the recognition that it's sort of inevitable. So it is this careful and very imprecise calibration between checking in with your internal world and the

things that you know very intuitively, very close to you, while also trying to ensure that the outcome of the study is not just an affirmation of what you thought you already knew.

Positionality

All of us are positioned and are actively positioning in many ways in relation to the world(s) we occupy. In research, we reflect specifically on how we are positioned/positioning in relation to the specific study we're engaging in. This anchors a process that could otherwise be endless. Some of the ways we're positioned/positioning relate to our identity. Positionality also relates to power dynamics rooted in intersecting identities. In their chapter on assessment in music therapy, Annette Whitehead-Pleaux et al. [22] highlighted different cultural facets that should be taken into account when working with service users. It's also a helpful framework that we can use when thinking of ourselves as a researcher as well as the cultural facets of our participants. Their model includes culture(s) of heritage, religion, gender identity and orientation, disability, location, socioeconomic cultures, survivor culture(s), and generational cultures. We're also positioned/positioning in terms of time (historically and in the unfolding of our personal and communal story), and in relation to worldviews (politically, philosophically, and morally), academic, professional, discursive and theoretical orientations and commitments. We're positioned/positioning psychologically and emotionally, musically, and as embodied beings living with other bodies. In our interview, Viggo Krüger described reflexivity as being visible to the reader in the text, helping them understand who you are, where you're coming from, and the values you bring. Where we're positioned/positioning informs what we see, hear and feel, what moves us or leaves us cold, where we feel a sense of belonging or alienation, and the behaviours we're motivated to engage in.

Some music therapy researchers identify their location and reflect on how they're mindful of it [23–27]. Some describe how they take ownership of their position [28, 29], explicitly acknowledging race, gender identification, sexual orientation, disability and ability, socioeconomic status and class [30], nationality and countries of residence and training [31], sociocultural contexts, educational background, disciplinary positionality and philosophical stances [4, 25], affiliations, physical and mental illness experiences, religious upbringing and current affiliation [32], values, land ownership and views thereof [33], family experiences [18, 34], work experiences [35], job status as well as degrees of privilege that may have been accrued. Have a look at the position statements by Kirsten Hillman et al. [25] and Ming Yuan Low et al. [36] as helpful examples.

We see authors in music therapy literature explain how positionality influences their ways of thinking [37, 38]. It moderates experiences, perspectives, judgements, and views of the topic they're investigating [7], their unconscious reactions [39], storytelling, data collection and analysis methods [31, 40]. Positionality shapes our interpretation [26, 32, 38, 41, 42] and findings [5], and the potential usefulness of the research [29]. Potvin et al. [29] acknowledged how their study was shaped by their homogeneity as white, cisgender, straight, non-disabled individuals. They recognised that their privileges influenced their perspectives, their ease of fitting within university cultures, and their ability to speak authentically from a position of security. They encouraged readers to consider their findings within the context of these privileges and the protections they afforded. Gro Trondalen mentioned, "I think it is important for me to tell the reader: 'this is where I come from'. And that also affords people [the opportunity] to disagree."

It's possible to broaden our understanding of what constitutes a meaningful positionality statement. This can involve examining what our location *does*—how being situated there influences our thoughts, feelings, and actions—or how we might resist certain ways of doing, thinking, and feeling [43]. What are the consequences of these aspects of positioning throughout the process of the research and did we work with them, use them as resources, critique, resist, mould, or celebrate them? Exploring our positioning also isn't just about sharing our story; it's about examining our role within it. As narrative therapist Michael Guilfoyle [44] asked, Where am I in the story? Who am I in this story? What choices have I made? Do I have agency? Have I exercised resistance? Am I excited about parts of the story? Am I working to write a new story? Has the story been painful? How am I using my story?

Posture

Not only do we need to explore where and how we're positioned/positioning, but we should also reflect on our posture. I may stand with my feet firmly planted in a particular place, and my posture may (metaphorically) be one of crossed arms with my back turned towards an alternative position. Alternatively, I could be rooted in a position, but still have a relaxed posture, a curious expression, and open hands as I engage with a different positionality or an individual who is differently positioned/positioning. Debates can get heated here, and a case can be made that there are some positions (in terms of beliefs or practices) that should never be entertained with any degree of openness because they cause harm. My view on this matter as a music therapist is that I am ethically required to be compassionately present with any service user regardless of any positions they hold—and that this can coexist with my own personal convictions. This is not a preferred stance; it is demanded of me as a registered health professional. As I integrate all aspects of myself to sustain personal integrity, I bring this approach into my research as well, seeing my task as being to transparently acknowledge and present my positionality, whilst also becoming aware of and attending to my posture of openness. A researcher using Lens Reflexivity is alert to both their positioning and their posture and accounts for the decisions they make regarding these.

Strategies for Exploring Oneself in Context

To be able to present insightful reflections on our positioning and posture, and the implications these may have had throughout a research study, work needs to happen. Reflexivity has been defined as "disciplined self-reflection" [45, p. 493] or "thoughtful, conscious self-awareness." [46, p. 532] In music therapy literature, reflexivity is described as critical reflection on one's attitudes and positions [47], detailed self-reflection [48], inquiry into one's gaze and its implications [49], examining one's feelings, reactions, and motives [30], exploring one's way of knowing [5], and doing so with intellectual humility. In our interview, Efrat Roginsky explained that she always tries to "consider as many possibilities as I can [remembering that] I might not have it all figured out".

Pausing and Slowing Down

Reflexivity takes time and deep work [50]. Trondalen [51] emphasised being fully present throughout the research process. This is challenging when we work in academic spaces that are pushing us to publish at speed. Maggie Berg and Barbara Seeber's [52] *The Slow Professor* encourages researchers to take more time, examine their profession's scripts, values, and norms, and make conscious choices within their institutions. Tríona McCaffrey also emphasised the importance of time, saying that sometimes research "...can be a really slow, reflexive process". In our interview, Gro Trondalen elaborated on her process of reflexivity presented in her article on Resource-oriented Bonny Method of Guided Imagery and Music as a creative health resource for musicians: [51] "I really needed to give it space...I really went deep". Reflexivity, she suggested, can allow music therapists to make a difference through genuine engagement.

Taking time within a research project to be reflexive is certainly not easy. If the research is for a degree, your university may have very strict cut-off points. When working in research teams with volunteers, expectations around the time required for reflexivity may also need to be managed sensitively. In relation to one of her projects, Tríona McCaffrey explained that "we were zero-funded project...And it's really, really hard when you've got people who are giving up their time voluntarily to be part of a research process...because they're interested and they're passionate about the field...There's a line then also that I suppose has to be drawn around people's time and boundaries around that."

Using a Journal

As we repeatedly pause to reflect throughout the research process, a reflexive journal serves as an invaluable too [4, 53, 54]. We can use it to develop initial ideas, draw images, and create mind maps. We can also record field observations, decisions, and interactions. It can serve as an analytical-theoretical tool for memoing and coding, or as a personal diary within which we can explore our inner life. The intended use may determine whether we keep it private or share it with others [55].

As an example, in her study on music therapy students' experiences of interactions with young clients during fieldwork placements, Elvie Miller [56] explained how she kept a reflexive journal because it offered her opportunities for self-inquiry. She explored how her research question reflected her personal and professional perspectives, and reflected on the process of ethical review, her interactions with clients during fieldwork and data collection, and the data analysis process.

Reflexive journals can also be used in team projects. In our interview, Tríona McCaffrey explained her process within her study on the role and impact of group songwriting with multiple stakeholders in recovery-oriented mental health services: [57] "I kept a weekly diary throughout... I found that a lot more of my reflexive process was actually on the team and the various different parts and the engagement with the hospital...

both the art psychotherapist and the music therapist who were involved in that study would have kept a reflexive journal also."

Novice researchers may find reflexive practices like keeping a journal challenging, as they can evoke feelings of ambivalence or anxiety [58]. Having some structure and prompts may be helpful (there are many throughout this book). Reflexive journals allow us to explore and document how messy research can actually be. While writing is common, arts-based methods (poetry, drawing, songwriting) can be enormously helpful. The arts can bring about nuanced self-reflexive awareness because they tap into preverbal, sensory, embodied, kinaesthetic, and imaginary ways of knowing [59]. We know this well as music therapists. These methods are not frivolous; they can be profoundly reflexive tools.

Engaging in Supervision and Mentorship

Academic supervision or peer supervision can be immensely helpful when we're exploring the lenses we bring to our studies [54, 60, 61]. In my conversation with Noah Potvin, we discussed how he experienced the value of supervision in his research on music therapy with informal hospice caregivers during pre-bereavement [21], a topic that was personally meaningful to him. He explained,

> I had to own the fact that this project was one that was going to be something of a corrective experience for me and that I wanted this to be an offering to clinicians who could support other 17-year-old, 16, 15-year-old versions of myself supporting their loved ones. So, I needed to head into it recognising how this is what I think I'm going to find and also preparing myself that maybe I'm not going to get the information I'm going to want. So, these were conversations I had with my dissertation chair, these were conversations I had with my clinical supervisor, and this was just stuff I needed to work out for myself at the same time in terms of recognising where the balance exists in between what's mine to own and what is theirs to own while maintaining the integrity of each of the participants' individual stories. We think about it as honouring the data and presenting findings in a way that the reader can trust and being faithful to the participants' perspectives, but no one seems to really own the fact that it can be a healing process for the researcher too...

In my interview with Gro Trondalen, we explored her experiences of supervision and mentoring students. I asked her how she creates spaces for her students to grow in their reflexivity (clinically and in research) and how she thinks about this. She replied,

> Being a practitioner in music therapy, I worked within different areas. And I try to really dig into what the music therapists are after and then support them in reflecting upon their question. For example: When do you ask that question? How do you ask that question? How does that question resonate in your body? Can you give that question a colour? Can you give that reflection, or question, or feeling a shape? Is it sharp? If it were an animal, what would that be? And then we discuss solutions in real life. And my ambition is that when they go out they have the experience: 'I have solved this. I did it myself'. If I'm supervising a PhD student or a Master's student about research methodology: What kind of research methodology would they like to have? How is it for you to talk with people? 'Oh, it's extremely difficult.' 'Okay, what is difficult? Tell me more about that.' And then maybe we think, 'what are you most concerned with? Would you like to do analysis of the music or are you concerned about the people playing the music?' And I think that questioning in different modes as a supervisor seems to afford the researcher to think in different ways. 'If you now should think in different kinds of research methodologies, what would that offer you?' That's where I introduce 'why'. I use all the other questions before the last one. I wait with the why. Because the 'why' is the really reflexive part. And then I ask, why would you choose that? And usually then they know. Then they know. Because then the researcher always comes back to herself or back to themselves and they could say, 'I haven't thought about this'. And then I can say, 'Isn't that interesting? I haven't thought about it either. We made ourselves wiser this time. Thank you for sharing'.

Going to Therapy

Sometimes we're drawn to study topics that are closely related to our own (perhaps difficult) life experiences. We may then find that we need personal support and additional professional guidance to proceed in an ethical way, a manner that safeguards and even nurtures our own well-being, and that respects the separate stories of our participants. Stephanie Thompson et al. [62] noted how personal therapy can enhance awareness of one's identity and cultural history. When Noah Potvin discussed how his research was motivated by personal experiences, he emphasised the importance of therapy and intensive self-reflection:

> I think without having gone into therapy, without having done intensive reflections for myself...In some ways it's organic, in some ways I think my

> unconscious wanted me to pay attention to it. But I also need to consciously say, 'Okay, I'm going to commit myself to doing the work'. Without that conscious commitment it would have just sat brewing underneath the surface.

When crafting a position statement, we might struggle with how much personal information to reveal. It's not necessary to exhaustively detail private matters. We can carefully choose what personal information we're comfortable sharing and how disclosing or not disclosing might affect the research [63], ourselves, and our personal relationships. We are all at different places in our journeys and we are allowed to respect that, while still being authentically reflexive.

Mindfully Noticing What You're Doing

In my interview with Viggo Krüger, he remarked, "It doesn't matter what you say, it's what you do…In the end, I think that it's action that matters." Mindfulness can help us recognise our actions in research, assess their effectiveness, and determine the next steps [64]. Reflexive processes are particularly crucial in guiding ethical actions. Creating a decision tree, as one might in clinical practice [65], can help map out our steps and choices. Reflexivity involves assessing the appropriateness and effectiveness of each action and their connections, as well as making necessary adjustments—especially in qualitative studies, where the process often evolves more organically.

Mindfully Noticing Your Thoughts and Where They Are Leading You

Claire O'Callaghan and Philippa Barry [66, p. 6] described reflexivity as the constant examination of "what we know and how we know it." One aspect that is central to examining our thought patterns is exploring our assumptions, which significantly influence our decisions and interpretations as researchers [54, 67, 68]. Assumptions are "taken-for-granted beliefs about the world and our place within it that guide our actions" [69, p. 5]. Assumptions can be paradigmatic (structuring our worldview), prescriptive (what we believe should happen), or causal (predictive beliefs about how the world functions). Kristin Ørjasæter and Ottar Ness [67] advocated for a phenomenological attitude of wonder and critical self-awareness towards challenging preconceptions. We draw on both academic and non-academic assumptions [70].

We don't only need to recognise our assumptions, we also need to challenge them [23, 71, 72]. Katrina McFerran et al. [23] explained how, whenever they recognised the appearance of their pre-existing assumptions in their research, they interrogated these carefully, being aware that humans tend to find what they're looking for. Recognising our assumptions can be a difficult and unsettling but necessary task [73]. Kerry Devlin explained an approach she uses when teaching music therapy students to help them reflect on the impact of the perspectives that they bring.

> Our values and who we are as people influence the way that we want to be in relationship with other people. There're not necessarily good and bad perspectives, they just have different implications for people. So if you're really focused on somebody's skills, you know, what they can and can't do, that *means* something for what you're going to work on. You're going to work on skills. But if someone comes to you and says, "I want to play, I want to learn to play guitar so I can play in a band and meet other people and connect"—that's a really different way of positioning yourself in relationship to another person. So the way I did that last year was to give [the students] a case folder. I have some amazing folks I've worked with who have given me permission to use video and documentation. So, they have a folder of information about somebody and then the students do a very skills-focused case presentation where they created goals and objectives and experiences that were focused on skills. And then I gave them an update on their scenario, giving them way more information about who the person is. For some of them—they were young kids—I aged them and said, "Oh, this person is now 20. They're queer and they're in a sheltered workshop and they don't really like it there, but their boyfriend is there. So they don't want to leave. And so what does that mean for what you're going to work on in sessions?" So they had to do another case presentation, and reconceptualise their understanding of that person…I asked them to include a reflexive component where they had to talk about what that meant for their understanding of the person— whether they had a sense of which perspective would be more meaningful for the person, based on who they are and what they wanted to work on, or the context of the environment. So, I guess I'm sort of talking about reflexivity both implicitly and explicitly through that process…And it's challenging, right?

Mindfully Noticing Your Emotions and Where They Are Leading You

Emotions can be valuable tools for knowledge production [74]. Qualitative researchers in particular have leeway to embrace emotions in their research (especially after what has become known as the "affective turn" [75]. Enhanced awareness of our emotional responses can make us more intentional in our decisions and problem-solving [64]. Rickson [5], for example, reflected on her personal experiences while researching, noting how her emotional journey influenced her relationships with participants and her interpretations. She highlighted the need for self-examination though, questioning her feelings in order to maintain a balanced view and remain open to new ideas. Hyejin So [76] emphasised the importance of managing their reactions to avoid overidentification with participants. In a critical interpretive synthesis, McFerran et al. [23] showed how music therapists often work with unspoken emotional material. They described how being carefully alert to and acknowledging emotional and bodily reactions can inform one's findings in helpful ways.

Emotions in research can be categorised into three interconnected components [77]. The first is the emotional labour of a researcher. During fieldwork, for example, we may face emotionally challenging situations, like observing a participant experiencing psychological distress. The research process can evoke complex, sometimes even overwhelming emotions, perhaps due to overporosity, emotional flooding, or being personally triggered [73]. Components of a study may drain our energy or block our progress. Through various encounters and experiences in the research process, we may find ourselves reflecting on our own personal life circumstances, which can generate emotional responses. Postgraduate students, in particular, may benefit from receiving emotional support within their supervision processes and going to therapy when necessary.

The second aspect is the role of "emotionally sensed knowledge." This is about the epistemology of emotion and how feelings enhance our understanding. As researchers, we draw on our emotions to better understand what's happening in our study. The third component involves the sociology of emotion. Here, we might explore how emotions are expressed and interpreted by participants and examine the underlying rules that drive how feelings are presented in a particular sociocultural context [77].

Asking Questions Critically About What You've Noticed

We need to critically examine our thoughts, emotions and actions, as well as the contexts within which these are designated value and appropriateness. Quoc Nguyen et al. [78, p. 1182] described reflection as "the process of engaging the self in attentive, critical, exploratory and iterative interactions with one's thoughts and actions, and their underlying conceptual frame, with a view to changing them and with a view on the change itself." This process can be improved through practice and guidance. To want to engage in critical thinking, we need motivation, attentiveness, self-confidence, courage, willingness to suspend judgment, and seek evidence. We then require persistence, flexibility, focused attention and fair-mindedness to do the actual work of critical thinking [79, 80].

To some degree, we're trapped within the frameworks we use to create meaning. Self-confirming cycles can develop through which our assumptions guide our behaviour, and then we use those same assumptions to interpret our actions, confirming the truth of the assumptions. Stephen Brookfield [69] suggested viewing our actions through unfamiliar angles to become aware of our assumptions. Some of the angles we can use are: observing (carefully, noticing, recognising what aspects to focus on); feeling (especially embracing perplexity and puzzlement); wondering (questioning and being able to formulate the question without assumptions), imagining (thinking up and exploring possible options), inferring (drawing solid conclusions from available information), drawing on stored knowledge, experimenting, consulting, identifying and analysing arguments, and judging on the basis of accumulated evidence.

In Karette Stensæth's [35] study on music therapy and interactive musical media, she discussed breaking free of her frame of reference by moving between sources of data. Kerry Devlin [28] allowed her reading of literature to change her perspectives in her autoethnograpy about her experiences of working with a client in music therapy, finding autistic self-advocates' writings very helpful in offering first-hand disability experiences.

According to Pascale Widmer et al. [81], reflexivity entails reflection, planning, and, importantly, action/adaptation. Rickson [34] explained how she was continually considering the lenses she was employing throughout the research process, examining how her beliefs and practices could be influencing her interactions and interpretations, and then adjusting them accordingly.

Thinking Together in Research Teams

Many music therapy researchers value engaging in reflexivity within a team context [4, 31, 32]. Viggo Krüger emphasised in our interview that reflexivity is not just an individual process; teamwork can be essential. Constructively exploring with other researchers and practitioners fosters openness to critique and developing new ideas. Collaboration can enhance quality and rigour of research, and diverse teams in particular bring a broader range of knowledge and perspectives, potentially leading to more innovative ideas [82].

In music therapy research, teams sometimes explore together or members start independently and then come together to compare their conclusions [9]. Often researchers use teams to develop codes and themes [21, 27, 31, 83–87]. In their arts-based duoethnography, Thomas and Blanc [88] described how their individual and collective art-making and reflexive journaling enriched their dialogue sessions. Katrina McFerran and Helen Shoemark [72] used their initial conversations to dismantle potential hegemonic stances and transcend their theoretical frameworks.

In our conversation, Anthony Meadows shared the following about working in research teams, with reference to a current study he was working on at the time:

> The reason that I work in teams is that I think other people have really interesting perspectives and so you put all these differences together and you let the other perspectives be present without trying to overwhelm them or say: 'Well no, mine's right, everybody fit in'. When I'm working with teams it's like, 'Okay, what is your perspective? Tell me about this.' And we all sit down, and we share the differences, and we grapple with the differences. And that helps to really get around blind spots and locking in before it's indicated. I'll say, 'Well, it seems to be really about this'. And then the person whose training is completely different will say, 'Well, no, I see it from this perspective'...'Oh, that's okay, let's work with that'. Because where we have to grapple with these sort of perspectives, in a sense they're theoretically driven ways of understanding something, then we have to really deal with what we're calling multiplicities of perspective. We're actually writing in a different kind of way where we're saying 'this is the way we understand it, but it's always changing'.

In another part of our conversation, Meadows said the following (highlighting also the value of self-awareness):

> I like reducing phenomena because it's the way my brain works. So that's why you'll see me doing a lot of categorisation in research. But there's a real limit to that. And I work with people who live in much more emotional experience, and they're less concerned about structures and categories and more about living a phenomenon and not through the space of structure and organisation. And so, when we put our heads together and the team works well, that's what you're grappling with. And I think that's what music therapy is as well in a lot of ways: these relationships between the process and the structure of the phenomenon, and the artistic beauty of it.

The emotional support provided by a well-functioning team can be another significant benefit [82]. Teamwork can alleviate feelings of loneliness and self-doubt among researchers, and it can enhance job satisfaction and morale. When there's trust and psychological safety in a team then people are usually more likely to share their thoughts and feelings openly.

Despite these advantages, team research can be time-consuming and financially demanding. Particularly in qualitative research, reaching consensus and exploring diverse ideas may take a long time. Variations in writing styles can also challenge the process of creating a final paper that reads cohesively [82]. In my interview with Tríona McCaffrey, I asked whether working in a research team necessitates greater reflexivity due to the many moving parts. She noted that while team members share responsibilities, the planning and coordination behind the scenes require significant reflexivity.

While we'll explore interactions with participants in an upcoming section, it's important to recognise here that we also think with participants, especially in collaborative research where they're viewed as co-researchers. In our interview, Viggo Krüger drew on his extensive experience in child welfare, highlighting the value of learning from young people about making practices more effective in their contexts.

Lens Reflexivity Throughout Methodological Steps

As we're being reflexive by exploring the implications of our perspectives and constructions as we engage in research, let's look at what that may entail throughout different phases of a study. We've been thinking of lenses (e.g., "glasses") that a researcher looks through and what makes up those lenses. Here, we can also think metaphorically of a researcher holding a camera lens as if they're a film director. They make choices about where to direct the lens and how to focus it. When the audience views the final film, they'll see what the director chooses to show them and will not see what has been excluded. Their gaze will also be directed to focus on specific aspects of a scene or to take in a scenario more expansively. As researchers, we select methods that work in this way. We cannot simply state what methods we used. To be reflexive, we need to explain why we selected them and why and how we are purposefully choosing to shape what the "audience" can and can't see.

Choosing a Topic

We're driven by a wide array of intrinsic and extrinsic agendas and motivations when selecting a topic to research. We may be fuelled internally by curiosity and passion for a specific subject or motivated by our commitment to generate impactful insights. External factors, like funding opportunities, institutional priorities, social responsibility and peer expectations also shape our work [89]. While some researchers have a clear understanding of their motivations, others may not. Reflexivity encourages a deeper awareness of our motivations.

Daryl Lindo [90] reflected on his experiences as a minority in music therapy training, which prompted him to explore the lack of diversity in the field. In a study by Ananya Muralidharan and Michael Silverman [91] on music therapy undergraduate students' sleep, the first author explained how she was drawn to the study because of problems with the quality and quantity of her own sleep. As we select a topic, we're already considering our perspectives on that topic. Our perspectives may be informed by experiences as therapy service users [92] or by our musical experiences [30]. Our disciplinary training [23] and work experiences [8, 57, 93] also shape how we approach our topics.

Developing Research Questions

Katrina McFerran and Michael Silverman [94] wrote a book about developing research questions in music therapy research. They encouraged researchers to start by identifying personally intriguing experiences related to music, health, and well-being. We can then refine the question(s) we're starting to develop by examining our beliefs and values. As we're exploring this, we're also thinking about which methods may be most appropriate and appealing, which also links to our values and beliefs. Our research questions then also take shape in relation to contextual factors (the communities in which we research, organisational policies, cultural features etc.).

Questions shape the study, and the study can influence how these questions evolve. Researchers may start with a broad, exploratory question, gradually refining it into more specific ones during data collection and analysis. For example, McFerran et al. [23] emphasised the iterative nature of this process, showing how intentions fostered through their critical interpretive synthesis reshaped questions as new experiences arose. The question can function as a compass rather than an anchor [95]. When framing qualitative questions, we're striking a balance. They should be specific enough to guide the study but not so narrow as to limit discovery [96].

Here are some prompts you may wish to explore in your reflexivity journal when developing research questions:

- How does my personal biography influence what I consider to be meaningful questions in this research area?
- How has my academic training shaped what I consider to be "important" research questions?
- What methodological preferences do I have, and how are these influencing my research questions?
- Whose interests are served by the questions I'm asking?
- How is the current political climate influencing which questions seem urgent or relevant?
- What implicit assumptions might be embedded in the language I'm using to frame my questions?
- What discomforts or resistances do I notice when considering certain questions?
- What literature or perspectives might offer alternative question framings?
- How might my emotional responses to this topic be influencing my question development?
- How am I balancing openness to new directions with maintaining focus in my research?
- What feedback have I received on my research questions, and how have I responded to this?
- How might my questions change if I were to start this research again from scratch?

Contextualising the Study in Relation to Published Literature

Just as I can explore how I, as a person, am positioned in context, I can examine how my study is placed within the context of other research studies that have been conducted within the area(s) I'm investigating. This involves asking, "Where does my study fit in relation to what has already been researched?" and "What literature do I want to draw on to position this study in particular ways?"

In a literature review, we do more than represent what's been studied; we actively engage in meaning-making. We select keywords, choose search engines, and decide which studies to include or exclude. We highlight certain aspects, define concepts (or elect to leave definitions to participants), and weave narratives that connect various studies. A reflexive process should include critical engagement with the voices present in the literature review [43]. We should consider which researchers we cite, who we deem credible, and how they are positioned. For example, in their study on institutional logics and the organisational context of music therapy, Ingelill Eide [97, p. 462] explained her process as involving "reading the music therapy literature while moving back and forth between my preconceived theoretical knowledge…and my interpretations and critical reflections on the findings in the music therapy literature."

Our understanding of the literature can inform our research questions, study design, participant interactions, and data analysis. Alternatively, in some research approaches, such as grounded theory, reading literature before conducting a study may be discouraged, as it can skew our thinking too much [98]. Barney Glaser [99] advised against consulting literature unless absolutely necessary. It's possible to employ a balanced approach, where we build on existing knowledge while still working inductively. Janice Morse [98] recommended not only describing the concepts you're studying, but deconstructing them; developing a tentative framework from the literature that can still be informed by your data; recognising the boundaries (the outline) of the phenomenon so that you still have the freedom to explore its internal structure (to "colour it in"). In this way, a study can be grounded but still malleable.

Dialogues Between Theory and Reality

A theory is a big idea that connects other ideas. It's based on sound assumptions and has some explanatory power [100]. Theories often follow narrative structures and, in this sense, theories are stories that we tell about the world [101]. Theory is also something that researchers *do*. We use theoretical tools to grapple with the practical realities of our research context(s) [102]. While theories typically provide a foundation for studies, they can evolve as research progresses, being challenged, revised, or expanded. Quantitative research often tests existing theories, whereas qualitative research may generate new ones [103].

Theory-free research is a myth [104]. If a researcher can't articulate their theoretical framework, they may not have unearthed their operating principles and preconceptions. When Gro Trondalen described her approach to supervision in our conversation, she explained how she asks her students,

> What kind of philosophy of science are you attracted to? Or what kind of theories? Do you like to go to postmodern theories, critical theories? Or do you think in more positivistic terms, or ethnographic terms, anthropology, suggesting different kinds of frameworks? Because many people come and they say, 'I don't have any theories.' But then I say, 'Of course you have theories, just listen to how you talk. That's your theory. Listen to how you talk about phenomenon'.

Without theory, it's almost impossible to decide what's important. However, theoretical assumptions can also limit what we see. Egon Guba [105, p. 87] cautioned that "no single viewpoint…provides more than a partial picture." According to Kenneth Bruscia [106], theories can't be strictly classified as true or false but rather as useful or not useful, depending on their ability to account for information and guide problem-solving.

Theories can emerge from disciplinary orientations, literature, and lived experiences. Bell hooks [107] celebrated theory makers who risk exploring painful experiences. Specifically related to our field, Brynjulf Stige [108] argued that the best place for music therapists to draw theories from is practice. A theoretical framework may already exist within the organisation or setting in which we work. For instance, in my interview with Viggo Krüger, he described how the child protection institution he joined had an inherent focus on children's human rights. This perspective was not something imposed later; it was part of the initial discussions about using music and the arts to empower young people, dating back long before the research project began.

When analysing data, connections to the theoretical framework need to be explicit. For example, in their paper on music therapists' views on copyrighted music, Amanda Reid and Sydney Nicolla [40] described how cognitive dissonance theory offered them a lens through which they could analyse the cognitive processes of their participants. We do need to continually assess the fit between theory and data, determining whether the theoretical framework is enhancing or detracting from our understanding [109].

We may be drawing on theory to inform our findings, or we may be analysing data to develop a theory. For example, I interviewed Claire Ghetti about her article published in 2012 entitled *Music therapy as procedural support for invasive medical procedures: Toward the development of music therapy theory* [110]. According to Ghetti, "the whole act of research is an interpretation". She explained that in this paper she was primarily aiming:

> to describe a theoretical concept that seemed to be quite important in the way the music therapists wrote about music therapy's procedural support. There was this element that they were hinting at without calling it that. So part of the work was to try to make sense of what it is that they're conceptually trying to depict. And is there some underlying set of concepts...that actually has an underlying structure?

In Ghett's process of formulating this, she needed to explore questions like

> Was it me co-constructing with the documents? Or was it something that would be reliable for another rater? Was I looking for this capital T truth or this one underlying essence of procedural support...or was I trying to come up with words and definitions that could be understood by several people? I wanted someone who was a music therapist but not from that setting who could be like 'Yeah I can use these words and concepts and I can see how they relate in a similar way as you do'.

Research outcomes that challenge established theoretical expectations are as valuable as those that align with them. As John Patrick Shanley wrote in the preface of his play *Doubt—a Parable*, "Doubt is nothing less than an opportunity to re-enter the present" [111, p., viii]. Katrina McFerran [112] urged us to reevaluate our assumptions and theoretical frameworks, suggesting that fresh perspectives could lead to significant discoveries.

Methodologies, Approaches, Designs, and Methods

In music therapy literature, we see examples of authors explaining why they selected certain designs and methods. For example, Tríona McCaffrey et al. [57] noted that their lead researcher's prior use of arts-based research methods (ABR) informed their choice, recognising how these methods held potential for creative and inclusive participant engagement in mental health research. Daryl Lindo [90] used Interpretative Phenomenological Analysis (IPA) to explore the accessibility of MA Music Therapy training in the UK for ethnic minority communities. He made this choice to gain deep insights into the experiences of music therapists from these backgrounds, focusing on their shared lived experiences.

Academic pressures also influence methodological choices. McFerran et al. [23, p. 14] observed that the "publish or perish" culture in Western universities drives researchers to produce extensive outputs. They noted that their increasing use of Critical Interpretive Synthesis (CIS) reflected this pressure, acknowledging that many of the authors of their article undertook a CIS to simultaneously generate a first publication from their doctoral research, as well as to foster their own capacity for critical reading and thinking.

We may decide on the methodology, design and methods in the early planning stages, but reflexivity could also prompt us to make changes as we go along [39, 113]. Potvin et al. [21] emphasised the importance of adapting to emergent conditions throughout the research process. Action research, for instance, inherently includes flexibility [5]. McFerran and Shoemark [72] discussed methodological responsiveness, and Haire and MacDonald [7] argued for a "playful, flexible and responsive" approach to methods. Researchers may adjust their approaches based on participants' needs [7, 47, 72]. For example, Guro Klyve and Randi Rolvsjord [39] changed their interview methods to accommodate children's needs, and Lindblad [112] extended the study duration based on participant feedback [39, 112]. Julie Krøier et al. [113] described challenges in capturing nonverbal interactions in focus groups, leading them to incorporate musical improvisation as an additional ABR method. Efrat Roginsky and Cochavit Elefant [53] found that combining qualitative approaches allowed them to adapt their study design to better fit participants' needs, replacing IPA with grounded theory methods.

Reflexive Ethical Considerations

Reflexivity is one of the most important items in our toolkit for recognising, carefully managing, and transparently reporting ethical considerations in our research [114, 115]. Sarah Tracy [116] proposed four domains for ethical reflection: procedural ethics (approval processes involving review boards), situational ethics (within the research context), ethical relationships (dynamics between researcher and participants), and ethical issues in exiting the study (completion and dissemination). In particular, qualitative research's inherent fluidity can lead to unexpected challenges, necessitating continuous adjustment of aims and procedures [117, 118].

Here are a few questions for ethical consideration when using Lens Reflexivity:

- What implicit values are embedded in institutional ethical frameworks, and how might they constrain or enable certain research approaches?
- What unanticipated ethical tensions have emerged in this study that weren't covered in my ethical planning?
- When faced with competing ethical principles, how am I prioritising which takes precedence?
- How am I navigating the tension between building rapport and maintaining appropriate boundaries with participants?
- How am I ensuring ongoing consent beyond the initial agreement, especially as the research evolves?
- In what ways might my research perpetuate or challenge harmful stereotypes?
- If I'm experiencing distress, how might this influence my ethical decision-making?
- What ongoing obligations do I have to participants after formal data collection ends?
- What considerations should guide decisions about returning to this research site in the future?

Engaging with Participants

Many of the threads of our discussion so far tie together here as we focus on participant engagement. Viggo Krüger and Brynjulf Stige [9] acknowledged that how we select participants is a choice that influences our findings. How we perceive and describe our participants also shapes our understanding, expectations, and engagements with them [24, 28]. According to Grace Thompson [119] in her editorial about *Respect-focused writing*, authors' words reveal the way they perceive the people with whom they work. This matters enormously.

As we interact with participants in a study, meaning is generated from the viewpoints of all involved [120]. In our interview, Claire Ghetti explained,

> I am making meaning of participants who are also making meaning when they're recounting events. That retrospection in itself is an interpretation, the revisiting is in some way influenced by what they know now and may be influenced by their interaction with me in the room, who they think I am as researcher.

Linking to the previous section on ethical considerations, reflexivity allows researchers to be sensitive to potential burdens and harm to participants [121], which is especially important when the power distance between researchers and participants is greater [122]. For example, in her study on sexism and cisgenderism in music therapy spaces, Kristen McSorley [123] explained how she was aware of the interactions between her own and her participant's social locations throughout the interviews because this could contribute to miscommunication and misunderstanding. Therefore, she aimed to listen instead of interpret, taking inventory of her worldview and its potential impact. She asked for ongoing clarification and used member checking during data analysis. In Michael Silverman's [41] study on change mechanisms in patient-preferred live music, he interviewed music therapists, interns, and students. He acknowledged his power within his relationship with the student participants and they had intentional discussions about this. He assured them that the study would not influence their grades or any future letters of recommendation and encouraged the participants to speak openly during the interviews.

Dual Relationships
In the previous chapter, we discussed how Sentinel Reflexivity can help us detect and minimise bias when dual roles are present in a research study, and how we may even elect not to include dual relationships because of how subjectivity can cloud the process too much when our quest is to let phenomena (and the people who are experiencing them) speak for themselves. In our current quest we wish to discover and share facets of what we're studying, knowing this is filtered through our perceptions. We acknowledge our subjectivity and work with it. We can value the benefits that dual relations offer, such as enhanced rapport [87] increased comfort and calm [47], deeper knowledge of participants while, crucially, reflecting on how our presence influences the information we are gathering [124].

We have to carefully think through power dynamics in the context of dual relationships especially. We need to work to ensure that participants don't feel coerced [125] (while recognising how this can be nuanced and difficult to eliminate altogether), and to reduce the likelihood that participants might experience the need to please the researcher [124] Sometimes, when there's a more mutual relationship, such as between colleagues, this can present challenges too. For example, Tríona McCaffrey [126] found that interviewing colleagues led to discussions in which participants' assumptions about shared knowledge could have limited their descriptions. Jeanette Kennelly et al. [127] interviewed fellow music therapists and explained how the first author was known professionally by all the interviewees. This required intentional, clear discussions about confidentiality in relation to issues participants raised about supervision practices in their area and how these discussions would be managed outside the research context.

Collecting Data

Lens Reflexivity during data collection is a cyclical process, not a once-off exercise. When we're selecting data collection methods, have we carefully thought through how they speak to our research questions? What do these methods afford in terms of highlighting certain facets of the phenomenon and blocking off others? Will our skill and comfort level (or inexperience and discomfort) with a certain tool impact the information we're able to gather? Have we got to know the research context and participants enough first to know that these methods will be appropriate? As we implement the data-gathering process, are we including reflexive pauses? Are we adjusting our strategies when necessary and documenting our decision-making processes in detail? Are we aware of our emotional responses as we interact with our participants?

Some authors explain the reasons behind their data collection choices. For example, Marie Skånland and Gro Trondalen [86] used joint interviews with service users and their music therapists, finding this dyadic approach more fruitful for generating shared narratives and creating a sense of safety for the service users (however, they were aware that they risked issues related to power dynamics). Shulamit Epstein et al. [124] employed semi-structured interviews for in-depth exploration and Interpersonal Process Recall because they wanted to access vivid descriptions of music therapy experiences.

Some authors also reflected on their process and experience of data collection. For example, McCaffrey [126] explained that individual interviews were successful in revealing participants' experiences, however, she was aware that she occasionally asked long-winded questions that could have confused participants. Reid and Nicolla [40] emphasised how the lead researcher's legal knowledge improved their understanding and interpretations of the music therapists' views on copyrighted music.

Analysing Data

On our current quest, we recognise that data does not reflect the world; we *make* meaning with the data we've gathered [128]. Both quantitative and qualitative researchers are actively interpreting when analysing data [129]. Many music therapy researchers acknowledge that they play an integral role in the analysis (e.g., Fairchild et al. [60], Hogan-Gibbons et al. [130], O'Callaghan and McDermott [49], Potvin et al. [29]) and (when there are participants in the study) that both the understandings of the participants and the researchers need to be taken into account [113]. A researcher's story can be organised in a variety of ways, and we need to know what they were looking for and why, how they conducted their research, what they found, and what they think this means [131].

As we're making sense of data, we may be using deductive, inductive, or abductive reasoning. Inductive reasoning moves from the specific to the general. Conclusions are built out of the data "building blocks". For example, researchers using qualitative methods immerse themselves in the data by coding and categorising information to generate patterns, themes, relationships, and, ultimately, theory [132]. Researchers using quantitative methods may use inductive reasoning to form hypotheses by observing patterns in preliminary data or previous research. They could also discover unexpected relationships or patterns in their datasets. Reflexivity matters when using inductive reasoning because we need to think critically about what is informing the patterns we see, the relationships we highlight, and the themes we create.

It's important to differentiate between inductive reasoning and inductive inference. Through inductive reasoning we're trying to identify generalisations, rules, or patterns. An inductive inference broadens the generalisation beyond the observed experience by making claims about unobserved or potentially unobservable objects [133]. For instance, if we look at a music therapist's instruments and see that they're all wooden, we have identified a generalisation or regularity. However, if we incorrectly expand this generalisation to claim that all instruments everywhere are made of wood, we'd be making an inductive inference, which is false in this case.

Deductive reasoning uses logical thinking to move from general principles and premises to specific conclusions. In data analysis, we're using deductive reasoning when we start with a theoretical framework or hypothesis and then systematically examine our data to see whether the framework or hypothesis is supported or needs rethinking [132]. A key limitation of deductive reasoning is that it can't uncover new insights; it relies on pre-existing assumptions or beliefs [134]. Reflexivity is crucial in deductive reasoning because as researchers we need to think through which established theories or hypotheses we're beginning with and how our professional commitments or cultural perspectives may be influencing this choice, as well as the motivations that may be driving us to confirm the hypothesis or support the theoretical framework.

Abductive reasoning involves forming educated hypotheses based on incomplete information with the aim of making reasonable inferences. Here we're choosing the most plausible explanation from a number of options by drawing on past experiences, creativity, and intuition. Abduction uses imagination to propose possibilities. Reflexivity is key here too because we need to be able to carefully think through and explain how we reached our conclusions. We evaluate the sources of our intuitive, creative insights, and consider how our professional backgrounds, cultural contexts, or personal experiences shaped our interpretations. We also need to consider how our comfort with ambiguity and uncertainty impacts our abductive reasoning process. We could keep a diary of alternative explanations that we've thought about but let go of, and which ones appeared more convincing and why. We could also speak with colleagues or participants as we question our tentative conclusions and embrace diverse viewpoints [135].

Pragmatism embraces abduction, deduction, and induction as interconnected. Through abduction, we can form a hunch or provisional hypothesis to start figuring out puzzling data; by deduction, we can convert this into a testable proposition; and by using induction, we actively collect new data to assess the hypothesis and deepen our understanding of cause-and-effect relationships [136]. As highlighted in the paragraphs above, reflexivity would be essential during every phase of this process.

Quantitative Analysis
Working with numerical data involves subjectivity [137]. Why have we selected certain variables over others? How are we operationalising these variables, and what theoretical frameworks inform this? Why did we select certain statistical approaches over others? How does our methodological training constrain these decisions and what are the impacts of this? What philosophical assumptions underlie the statistical approach we're using? Are we critically reflecting on our decisions about handling outliers and missing data? How do our expectations influence our interpretation of statistical findings? How do funding sources or institutional pressures influence our analytical decisions? What assumptions underlie our datasets? Could our analysis be reproducing existing inequalities? [43]

Qualitative Data Analysis
It's more common in qualitative data analysis to find researchers explicitly owning how their findings are a product of the interplay between themselves and the topic/participants in their study. Some start by explaining how they reflexively made decisions about what data to focus on for analysis. For example, in their study on music as a structuring resource in child welfare, Viggo Krüger and Brynjulf Stige [9] interviewed adolescents and young adults. They explained how they didn't analyse the text from all the transcripts but focussed on the aspects that were especially relevant to their emerging theoretical discussion. They wrote that they used participants' quotes as a way of letting the participants' voices be heard most clearly. However, they acknowledged that, by selecting certain quotes, they were already performing an interpretation. Claire O'Callaghan and Fiona

McDermott [49] also explained that deciding what is relevant to analyse is ultimately a judgement based on one's theories about the phenomenon being analysed.

Researchers also decide which analytic technique to use. Qualitative music therapy researchers using (what I'm calling) Lens Reflexivity employ various analytical approaches. For example, Potvin et al. [21] used initial, focused, and selective coding alongside situational analysis, embracing the "messy complexities" of data. In descriptive phenomenological studies, researchers immerse themselves in participants' experiences while remaining critically reflexive. Horizonalising can help address our assumptions by assigning equal value to all meaning units. Interpretative Phenomenological Analysis is also chosen for its alignment with a quest that explores reality while recognising that one sees through one's own lenses [38, 125].

Qualitative researchers sometimes adapt their approaches during the course of their studies. Danielle Jakubiak [68] initially planned to use Guest's Laban movement analysis (LMA) for examining gestures but later found music analysis more suitable. Nerdinga Snape et al. [138] adjusted their coding approach by deciding only to analyse codes mentioned by at least two participants. This decision was made for manageability rather than reliability and allowed for a coherent overview of diverse experiences.

Pattern Recognition

When analysing qualitative data, researchers are essentially looking for patterns that can help explain or illuminate the phenomenon they're studying. In inductive qualitative data analysis, identifying patterns involves breaking data down into smaller units, categorising and reassembling them to develop underlying structures. We don't just spot patterns that are lying there waiting to be found. The process is subjective, interpretive, and iterative. We revisit our data multiple times, and each iteration can unveil new insights. It's also a dialectical process in that we're continuously balancing developing insights while being guided by our research aims and being informed by our theoretical frameworks. Pattern recognition is also informed by culture. For example, a person's cultural background can influence whether they see the trees before the forest or the forest before the trees [139].

When we're looking for patterns, we're relating something to something else. We're looking for (a) the "this" (e.g., a code, category, concept, or theory), (b) the "that" (e.g., a unit of analysis, like a sentence from a transcript or thick description), (c) the juxtapositioning of the this and the that, and (d) the suggested meanings that arise from their relationship [140]. Without this process there is no qualitative data analysis. What we're required to do is explain the relationship between the code ("this") and its supporting evidence ("that"). Simply listing codes or categories without showing their connection to the data results in a weak analysis. Of course, pattern recognition in qualitative research isn't only about identifying similarities. We also need to be attuned to differences, contradictions, and negative cases that can challenge patterns or provide alternative explanations. Doing so can help us create a more comprehensive and nuanced understanding of the phenomenon we're studying.

Balancing What Is There with How You Perceive What Is There
On this quest, we believe that there's a real world outside of our subjective perceptions, but we can only know it *through* our perceptions and interpretations of it. As we discussed earlier in this chapter, this invites us into a balancing act: we're analysing something in the world and our interpretations shape how we see and explain it. This balancing act was one of the thorniest aspects that I needed to grapple with in this study as I read the music therapy literature and spoke with researchers.

In my conversation with Noah Potvin, he explained his interviews with informal hospice caregivers who struggled to describe their music therapy experiences. Potvin emphasised how he needed to ensure that he didn't fill in the gaps for them, staying true to the data while recognising that grounded theory also required him as the researcher to become an analytical tool. He discussed balancing personal interpretation with maintaining the integrity of participants' stories. In our interview, Gro Trondalen described using various methods to triangulation analysis, such as watching video recordings and listening to the music, noting that while these approaches might bring her closer to the material, they also risked drawing her closer to her interpretation. She reflected on the tension inherent in this process.

Presenting Findings

After doing the reflexive work explored in this chapter, how do we communicate our process to readers and present our findings in reflexive ways? Aigen [141] highlighted that reflexivity involves the researcher being aware of and *conveying* their beliefs, interests, preconceptions, prior experiences, and sociocultural influences that may have impacted the study.

The struggle is also to juggle our reflexive descriptions with the word limitation imposed by a journal or faculty.

Let's think about writing style. Writing in the first person is a deliberate choice that conveys our personal engagement with the data and our inseparability from the knowledge that we've generated during the research [142]. Our language also conveys how we perceive participants. For example, Low et al. [36] addressed the importance of language choice regarding balancing identity-first language preferred by the autistic community with person-first language used by cited researchers.

When we present our findings, we need to carefully consider whose voice is being heard. This is another tricky balancing act [56], particularly in qualitative research where paraphrasing can risk losing the essence of respondents' experiences. Transparency really matters here, as we're clear about whose interpretations are presented. In my interview with Tríona McCaffrey, we discussed her paper on arts-based methods with mental health service users [143], where group members created songs and a visual image. McCaffrey then wrote a song in response. She explained, "I was really aware that I didn't want my voice to overpower or detract from someone else's, because the heart of this was listening to people's experiences of music therapy in mental health". She therefore elected to use italics for the words of the person who drew the image and red font for her own reflections in her lyrics. She did this for transparency and to show her awareness of power dynamics.

In my interview with Anthony Meadows, we discussed the importance of writing that invites reader engagement. He suggested that reflexive writing not only communicates findings but also invites readers into a relational and potentially disruptive experience, encouraging them to question and reflect on the material.

Trustworthiness in a Study Employing Lens Reflexivity

Brynjulf Stige [131] argued that there must be a logical and systematic approach to how researchers interact with and collect empirical material. When researchers present their findings by clarifying how their thinking, position, and experiences have shaped their interpretations, this clarity allows readers to trace the logic of the study, fostering trustworthiness [46]. Many music therapy researchers emphasise the importance of transparency regarding their thought processes, experiences, and positioning [6, 23, 25, 29, 36, 60, 68, 125, 143]. Bibb et al. [144] stated that transparency helps readers understand the potential influence of the researchers' perspectives on the findings, and this enables them to assess critically whether they agree with the conclusions reached.

In our interview, Tríona McCaffrey reflected on the importance of transparency for the integrity of a study. By critically examining their decisions throughout a study, researchers can ensure that their work is grounded and defensible, making it more robust and credible. Gro Trondalen also stressed the importance of being able to document and justify each step of the research process. This reflexive stance allows her to offer her insights while remaining honest about the limitations of her perspectives. In a study employing Lens Reflexivity, the researchers work to gain the reader's trust that the findings are a logical interpretation that has taken into account the researcher's positionality and perspectives.

An Accessible Summary

Lens Reflexivity involves consciously recognising and examining the active role we play in forming and influencing knowledge through our personal viewpoints. Unlike trying to step aside completely, this approach recognises that we always see through "clouded lenses." The task is to purposefully explore, monitor, and report on how these lenses influence our research whilst being transparent about our perspectives and challenging them when necessary.

Positionality refers to how we actively position ourselves in relation to the world and our specific research study and how we are positioned by others. This includes aspects of our identity such as culture, religion, gender, disability, location, and socioeconomic status, as well as our positioning in terms of time, worldviews, academic orientations, and emotional and embodied experiences. Where we're positioned influences what we see, hear, and feel, what moves us or leaves us cold, and the behaviours we're motivated to engage in. In addition to positioning, we also need to consider our posture—the stance we take towards different perspectives.

In Lens Reflexivity, we maintain the belief in an independent reality while also acknowledging that we can never fully step out of our own meaning-making systems. Contemporary scholars recognise that com-

(*continued*)

(continued)

pletely setting aside all preconceived ideas and past experiences is neither possible nor desirable. Humans are always situated within historical and cultural contexts. So, rather than trying to bracket everything, we hold back some preunderstandings while using other aspects as sources of insight. This leads to an intricate balancing act between being restrained yet responsive, rooted in our personal values while exploring participants' values, and presenting convincing arguments while recognising they represent just one of many possible perspectives. There is constant movement and adjustment.

Practical strategies for exploring ourselves in context include pausing and slowing down to allow deep, reflexive work. We can mindfully notice our actions, thoughts, and emotions, and ask ourselves critical questions about what we've observed and how our assumptions might be guiding our interpretations. We can use reflexivity journals to develop ideas and record our decisions, engage in academic supervision or mentorship, and we may also choose to seek personal therapy when research topics connect closely to our own experiences. Working in research teams can also enhance reflexivity by bringing multiple perspectives together, helping identify blind spots, and providing emotional support throughout the research process.

In terms of the methodological steps we take, our perspectives can influence each decision. As a result, we need to carefully consider and explain what we are looking for and why, how we conducted our research, what we found, and what we think it means. We recognise that data doesn't reflect the world directly; we make meaning with the data we've gathered. Both researchers and participants are actively interpreting throughout the process. When presenting findings, we carefully consider whose voice is being heard, balance transparency about our interpretations with word limitations, and choose a writing style that conveys our personal engagement with the data. When using Lens Reflexivity, we may elect to write in first person to acknowledge how we are inseparable from the knowledge we've presented.

As we use Lens Reflexivity, we build trustworthiness by being transparent about our thought processes, experiences, and positioning. When we clarify how our thinking, position, and experiences have informed our interpretations, we allow readers to follow the logic of our study and decide whether they agree with our conclusions.

References

1. Kenny CB. The field of play: a guide for the theory and practice of music therapy. Atascadero, CA: Ridgeview Publishing Company; 1989.
2. Campbell S, Millán EF, Wolf O, Thornton R, Riva S. Collective writing as survival tool: mechanisms of reflexivity against neoliberal academia. Emot Space Soc. 2024;50:101007.
3. Freeman D. Use of reflexive thinking in music therapy to understand the therapeutic process; Moments of clarity, self-criticism: an autoethnography. Qualitative Inquir Music Therapy. 2018;13(1):1–43.
4. Meadows A, Wimpenny K. Core themes in music therapy clinical improvisation: an arts-informed qualitative research synthesis. J Music Ther. 2017;54(2):161–95.
5. Rickson D. Researching one's own clinical practice: managing multiple roles in an action research project. Voices: A World Forum for Music Therapy [Internet]. 2009 Mar [cited 2024 Jul 18];9(1). Available from: https://voices.no/index.php/voices/article/view/33.
6. Tuastad L, Stige B. The revenge of Me and THE BAND'its: a narrative inquiry of identity constructions in a rock band of ex-inmates. Nord J Music Ther. 2015;24(3):252–75.
7. Haire N, MacDonald R. Thinking through improvisation: how arts-based reflexivity can offer new knowing about music therapists' experiences of humour in music therapy. Voices: a World Forum for Music Therapy [Internet]. 2021 Jun [cited 2024 Jul 18];21(2). Available from: https://voices.no/index.php/voices/article/view/3156.
8. West R, Furman A, Silverman MJ. Individualized education program team members' perceptions of music therapy: an interpretivist investigation. J Music Ther. 2021;58(4):437–62.
9. Krüger V, Stige B. Between rights and realities–music as a structuring resource in child welfare everyday life: a qualitative study. Nord J Music Ther. 2015;24(2):99–122.
10. Short H. Say what you say (Eminem): managing verbal boundaries when using rap in music therapy, a qualitative study. Voices: A World Forum for Music Therapy [Internet]. 2013 Jan [cited 2024 Jul 18];13(1). Available from: https://voices.no/index.php/voices/article/view/668.
11. Carroll D. Portraiture and the role of researcher: reflections and questions/ La méthode de l'art du portrait et le rôle du chercheur: réflexions et questions. Canadian J Music Ther. 2007;13(2):148–59.
12. Cohen MZ, Omery A. Schools of phenomenology: implications for research. Critical Issue Qualit Resear Meth. 1994;2:136–53.
13. Heidegger M. Being and time. Macquarrie J, Robinson E, translators. New York: Harper; 1962. (Original work published 1927)

14. LeVasseur JJ. The problem of bracketing in phenomenology. Qual Health Res. 2003;13(3):408–20.
15. Koch T. Interpretive approaches in nursing research: the influence of Husserl and Heidegger. J Adv Nurs. 1995;21(5):827–36.
16. Merleau-Ponty M. Phenomenology of perception. London: Routledge; 1962. (Original work published 1945)
17. Tracy S. Qualitative research methods. 2nd ed. Hoboken, NJ: John Wiley; 2020.
18. Gottfried T, Elefant C, Gold C. Music-oriented parent counseling to promote improvement in level of parental stress, quality of life and the use of music in everyday life among parents of children with autism: a mixed-methods randomized controlled study. Nord J Music Ther. 2023;32(5):397–422.
19. Finlay L. Engaging phenomenological analysis. Qual Res Psychol. 2014;11(2):121–41.
20. Ladkin D. 'The enigma of subjectivity': how might phenomenology help action researchers negotiate the relationship between 'self', 'other' and 'truth'? Action Res. 2005;3(1):108–26.
21. Potvin N, Bradt J, Ghetti C. A theoretical model of resource-oriented music therapy with informal hospice caregivers during pre-bereavement. J Music Ther. 2018;55(1):27–61.
22. Whitehead-Pleaux A, Brink S, Tan X. Culturally competent music therapy assessments. In: Whitehead-Pleaux A, editor. Cultural intersections in music therapy. Barcelona: Barcelona Publishers; 2017. p. 271–84.
23. McFerran KS, Hense C, Medcalf L, Murphy M, Fairchild R. Integrating emotions into the critical interpretive synthesis. Qual Health Res. 2017;27(1):13–23.
24. Epstein S, Elefant C, Thompson G. Music therapists' perceptions of the therapeutic potentials using music when working with verbal children on the autism spectrum: a qualitative analysis. J Music Ther. 2020;57(1):66–90.
25. Hillman KB, Bolger L, McFerran KS. Deconstructing trauma narratives: a critical interpretive synthesis of research into music therapy and psychological trauma in adults. Arts Psychother. 2022;77:101863.
26. Silverman MJ. Songwriting, professional studio recording, and a CD release party: interviews with two adults with mental health conditions. Arts Psychother. 2022;80:101915.
27. Bensimon M. Perceptions of music therapists regarding their work with children living under continuous war threat: experiential reframing of trauma through songs. Nord J Music Ther. 2020;29(4):300–16.
28. Devlin K. How do I see you and what does that mean for us? An autoethnographic study. Music Ther Perspect. 2018;36(2):234–42.

29. Potvin N, Belt C, Moore C. New music therapy faculty and the pursuit of fulfillment, success, and identity: a collective autoethnography. Arts Psychother. 2021;74:101781.
30. Campbell KS. A qualitative exploration of music therapist beliefs, education, and uses of hip hop in clinical practice. Music Ther Perspect. 2023;41(1).
31. Silverman MJ, Bibb J. Acute care mental health workers' assumptions and expectations of music therapy: a qualitative investigation. Arts Psychother. 2018;59:94–100.
32. dos Santos A, Brown T. Music therapists' empathic experiences of shared and differing orientations to religion and spirituality in the client-therapist relationship. Arts Psychother. 2021;74:101786.
33. Biedka S. Music therapists' experiences of therapeutic relationships with clients with marginalized gender identities and sexual orientations. Music Ther Perspect. 2022;40(2):152–63.
34. Rickson D. Family members' and other experts' perceptions of music therapy with children on the autism spectrum in New Zealand: findings from multiple case studies. Arts Psychother. 2021;75:101833.
35. Stensæth K. Music therapy and interactive musical media in the future: reflections on the subject-object interaction. Nord J Music Ther. 2018;27(4):312–27.
36. Low MY, McFerran KS, Viega M, Carroll-Scott A, McGhee Hassrick E, Bradt J. Exploring the lived experiences of young autistic adults in Nordoff-Robbins music therapy: an interpretative phenomenological analysis. Nord J Music Ther. 2023;32(5):432–55.
37. Thompson GA. A grounded theory of music therapists' approach to goal processes within their clinical practice. Arts Psychother. 2020;70:101680.
38. Silverman MJ, Segall LE, Edmonds T. "I've lost my callouses:" A phenomenological investigation of music therapists who left the profession. J Music Ther. 2022;59(4):394–429.
39. Klyve GP, Rolvsjord R. Moments of fun: narratives of children's experiences of music therapy in mental health care. Nord J Music Ther. 2023;32(2):100–20.
40. Reid A, Nicolla SK. Exploring music therapists' experiences with and perceptions about copyrighted music: a thematic analysis. J Music Ther. 2022;59(3):269–306.
41. Silverman MJ. Change mechanisms in patient-preferred live music: an exploratory interpretivist study. J Music Ther. 2021;58(3):310–44.
42. Silverman MJ, West R, Schwartzberg ET, Hunt C, Peterson MR, Shibley L. Experiences of music therapy students working as camp counselors for individuals with autism spectrum disorder: a thematic analysis. Nord J Music Ther. 2018;27(5):431–47.
43. Jamieson MK, Govaart GH, Pownall M. Reflexivity in quantitative research: a rationale and beginner's guide. Soc Personal Psychol Compass. 2023;17(8).

44. Guilfoyle M. Listening in narrative therapy: double listening and empathic positioning. S Afr J Psychol. 2015;45(1):36–49.
45. Wilkinson S. The role of reflexivity in feminist psychology. Women's Stud Int Forum. 1988;11(5):493–502.
46. Finlay L. 'Outing' the researcher: the provenance, process, and practice of reflexivity. Qual Health Res. 2002;12(4):531–45.
47. Solli HP. Battling illness with wellness: a qualitative case study of a young rapper's experiences with music therapy. Nord J Music Ther. 2015;24(3):204–31.
48. O'Callaghan C, McDermott F. Music therapy's relevance in a cancer hospital researched through a constructivist lens. J Music Ther. 2004;41(2):151–85.
49. O'Callaghan C, McDermott F. Discourse analysis reframes oncologic music therapy research findings. Arts Psychother. 2007;34(5):398–408.
50. Newport C. Deep work: rules for focused success in a distracted world. New York: Hachette UK; 2016.
51. Trondalen G. Resource-oriented Bonny Method of Guided Imagery and Music (R-oGIM) as a creative health resource for musicians. Nord J Music Ther. 2016;25(1):5–31.
52. Berg M, Seeber BK. The slow professor: challenging the culture of speed in the academy. Toronto: University of Toronto Press; 2016.
53. Roginsky E, Elefant C. Silent sounding: communicability, musicality, and the use of music with nonspeaking individuals with cerebral palsies and multiple disabilities. Nord J Music Ther. 2021;30(1):61–78.
54. Annesley L, Curtis-Tyler K, McKeown E. Parents' perspectives on their child's music therapy: a qualitative study. J Music Ther. 2020;57(1):91–119.
55. Luescher TM. Academic rigour as praxis: what place for reflexive journaling? [Internet]. 2010 [cited 2024 Jul 18]. Available from: https://www.researchgate.net/publication/303738563_Academic_Rigour_as_Praxis_What_Place_for_Reflexive_Journaling.
56. Miller E. Music therapy students' experiences of interactions with young clients during fieldwork placements. Voices: A World Forum for Music Therapy [Internet]. 2012 Jun [cited 2024 Jul 18];12(2). Available from: https://voices.no/index.php/voices/article/view/617.
57. McCaffrey T, Higgins P, Monahan C, Moloney S, Nelligan S, Clancy A, et al. Exploring the role and impact of group songwriting with multiple stakeholders in recovery-oriented mental health services. Nord J Music Ther. 2021;30(1):41–60.
58. Meyer K, Willis R. Looking back to move forward: the value of reflexive journaling for novice researchers. J Gerontol Soc Work. 2019;62(5):578–85.
59. Gerber N, Templeton E, Chilton G, Cohen Liebman M, Manders E, Shim M. Art-based research as a pedagogical approach to studying intersubjectivity in the creative arts therapies. J Appl Arts Health. 2012;3(1):39–48.

60. Fairchild R, Thompson G, McFerran KS. Exploring the meaning of a performance in music therapy for children and their families experiencing homelessness and family violence. Music Ther Perspect. 2017;35(1):36–49.
61. Aitchison KA, McFerran KS. Six adolescents' lived experiences of resource-oriented music therapy assessment in a community-based mental health day program. Arts Psychother. 2023;82:101991.
62. Thompson S, Grocke D, Dileo C. The use of group descriptive phenomenology within a mixed methods study to understand the experience of music therapy for women with breast cancer. Nord J Music Ther. 2017;26(4):320–37.
63. Lazard L, McAvoy J. Doing reflexivity in psychological research: what's the point? What's the practice? Qual Res Psychol. 2020;17(2):159–77.
64. Ulibarri N, Cravens A, Nabergoj A, Kernbach S, Royalty A. Creativity in research. Cambridge: Cambridge University Press; 2019.
65. Thompson S, O'Callaghan C. Decision making in music therapy: the use of a decision tree. Aust J Music Ther. 2013;24:48–66.
66. O'Callaghan C, Barry P. Music therapists' practice-based research in cancer and palliative care: creative methods and situated findings. Voices: A World Forum for Music Therapy [Internet]. 2009 [cited 2024 Jul 18];9(3). Available from: https://voices.no/index.php/voices/article/view/257.
67. Ørjasæter KB, Ness O. Acting out: enabling meaningful participation among people with long-term mental health problems in a music and theater workshop. Qual Health Res. 2017;27(11):1600–13.
68. Jakubiak D. Hermeneutic inquiry on musical gestures in a music therapy context/Recherche herméneutique sur le geste musical dans un contexte musicothérapeutique. Canadian J Music Ther. 2014;20(2):134–59.
69. Brookfield SD. Becoming a critically reflective teacher. 2nd ed. San Francisco: John Wiley & Sons; 2017.
70. Alvesson M, Sandberg J. Pre-understanding: an interpretation-enhancer and horizon-expander in research. Organ Stud. 2022;43(3):395–412.
71. Abrams B. Evidence-based music therapy practice: an integral understanding. J Music Ther. 2010;47(4):351–79.
72. McFerran KS, Shoemark H. How musical engagement promotes well-being in education contexts: the case of a young man with profound and multiple disabilities. Int J Qual Stud Health Well Being. 2013;8(1):20570.
73. Probst B. The eye regards itself: benefits and challenges of reflexivity in qualitative social work research. Soc Work Res. 2015;39(1):37–48.
74. Askins K, Swanson K. Holding onto emotions: a call to action in academia. Emot Space Soc. 2019;33:100617.
75. Knight V, Zempi I. Embracing the emotional turn: responding to researchers' emotions. Emotion Soc. 2020;2(2):139–56.
76. So H. Korean music therapy students' experience of group music therapy: a qualitative case study. Front Psychol. 2019;10:636.

77. Hubbard G, Backett-Milburn K, Kemmer D. Working with emotion: issues for the researcher in fieldwork and teamwork. Int J Soc Res Methodol. 2001;4(2):119–37.
78. Nguyen QD, Fernandez N, Karsenti T, Charlin B. What is reflection? A conceptual analysis of major definitions and a proposal of a five-component model. Med Educ. 2014;48(12):1176–89.
79. Hitchcock D, Hitchcock D. Critical thinking as an educational ideal. In: On reasoning and argument: essays in informal logic and on critical thinking. Cham: Springer; 2017. p. 477–97.
80. Hanscomb S. Critical thinking: the basics. 2nd ed. London: Routledge; 2023.
81. Widmer PS, Schippers MC, West MA. Recent developments in reflexivity research: a review. Psychol Everyday Activity. 2009;2(2):2–11.
82. Barry CA, Britten N, Barber N, Bradley C, Stevenson F. Using reflexivity to optimize teamwork in qualitative research. Qual Health Res. 1999;9(1):26–44.
83. Selle EW, Silverman MJ. Cardiovascular patients' perceptions of music therapy in the form of patient-preferred live music: exploring service user experiences. Nord J Music Ther. 2020;29(1):57–74.
84. Von Fritschen C, Dos Santos A. Perspectives on music healing by traditional healers and music therapists. Music Ther Perspect. 2023;41(2):152–8.
85. Tuastad L, Johansen B, Østerholt AL, Nielsen I, McIvor DSH. Being a person who plays in a band rather than being a person with a mental illness playing in a band: a qualitative study of stigma in the context of music therapy in mental health aftercare. Nord J Music Ther. 2023;32(2):121–39.
86. Skånland MS, Trondalen G. The therapeutic relationship in music therapy in a Flexible Assertive Community Treatment team: a joint interview study of service users and their music therapist. British J Music Ther. 2023;37(2):108–22.
87. McMahon K, McFerran K, Clark IN, Odell-Miller H, Stensæth K, Tamplin J, et al. Learning to use music as a resource: the experiences of people with dementia and their family care partners participating in a home-based skill-sharing music intervention: a HOMESIDE sub-study. Front Med. 2023;10:1205784.
88. Thomas N, Blanc V. Break it then build again: an arts based duoethnographic pilot reconstructing music therapy and dance/movement therapy histories. Arts Psychother. 2021;73:101765.
89. Adams J. The dynamics of research motivation: a comprehensive framework for understanding why researchers pursue specific questions. J Resear Pract. 2019;15(3):245–67.
90. Lindo D. Examining the accessibility of MA Music Therapy training in the United Kingdom for ethnic minority communities. British J Music Ther. 2023;37(1):5–16.

91. Muralidharan A, Silverman MJ. An exploratory thematic analysis of factors that influence sleep in music therapy undergraduate students. Music Ther Perspect. 2023;41(1).
92. Brand M, Clarke V, Warner C. "Surprisingly helpful": an exploration of trainee and registered music therapists' perspectives on the current role of personal therapy in music therapy training in the United Kingdom. Approach: Interdiscip J Mus Ther. 2023;15(2):200–16.
93. McCaffrey T. Evaluating music therapy in adult mental health services: tuning into service user perspectives. Nord J Music Ther. 2018;27(1):28–43.
94. McFerran K, Silverman MJ. A guide to designing research questions for beginning music therapy researchers. Silver Spring, MD: American Music Therapy Association; 2018.
95. Dixon-Woods M, Bonas S, Booth A, Jones DR, Miller T, Sutton AJ, et al. How can systematic reviews incorporate qualitative research? A critical perspective. Qualitat Resear. 2006;6(1):27–44.
96. Agee J. Developing qualitative research questions: a reflective process. Int J Qual Stud Educ. 2009;22(4):431–47.
97. Eide ISB. Institutional logics and the organizational context of music therapy. Nord J Music Ther. 2020;29(5):460–75.
98. Morse JM. Theory innocent or theory smart? Qual Health Res. 2002;12(3):295–6.
99. Glaser BG. Doing grounded theory: issues and discussions. Mill Valley, CA: Sociology Press; 1998.
100. Collins CS, Stockton CM. The central role of theory in qualitative research. Int J Qual Methods. 2018;17(1):1609406918797475.
101. Goodson P. Theory in health promotion research and practice: thinking outside the box. Sudbury, MA: Jones & Bartlett Learning; 2010.
102. Bruce T. Using theory to escape the descriptive impasse. Waikato J Edu. 2010;15(2):7–19.
103. Wu HL, Volker DL. The use of theory in qualitative approaches to research: application in end-of-life studies. J Adv Nurs. 2009;65(12):2719–32.
104. Lincoln YS, Guba GE. Naturalistic inquiry. Beverly Hills, CA: Sage; 1985.
105. Guba EG. The context of emergent paradigm research. In: Lincoln YS, editor. Organizational theory and inquiry: the paradigm revolution. Beverly Hills, CA: Sage; 1985. p. 79–104.
106. Bruscia KE. Defining music therapy. 3rd ed. Gilsum, NH: Barcelona Publishers; 2014.
107. hooks b. Teaching to transgress: education as the practice of freedom. New York: Routledge; 1994.
108. Stige B. The practice turn in music therapy theory. Music Ther Perspect. 2015;33(1):3–11.

109. Sandelowski M. Rigor or rigor mortis: the problem of rigor in qualitative research revisited. Adv Nurs Sci. 1993;16(2):1–8.
110. Ghetti CM. Music therapy as procedural support for invasive medical procedures: toward the development of music therapy theory. Nord J Music Ther. 2012;21(1):3–35.
111. Shanley JP. Doubt: a parable. New York: Theatre Communications Group; 2005.
112. McFerran K. Reconsidering the dominant narratives of the music therapy profession for the future. Canad J Music Ther. 2021;27(1):24–37.
113. Schwantes M, Rivera E. "A team working together to make a big, nice, sound": an action research pilot study in an inclusive college setting. Arts Psychother. 2017;55:1–10.
114. Etherington K. Ethical research in reflexive relationships. Qual Inq. 2007;13(5):599–616.
115. Vears D, Hiller A. Reflexivity and the clinician-researcher: managing participant misconceptions in qualitative research. Int J Qual Methods. 2016;15(1):1–10.
116. Tracy SJ. Qualitative quality: eight "big-tent" criteria for excellent qualitative research. Qual Inq. 2010;16(10):837–51.
117. Hesse-Biber SN, Leavy P, editors. Emergent methods in social research. Thousand Oaks, CA: Sage; 2006.
118. Takeda A. Uncovering ethical concerns through reflexivity—ethics in practice in fieldwork. Int J Soc Res Methodol. 2022;25(3):419–24.
119. Thompson G. Respect-focused writing: an invitation to reflexivity in the use of terminology. Nord J Music Ther. 2022;31(5):383–6.
120. O'Callaghan C. Lullament: lullaby and lament therapeutic qualities actualized through music therapy. Am J Hosp Palliat Med. 2008;25(2):93–9.
121. Guillemin M, Gillam L. Ethics, reflexivity, and "ethically important moments" in research. Qual Inq. 2004;10(2):261–80.
122. Berger R. Now I see it, now I don't: researcher's position and reflexivity in qualitative research. Qual Res. 2013;15(2):219–34.
123. McSorley K. Sexism and cisgenderism in music therapy spaces: an exploration of gender microaggressions experienced by music therapists. Arts Psychother. 2020;71:101707.
124. Epstein S, Elefant C, Arnon S, Ghetti C. Music therapy spanning from NICU to home: an interpretative phenomenological analysis of Israeli parents' experiences in the LongSTEP Trial. Nord J Music Ther. 2023;32(4):350–73.
125. Epstein S, Elefant C, Ghetti C. Israeli parents' lived experiences of music therapy with their preterm infants post-hospitalization. J Music Ther. 2022;59(3):239–68.

126. McCaffrey T. Music therapists' experience of self in clinical improvisation in music therapy: a phenomenological investigation. Arts Psychother. 2013;40(3):306–11.
127. Kennelly JD, Baker FA, Daveson BA. Professional supervision as storied experience: narrative analysis findings for Australian-based registered music therapists. J Music Ther. 2017;54(1):80–107.
128. Alvesson M, Sköldberg K. Reflexive methodology: new vistas for qualitative research. Thousand Oaks, CA: Sage; 2000.
129. Greiffenhagen C, Mair M, Sharrock W. From methodology to methodography: a study of qualitative and quantitative reasoning in practice. Methodological Innovat Online. 2011;6(3):93–107.
130. Hogan-Gibbons C, Short AE, Isobel S. Mental health inpatient experiences of song-writing: a qualitative study. Aust J Music Ther. 2020;31:29–44.
131. Stige B. Do we need general criteria for the evaluation of qualitative research articles, and if we do, how could such criteria be formulated? Nord J Music Ther. 2002;11(1):65–71.
132. Bryman A. Social research methods. 5th ed. Oxford: Oxford University Press; 2016.
133. Klauer KJ, Phye GD. Inductive reasoning: a training approach. Rev Educ Res. 2008;78(1):85–123.
134. Evans J. Deductive reasoning. In: Holyoak K, Morrison R, editors. The Cambridge handbook of thinking and reasoning. Cambridge: Cambridge University Press; 2005. p. 169–84.
135. Locke K, Golden-Biddle K, Feldman MS. Perspective—Making doubt generative: rethinking the role of doubt in the research process. Organ Sci. 2008;19(6):907–18.
136. Kistruck GM, Shantz AS. Research on grand challenges: adopting an abductive experimentation methodology. Organ Stud. 2021;43(9):1479–505.
137. Lakew Y. Statistical tales: bringing in reflexivity to make sense of quantitative data. In: Present scenarios of media production and engagement. Bremen: edition Lumiere; 2017. p. 225–38.
138. Snape N, Saarikallio S, Ala-Ruona E, Hartmann M, Brabant O, Erkkilä J. Depressed adults' experiences of listening to their own clinical improvisations at home: a process evaluation of the music therapy homework. Nord J Music Ther. 2023;32(2):139–59.
139. Prinz J. Beyond human nature: how culture and experience shape the human mind. New York: W.W. Norton & Company; 2012.
140. Chenail RJ. Conducting qualitative data analysis: qualitative data analysis as a metaphoric process. Qual Rep. 2012;17(1):248–53.
141. Aigen K. An analysis of qualitative music therapy research reports 1987–2006: doctoral studies. Arts Psychother. 2008;35(5):307–19.

142. Arns B, Thompson GA. Music therapy teaming and learning: how transdisciplinary experience shapes practice in a specialist school for students with autism. Aust J Music Ther. 2019;30:31–52.
143. McCaffrey T, Edwards J. Meeting art with art: arts-based methods enhance researcher reflexivity in research with mental health service users. J Music Ther. 2015;52(4):515–32.
144. Bibb J, Howden A, McFerran KS. Exploring the experiences of professional practice for Australian based registered music therapists. Aust J Music Ther. 2021;32(2):79–98.

CHAPTER 5

Authorial Reflexivity

What if the truth isn't out there, rather there are "only stories yet to be constructed" [1, p. 267]? A researcher working with Authorial Reflexivity is saying: "I can only tell you how I see this. No matter how hard I've worked to get to know this topic, the context, and these participants' experiences, I cannot claim to have climbed inside their reality. I'm perceiving their experiences from within the confines of my own, so that's what I will share with you". Gro Trondalen [2, p. 24] wrote about "the assumptions that it is only the researcher's experiences and intuition of the phenomenon that is available to the researcher herself, after all."

This researcher may be focusing their gaze inwards, outwards or both, as captured perfectly in the title of Kerry Devlin's [3] autoethnography *How do I see you, and what does that mean for us?* In our interview, Devlin explained how, in this paper, she explored her relationship with a child she worked with in music therapy:

> I was reflecting on a relationship just from my perspective at a different point in time and so it's always one-sided in that way. This is just my

---

Deliberately acknowledging and exploring our active participation in creating and shaping knowledge in our study *because we can only see the world from our own vantage point* and responding to these insights *by recognising that this is one of many possible stories.*

A. dos Santos, *Reflexive Research in Music Therapy*,
https://doi.org/10.1007/978-3-032-02033-8_5

> rendering of an experience and it's forever one-sided because it's only how I perceive that relationship.

We can embrace the fact that we'll never have the full picture or final understanding. As Devlin said in relation to music therapy in particular, "I think when you're in music with someone, there is something that's just unknowable".

If we tried to get rid of our personal perspectives we'd lose all ways of knowing the world. We gather knowledge of the world as we *assemble* our perspectives [4]. We *are* subjective and we can value and celebrate this. There are ways of producing excellent research that makes a helpful contribution to the world, within which we embrace our originality, uniqueness, and plurality (as opposed to standardisation, control, and generalisation). Our imagination and creativity can enrich our research. Imagination here is not about fantasy and fiction; it is, as Brian Abrams [5, p. 369] described, "the capacity for envisioning reality in uniquely expressive ways that construct and convey its experiential essence."

Acknowledging that we're grounded in our own experience doesn't cut us off from others. We can be moved and changed by reading another researcher's account of their experience. In my interview with Michael Viega, he explained this in relation to his experience with music in general, giving the example of his response to the singer-songwriter Ani DiFranco. While knowing that her feminist lyrics don't directly reflect his own experience, the truth of what they conveyed "felt profoundly emotional to me…I can't help but assimilate them into my awareness and experience and be completely and utterly moved by it…She's relating within her own femininity and I don't think me assimilating it takes away from it. I can incorporate that into my own consciousness…"

In their book *Where research begins*, Thomas Mullaney and Christopher Rea [6] explained how research starts as the researcher identifies the problem they carry inside them and figures out what to do with it. Conducting self-centred research doesn't mean simply letting your ego run amok. It's not self-consumed, self-indulgent, self-serving, or self-congratulatory. It is the opposite: self-centred researchers are reflexive, self-aware, self-critical, honest, and open. By developing our self-awareness we can gain a better sense of the distinction between our own and others' points of view [7, 8]. In our conversation, Viega said, "I think the initial impetus of reflexivity is to notice any defences you have and anything related to ego that's getting in the way…A feeling of defensiveness is a signal that a new perspective is necessary."

As we gather "self-evidence" about our research, we can ask ourselves:

- Why do I care about this topic?
- What is it about this topic that I think holds the key to a larger issue?
- Why does this text jump out at me?
- Why does this topic call to me, given that there are so many other possibilities I could pursue?
- What is the problem that matters to me so much that I wish to address it through my study?

As we explore these questions, we need to really listen to ourselves and welcome our vulnerability. Our task is to notice what we're noticing about ourselves [6].

Theoretical Options that Can Underpin Authorial Reflexivity

There is a range of theoretical and philosophical frameworks that could underpin a researcher's claim that their findings are shaped by their perspectives and informed by their experiences as opposed to presenting Truth about the external world. Here I'll mention three: interpretivism, radical constructivism, and field theory.

Interpretivism

We can build a study on an interpretivist epistemology foundation by holding onto the notion of a shared external reality, but one that may be interpreted differently as we make meaning from within our own contexts. Therefore, instead of a single, universal Truth, we focus on numerous smaller truths shaped by human subjectivities. Wilhelm Dilthey, an early advocate of this perspective, noted that inner experience and consciousness serve as the foundation for thought: "all experience must be related back to and derives its validity from the conditions and context of consciousness in which it arises" [9, p. 52]. All knowledge is located within particular communities and certain knowledge can claim no greater worth (as knowledge) than any other competing claims to truth [10].

Radical Constructivism

Another option that can theoretically underpin Authorial Reflexivity is radical constructivism, articulated by Ernst von Glasersfeld [11]. This perspective makes an even stronger claim: all knowledge is purely constructed. Radical constructivism is radical because of this departure from "objective" ontological reality. Each person creates their own unique understanding based on their personal experience [12].

Von Glaserfeld [13] differentiated between "matching" and "fitting." The metaphysical realist seeks knowledge that corresponds with reality, much like selecting paint that matches the existing colour on a wall that needs repairing. However, when we say something fits, we refer to a different kind of relationship. Consider a smartphone charger. A charger fits when it powers the device, even if it's not the original charger designed for that phone model. The fit pertains to the charger's ability to achieve the goal—charging the phone—rather than matching the phone's original specifications or brand. Knowledge (what is "known") isn't passively received as we discover aspects of the world. It originates through our activity in the world. Epistemology is then the study of how the mind operates and how it constructs a relatively regular world out of the flow of its experience. Our activity of knowing is like creating the charger that will fit the phone, turn it on, and enable us to use it to accomplish the goals we've chosen.

Field Theory

I suggest that field theory can also serve as a theoretical framework for Authorial Reflexivity. We find this theory in texts on Gestalt therapy. Field theory has multiple interpretations [14], just as the term "field" is defined in various ways [15]. Psychologist Kurt Lewin [16] first proposed this theory, arguing that to truly comprehend a situation or life space (the field), we need to view it holistically instead of focusing on isolated components. A person is inseparable from their context, and so the interplay between a person and their environment becomes the focal point. The field includes only those environmental factors that the individual perceives at some level, either consciously or unconsciously [17]. It is a phenomenal field in the sense that there's always a horizon of possibilities that can arise or be focused on in any situation [14].

Dave Mann [18] gave an example of a river. A thirsty hiker comes across a rushing freshwater river. With relief, he gulps down some of the water. Across the bank, a fisherman casts his line, intently observing the river for the chance of a salmon bite. Meanwhile, an ecologist gauges the river's depth and flow to determine if the water level has decreased and if there's potential for harnessing energy. Nearby, two young children splash in the river's shallows, while their father enjoys a moment of peace and quiet. This same river is experienced in vastly different ways depending on each individual's needs in that specific moment. Each individual's situation and perception are distinct [14]. By listening to each person's story we get a fuller picture of the river and its potentials—just like we do when we read multiple researcher's accounts of a phenomenon.

If we're working in a Gestalt-informed manner in a therapeutic context, we may be exploring with clients how they organise their field and what is causing them to do so. For a researcher, the questions become: How am I operating within, navigating and arranging this research situation? Why am I doing so in this way? What does how I'm navigating the field afford in terms of what I notice and what I don't? How can I organise the field more intentionally by actively stepping back, observing, and structuring its dynamics to make the relationships between its elements more explicit? This may still seem a bit abstract so let's look at an example.

Imagine you're conducting a qualitative study on music therapy with teenagers in a children's home. You're hoping to develop a long-term relationship with this organisation and potentially gain some employment there once the study is finished. The research involves collaboration with the home's staff, the teenagers, and other stakeholders. As you intentionally reflect on aspects of the field as it relates to this project, you might ask yourself: "How am I operating within, navigating, and arranging this research situation?" You notice that you tend to defer to the staff's opinions about what approaches might work best for the teenagers ("Don't work in a group, they'll just be disruptive and give you a hard time"). As you ask yourself, "Why am I doing this?" and "What is this affording?" through reflexive journalling, you realise that your decisions are understandably driven by a belief that the staff's support is essential for the research's success and for your potential job prospects at this organisation.

You acknowledge their years of experience in this context. However, you also recognise that this plan is leading you to overlook the essential voices of the teenagers and your knowledge of how group music therapy could be potentially helpful (and fun). You then ask yourself, "How can I organise the field more intentionally?" This might involve addressing power imbalances by restructuring group meetings and creating spaces to explore how the teenagers may wish to engage in music therapy, creating a field where participants' roles and contributions are embraced in a more balanced way.

Embracing Self-Exploration and Expression

When we're self-aware, we notice and attend to our thoughts, emotions, beliefs, behaviours, and attitudes, and we can see the links between these and aspects of our developmental and social background [19]. We can engage in self-awareness to access inner insights but we can also think of self-awareness as self-storying [20]. We have many possible self-narratives and fluid storylines. In my interview with Nicky Haire, she explained that "there's a kind of self-awareness in reflexivity which requires time. But it's not just about self-awareness…it's a multi-layered *being*".

Exploring Layers of Self

In his book *How our lives become stories,* Paul Eakin [21] distinguished between five (often intertwined) types of self: ecological, interpersonal, extended, private, and conceptual. In research terms, reflecting on my ecological self would entail exploring who I am here in this place, participating in this activity. In terms of my interpersonal self, I would explore how I'm engaged in social interactions with others. My extended self expands over time, and I would look at how my memories and past experiences, as well as my anticipation of the future, are shaping who I am and how I'm thinking, feeling, and engaging. In relation to my private self, I'd explore the nature, qualities and implications of my inner conscious experiences that aren't necessarily available to others but may be shaping the research process. In terms of my conceptual self, I would examine notions of social roles, personality, and perceptions of self as a category.

There are endless ways of exploring these layers. You could create musical self-portraits or use guided imagery sessions followed by free writing to reflect on how each self appears in your research. You could document the sounds of environments where you're conducting your study and look at how these spaces shape your presence and approach, and how your ecological self responds differently in various settings. If you're part of a class of students you could experiment with role-playing to embody different researcher personas as you explore your conceptual self. Reflect on how each role feels and what it reveals about your assumptions regarding what a researcher "should" be. You could symbolise your private self using clay or by creating a playlist, or make a collage of your cultural influences and examine how these shape your conceptual self and research paradigms. You could rewrite your researcher biography from the perspective of each type of self, noting how the story changes depending on which self is narrating.

Introspection

If we value conducting research that seeks participants' experiences, then it's rather inconsistent to reject researchers' introspection as "unscientific" [22, p. 100]. The term introspection originates from the Latin *introspicere*, meaning "to look within" [23]. Historically, introspection has deep roots in both Eastern and Western philosophical traditions. In Eastern thought, introspection developed within Confucianism, Taoism, and Buddhism, shaping philosophies of self-observation and internal understanding. In the West, philosophers like Plato, Descartes, Locke, and Hume also explored the value of introspection [24].

In everyday life, introspection is a natural, often automatic, process. It emerges as we engage with questions like "Why am I feeling this way?" or "What do I think about this?" As researchers, our introspection is often more structured and transparent so that we can generate and examine a first-person perspective. Researcher introspection can provide unique access to subjective experiential or phenomenological data that can't be tapped into through other methods [24]. Researcher introspection has been described as the "ultimate participant observation" [25, p. 188]. Through introspection, we adopt the role of an informer regarding our own lived experiences. We may also be inviting and guiding participants to introspect. A combination of both may also occur [24].

Introspection in research encompasses three time-related approaches. Retrospective introspection entails reflecting on past experiences. Concurrent introspection emphasises real-time self-observation, allowing us to capture experiences as they occur. Imaginary introspection envisions potential futures [26]. While introspection can offer valuable insights, it also has some limitations. It's dependent on memory, especially in retrospective analysis. Memory is reconstructive and susceptible to distortions. Introspection also tends to emphasise extraordinary events while downplaying everyday happenings. However, if we're aware of this we can work to mitigate these limitations [27].

Lived Experience

Phenomenological researchers often mention the "lifeworld" and "lived experience". Edmund Husserl [28, p. 50] first used the term lifeworld (*Lebenswelt*) in 1936 to refer to the "actually intuited, actually experienced and experienceable world, in which practically our whole life takes place." The lifeworld is the background to our experiences, the taken-for-granted familiar world that we inhabit before we try to analyse it. Within this context, we experience phenomena as they present themselves to our consciousness. A number of lifeworld themes or dimensions can be used as guides for research reflection: selfhood, the lived body, place and space, lived time, relations, experiences of one's research project, and language [29–31].

Selfhood:

- How does my personal identity influence what I notice or value in this research?
- How am I experiencing my sense of agency in this research?
- What are my feelings around my presence and voice here?
- How is my identity connecting me to others here and how is it created through my interactions with others?
- In what ways have my life experiences shaped my interpretation of participants' stories?
- What aspects of my background might create both insights and blind spots in this work?

The lived body:

- How do I physically respond when engaging with certain aspects of this research?
- What embodied knowledge am I drawing upon when making sense of participants' experiences?
- In what ways does my physical presence impact data collection situations?
- How might my own bodily experiences of comfort/discomfort be informing my analysis?
- How does my own experience of health, ability, embodiment, race, or gender inform my understanding of others?

Place and space:

- How do the physical environments where I'm conducting my research influence interactions?
- What meanings do I associate with the spaces where this research takes place?
- How might different research settings affect what participants feel comfortable sharing?
- What boundaries between personal and research spaces am I maintaining or crossing?
- How does my cultural relationship to this place differ from those of my participants?

Time:

- How do my own temporal rhythms affect how I structure and pace this research?
- How does my own life phase influence my understanding of participants at different life stages?
- In an interview, does time feel like it's moving slowly or whizzing by?
- Are past experiences of conversations with other participants becoming superimposed on the present moment?
- Is the anticipation of how the conversation will be analysed in the future impacting how the engagement is unfolding now?

Relations:

- How do my personal relationships influence my understanding of relationships in the research context?
- How do power differences between myself and participants shape our interactions?
- How do my cultural backgrounds regarding relationships differ from those of my participants?

The project:

- What emotions arise for me during different phases of this research?
- How do I feel when encountering data that challenge my initial assumptions?
- What aspects of this research do I find most engaging or meaningful, and why?
- How am I changed by the process of conducting this research?
- What tensions or contradictions am I experiencing in my role as researcher?

Language:

- What assumptions might be embedded in the terminology I use to describe phenomena?
- How might my academic language differ from the everyday language of participants?
- What metaphors do I naturally reach for when describing this research, and what do they reveal?
- In what ways might translation (between languages or between everyday and academic language) be influencing meaning in my research?

Embodied Knowing

Embodiment refers to how we experience and make sense of the world through our bodies [32]. Within my interview with Nicky Haire, I asked her how she would describe reflexivity and she highlighted the role of the senses. She answered: "All over my PhD I was writing 'reflexivity as a method of sense-making' and I only just realised now that actually I meant 'feeling', like *sense* making...So not just intellectualising or analysing; it's a method of actually taking it into my body but still somehow processing it. And…that wasn't a…tidy process…and it definitely wasn't a linear process. But it was an embodiment and an enriching process."

Embodied self-awareness, as defined by Alan Fogel [33], is a mindful focus on sensations, emotions, and movements in the present moment, free from judgement. This differs from conceptual self-awareness, which classifies and dissects experiences through language and logic. We are interconnected beings, of course. Although embodied self-awareness exists before language, expressive or evocative words can enhance it. Embodied Inquiry is a qualitative research method that highlights the importance of the body in reflexivity and positionality. It sees the body as a means of communication as well as a focal point for investigation [34].

When we experience or think about a significant life event, we might first have an ambiguous bodily awareness—a "sense" of the circumstance—before developing a conceptual understanding. Eugene Gendlin [35] introduced the concept of the felt sense in 1964. The felt sense is a bodily experience that's preverbal and linked to a specific situation. It's distinct from emotions, thoughts, or sensory information. Through his research and collaboration with Carl Rogers, Gendlin noticed that some individuals responded better to psychotherapy when they focussed on the felt sense of their challenges [36].

Engaging with our felt sense as a researcher offers a valuable approach to access embodied knowledge that's often overlooked in favour of direct reasoning. Let's imagine an example where a researcher in a dual role is writing up their process of music therapy with a participant, Mia. In their reflexive journal, they write the following:

> *During today's session with Mia, there was a moment when she shifted from jagged, disconnected piano notes to a flowing melodic line. Before I could intellectually process this change, my breathing already deepened and my shoulders relaxed. There was a feeling of expansion in my chest and a sense of being*

"carried" by her music. When I looked at the video later, I realised this "felt sense" had guided my clinical response as I matched her with more fluid accompaniment. The feeling in my body was then one of "rightness" or "coherence"—that bodily "yes". I saw that when there was a tonal resolution I closed my eyes peacefully. Because I'm researching this process with Mia, I'm also wondering how this felt sense informs my interpretation of our musical interactions? My body seemed to recognise a meaningful therapeutic moment before my conscious mind could explain it. When coding my data, I need to think about how these embodied responses might be guiding my attention toward certain moments and away from others. How can I lean into this somatic knowledge? Maybe my methodology needs to include ways to document these felt sensations along with my video data. This experience also makes me reflect on how my own musical training has honed certain sensitivities in my felt sense. My years of classical training could be making me especially responsive to tonal resolution and phrase structure. I have an embodied response to tonal resolution. It's a felt sense of "completion", "rightness" and warmth. I feel it in my stomach. I wonder if I potentially overvalue these elements in my research at the expense of other qualities that might matter more to participants with different musical backgrounds?

Arts-based researchers, in particular, have a range of tools at their disposal to explore felt sense. A felt sense could be vague, ephemera,l and easy to miss, so it takes intentionality and care to tune into it. When we do this with curiosity and patience, we can awaken new insights.

Here are some more ideas for how you could explore embodied self-awareness in your own study:

- Through body mapping you can create a detailed drawing of your body, highlighting areas of tension, comfort, or energy that emerge during different research activities.
- In your reflexive journal, document physical sensations that occurred in response to specific moments, exploring how your body "knew" before your conscious mind did.
- Use free movement improvisations with music of your choice to physically express your experiences as a researcher, followed by (if you want to and feel it's necessary) writing about what your movement patterns tell you about your embodied understanding.

(*continued*)

(**continued**)

- Monitor your breathing patterns during different research activities and interactions, noticing how your breathing changes with different emotional states and research decisions.
- Create regular "sensory check-ins" during your research project, documenting what you're seeing, hearing, feeling, tasting, and smelling to develop a heightened awareness of how sensory experiences are forming your understanding.
- Document how different research environments (rooms, acoustics, temperatures, seating arrangements) affect your physical comfort and presence as a researcher.
- Translate physical sensations experienced during research cross-modally into music, colours, or textures, exploring the interconnection between different sensory modalities in your embodied knowing.
- Explore how ethical dilemmas in research manifest as physical sensations, developing awareness of how your body signals alignment or conflict with your values.

Knowing Through Emotions

Emotional dimensions of research studies can be viewed as "epistemologically productive" [37, p. 37]. "Much richness can arise when we research with feeling" [38]. The "affective turn" marked an intellectual shift in recent decades towards valuing emotions as essential areas of academic inquiry [39]. Rationality and emotion coexist symbiotically, with all reasoning shaped by feelings and vice versa. In *Research is ceremony*, Shawn Wilson [40] critiqued the idea that research must be purely intellectual and objective, arguing that such approaches deny the emotional and relational nature of human inquiry. Indigenous scholar Eber Hampton [41] also argued that research is inherently emotional because it's driven by human feelings. Attempting to separate intellect from emotion in research can be dishonest and dangerous, leading to dehumanising practices that harm researchers and those around them. Research outputs can also then often come across as overly sanitised with the challenges of research becoming invisible. Feminist scholars have also worked to show how knowledge is intrinsically influenced by situated, embodied experiences: "to know differently, we have to feel differently" [42].

Knowing Through Writing

Traditional academic writing often marginalises creative and experiential approaches. Ilaria Boncori [43] argued that by embracing slowness, emotion, and vulnerability, we can reshape academic practices and discourses for the better. We can breathe creativity and life back into our work and the process can become more dynamic when we write "through, with, and despite" [43, p. 71] our bodies. When our writing is raw and honest we invite our readers to identify with us and the stories we're sharing [44]. In competitive academic contexts it's often individual success that's celebrated. One way of resisting this and placing relationality in a more central position is to write with our emotions in ways that invite connection [45]. Writing differently can be risky, though, because when we do this we may feel exposed.

Instead of only first having ideas and then writing them down, the act of writing can bring us new insights. (We know this about music too. We don't just play music that represents what we already know; music also speaks back to us and brings us new ideas.) Laurel Richardson [46, p. 179] stated, "I consider writing as a method of inquiry, a way of finding out about yourself and your topic." When Claire O'Callaghan [47] employed practice-based research to examine her interpretations of her programme's relevance in a cancer hospital through reflexive journal analysis, she drew on Laurel Richardson's [48] assertion that writing is a way of knowing. (I also recommend looking at the book *Departing radically in academic writing* edited by Elizabeth Mackinlay and Karen Madden [49].)

In music therapy literature, we often see researchers making use of reflexive journals to think through writing. For example, in their examination of clinical applications of feminist music therapy, Kendra Bodry and Melody Schwantes [50] wrote about how they kept reflexive journals to examine their emotions and process. In Bill Ahessy's [51] study on online music therapy with children and adolescents with visual impairment, he was both the music therapist and the researcher. He kept a reflexive journal throughout the process to bring his personal and professional perspectives into awareness.

Laura Beer [52] explained how keeping a journal can help track one's dilemmas, thoughts, and potential areas for additional investigation. It can help us see which strands of thought are most important to pursue and which ones can be set aside. She found that writing in an electronic journal offered a way of writing freely without becoming bogged down with perfecting flow, grammar, and cohesiveness. Her inner critic didn't get in the way. She could simply focus on untangling her interior arguments and inclinations. Through this kind of creative, free-style writing she could also separate out the participants' voices from her own. Often, before or after writing, she would also play musically to further explore her inner world. Beer reminded us that it's never too early for qualitative researchers to begin writing a personal account in their projects. In a study by Philippa Barry and colleagues [53] on the creation of music therapy CDs for initial paediatric radiation therapy, their clinical reflexive journal served as data.

Laurel Richardson [46] offered creative writing techniques that can help researchers. We can join or start a writing group, work through a creative writing guidebook, or take part in writing workshops or classes. We can transform our field notes into dramatic pieces or experiment with poetic representations of in-depth interviews. Poetry serves as not only a tool and method for presenting research data but also a source of data and a means for data analysis [54]. We could write an article as a more seamless narrative that integrates literature, theory, and methods, rather than presenting disjointed sections. We might choose to write about specific settings or events from the perspectives of different role players, exploring what insights arise from each role. These different viewpoints could be presented in dialogue. When reviewing a previous paper or field notes, one could identify anyone left out or marginalised. The text could then be rewritten to imagine these potential perspectives. Collaborative writing can enhance our awareness of personal stylistic tendencies. Memory work is an example of a collaborative strategy where people share and retell their stories, enhancing their memories as they do so or creating new narratives, as well as discovering commonalities in their experiences.

Jasmine Ulmer [55] examined how movement, creativity, and exploration in dance could inform the academic writing process. I encourage you to take a look at her paper *Embodied writing: choreographic composition as methodology*. Ulmer explored writing where words dynamically move, pause, emphasise, and flow like dancers across a blank page. She explained how altering our writing approaches can also transform our thinking processes.

We'll discuss autoethnographies momentarily, but it's important to mention autoethnographic writing here as we're placing a spotlight on thinking through writing. Kerry Devlin [3] explained that autoethnographers can draw on the adaptability of creative writing strategies. In her paper, she described how she isn't always sure what will surface when she sits down to write. Sometimes, she feels emotional; for hours she may sit and think and struggle with questions. On other occasions, words may flow easily, "as though my fingers knew the answer to a question that my brain hadn't quite figured out yet" [3, p. 235]. In her autoethnography there were many moments in the process when she felt stuck. After about 50 revisions of her paper, only then did she feel that it flowed like a story but, "like many good stories, mine may leave you with more questions than answers…This is simply the nature of storytelling" [3, p. 235].

Knowing Through the Sounding Board of Supervision and Mentorship

In our interview, Kerry Devlin shared the following (in relation to her autoethnographic study "How do I see you and what does that mean for us? [3]):

> I like to get connected with my felt experience of something. I've had really good supervisors, research mentors, especially for that autoethnography. That was not my first idea for a project. I came in thinking, "Oh, I should do, like, 'real research'". …I kept talking about how: "I'm really grappling with working in the education system…I don't know what I'm having, like a crisis as a new-ish clinician trying to understand my own identity and the spaces I want to be in." And I had a really good mentor who was the one who helped me understand *that* is the thing I should research and that it's just as valuable to research yourself, you know? It's just as valuable as doing quantitative research or more traditional research methodologies. And so the process of doing that and having somebody who gave me the space and helped me give myself the permission to work in that way I think completely changed the trajectory of the kind of research I'll do moving forward.

While there's often time pressure on research supervision, it may be beneficial to create meetings that focus specifically on helping students explore their experiences, or to have student groups with this as the agenda. In supervision groups, students could be invited to create timelines of significant moments in their study and how they experienced these. They could examine together how their core values are sculpting their study; or improvise musically as they reflect on why a study matters to them and how they hope it will contribute. There are endless creative options. The supervisor's role is to invite, prompt, probe deeper, while holding open an explorative and non-judgemental space.

Being Present in the Text as the Storyteller

We are present in our research just as we're present as music therapists in our encounters with service users. In our interview, where we discussed her autoethnography, Devlin explained that she valued being able to write an article that tells a story and that this

> impacted the way I think about research moving forward—the process of telling that story and having the experience of reflecting as a clinician on my clinical work, but also as a researcher looking at my clinical work in reflection…And when I wrote that, I was having a big identity crisis development moment where I was coming to terms with the fact that *I* was identifying as disabled myself and not quite sure what that meant for me as a clinician, me as a researcher. And I think the process of actually engaging reflexively as a clinician, as a researcher, in those similar overlapping ways, has also really helped me personally and developed my own reflexivity as I was writing about this process. I was like, 'wait a second, I'm going through this parallel process in my personal life and of course it can't be separated from my clinical self from my therapist self, from my researcher self'.

In our interview, Michael Viega explained reflexivity as "not merely practice or research; it's fundamentally a human growth activity that prompts the question, 'where am I situated in the midst of this?'…so that I can be aware of what uniqueness I bring and enhance what's happening within the community because we're all mutual stakeholders, trying to support the growth of something".

Stephen Venkatarangam [56] published a paper on participants' experiences of a receptive music therapy intervention that incorporated raga. He wrote about how he identifies as a first-generation Canadian of East Indian ethnicity. He described his musical training in Western classical music, experimental rock and improvisational jazz, and then Hindustani classical Indian music (raga). Raga had a transformative effect on him, which led him to introduce live receptive raga sitar experiences in sessions as a music therapist and to investigate whether people who don't usually listen to classical Indian music could have meaningful experiences during receptive raga interventions. In his paper he also drew on his perspective as a musician.

In Bodry and Schwantes' [48] paper on the clinical applications of feminist music therapy, they vividly presented themselves as active storytellers, specifically noting how they defined feminist music therapy and how they see it functioning. They articulated what they believe, what they think, and why they use this way of thinking. They richly described their positioning as well as their relationship with each other and how they explored ways of working together in this project. I'd strongly encourage you to read their full description of themselves in their paper.

Debbie Carroll [57] wrote about portraiture and the role of the researcher. Portraiture draws on aspects of case studies, narratives, phenomenology, and ethnography. The portraitist and the participant both negotiate the conversation and influence the emerging image [58]. In portraiture, the researcher's voice is pervasive. We see it reflected in Carroll's assumptions, concerns, and framework, in the questions she poses, the data she collects, the narratives she chooses to share, and in the tone, rhythm, and style of her storytelling. Voice serves as the research instrument.

Authorial Reflexivity Throughout the Research Stages

Research Problems and Questions

Mullaney and Rea [6, p. 4] argued that "the better (and faster) you figure out your own concerns and motivations as a researcher, the better (and faster) you will discover a research problem that is deeply meaningful both to you and to the world at large." Katrina McFerran and Michael Silverman's [59] model for developing research questions in music therapy also begins with identifying intriguing personal experiences. To first tune into what matters to you, Mullaney and Rea recommended some helpful introspective exercises, such as noting all the research topics you are drawn to, choosing one and running a search in a database. When clicking on results that interest you, the goal is first to "read yourself" as you read the texts that are identified. Which titles spark curiosity, speculation, or boredom? Becoming more aware of what you're noticing can be surprisingly challenging. Something may stand out to you, but in a subtle way.

Mullaney and Rea [6] encouraged researchers to stress test the questions they start to develop. One of the ways to do this is to explore our assumptions. We arrive at our topic and questions "with a whole mess of assumptions", which is natural and good because these are the reasons we thought that our topic was interesting and meaningful for us to explore. We all bring our "baggage" to our studies. What's important is that we make our assumptions visible and vulnerable instead of judging them and "driving them underground" [6, p. 62] where we may land up holding onto them even tighter. Assumptions shape our expectations about reality. When these expectations are not met, it's in this gap that we start to notice what needs to be questioned.

Methodologies

While autoethnography could be seen as the quintessential approach to reflexivity that entails exploring one's own experiences of meaning-making, there are also other methodological approaches within which Authorial Reflexivity can be used. Let's look at autoethnography first (as well as collaborative autoethnographies), and then discuss heuristic research and arts-based research.

Autoethnography

To grasp autoethnography, we need to dissect it into its components. The prefix "auto" signifies that the narrative should be self-reflective, focusing on our own experience as the author, rather than those of others. "Ethno" indicates that the narrative should connect to broader themes concerning a culture or subgroup. Autoethnography values the context of research, allowing the author to weave in personal and cultural influences through their self-narrative [60]. Autoethnography is different from autobiography, which centres on individual narratives. Autoethnographers view personal stories as lenses to interpret the connections between themselves and their sociocultural contexts, exploring how these contexts shape the meanings of their experiences and viewpoints [61]. "Graphy" means that we're creating a narrative that will add to existing knowledge.

In music therapy literature, we find a number of autoethnographies, including explorations of developing post-ableist music therapy [62], navigating oppression, power, and privilege in music therapy spaces [63], understanding the therapeutic process [64], integrating ethnomusicology into music therapy [65], finding empathy through music therapy techniques during experiences of family trauma [66], gender-affirming voice-work in music therapy [67], clinical intuition in work with young children living in urban poverty [68], playing the guitar for self-care [69], experiences of music during recovery from laser eye surgery [70]. Allison Echard

[71] argued that autoethnography can be understood as a form of clinical reflexivity.

Building repositories of research that include stories from many different people groups matters enormously [72]. For example, Toyin Falola [60] argued for the value of autoethnography within Afrocentric research. He highlighted how science in the West adheres to the empirical method, with researchers typically refraining from sharing interpretations that extend beyond what can be substantiated through scientific investigation. This reflects a Eurocentric conception of knowledge as distinct from personal experience, opinion, or emotion. Afrocentric social science research highlights cultural centredness, knowledge pluralism, and a holistic perspective. Falola argued that the ideal Afrocentric social science study is conducted by a community member who understands and accurately reflects the culture and aligns with local philosophies. This researcher engages in methodological reflexivity, exploring how their personal experiences and community position influence their research. Autoethnography fits into this approach well. It promotes a pluriversal understanding of knowledge, as no single system of knowledge can capture the entirety of the human experience. Autoethnography encourages researchers to voice their own truths while honouring the truths of others.

Critical autoethnographers focus on exploring how power dynamics enhance or restrict experiences [73]. These researchers often consider intersectionality [74, 75] as they examine the interconnectedness of oppressive systems like racism, xenophobia, sexism, heteronormativity, classism, religious extremism, ageism, and ableism.

Collaborative Autoethnographies

In collaborative autoethnography (CAE) multiple researchers work together to explore shared and differing meaning about a social phenomenon [76, 77]. Sometimes researchers cycle between working collaboratively and alone throughout a CAE process, as they connect their stories to broader issues, relate to and critique existing literature, and maintain a balance that prevents the process and findings from becoming too inward-looking [61].

In performative CAE [76], researchers write about and analyse their experiences together and also present their findings through performances, like musical or theatrical presentations, readings, dance, digital media, or other artistic expressions [77]. One of the goals is to challenge standard assumptions about how knowledge is generated, analysed, and shared

[76]. Michael Viega and his colleagues [78] used digital music improvisation as their primary performative method for exploring their research questions. They took part in an ongoing group process of six improvisation sessions in which they built interpersonal rapport, selected thematic elements to investigate, and reflected on their experiences. In their paper there were times when they wrote individually and specified which author was contributing. At other points, we as readers are asked to interpret their contributions as a collective voice.

Duoethnography—autoethnography with two researchers working together—emerged through the work of Richard Sawyer and Joe Norris [79]. They wanted to embrace the power of dialogue. Duoethnographers need to be able to openly and critically examine themselves and their co-researchers in a supportive manner. Dialogues don't only take place among the researchers but also with cultural artifacts like photographs, songs, and even the duoethnographic text itself [80, 81]. Each duoethnographer's voice is clearly articulated throughout, often in a script-like format. It takes vulnerability to engage in duoethnography because researchers are deeply questioning themselves, they're open to critique from their co-researcher, and then they seek to share their perspective shifts with their readers [82].

A few music therapists have published duoethnographies and trioethnographies (with three researchers working together). For example, Amy Thomas and Fiona Sham [83] used duoethnography to explore the impact of culture on their clinical practice. Xiyu Zhang et al. [84] examined the experiences of three international music therapy interns during their clinical training, and Petra Jerling and colleagues' [85] trioethnography focused on exploring how to select the best music for the moment in a music and imagery session. In their arts-based duoethnography, Thomas and Blanc [86, p. 3] explained that their goal was "to resituate a more inclusive and personal history in both our own bodies and professional practices, while avoiding a singular, essentialist, or obscurance of non-dominant narratives."

Heuristic Research

When using the heuristic research model of Clark Moustakas [87], a researcher seeks to uncover the essence of a phenomenon while also engaging in deep self-reflection [88, 89]. The term "heuristic" derives from Greek, meaning to discover or find. It's related to the Greek term "Eureka," which symbolises the "aha" moment. The heuristic model is fundamentally phenomenological, aiming to reveal the meaning and essence of human experiences from the perspective of the individual experiencing them. We bring our primary subjective experiences into conscious awareness and welcome them into the inquiry process (but we ensure that we aren't overwhelmed by them). Heuristic research focuses on lived experience, and the researcher engages in an internal search as well as in-depth interviews with participants. In both aspects, the researcher's self is always present [88].

Heuristic research involves six phases: initial engagement (self-inquiry: what am I interested in researching and why?); immersion (intensive exploration of the topic through self-investigation and exploring with others); incubation (stepping away so that tacit knowledge can unfold); illumination (awakening of new knowledge after this incubation period); explication (articulating and refining the knowledge that has been gathered); and creative synthesis (which can take a creative form) [88].

In music therapy literature specifically, Amanda Schenstead [90, p. 2] wrote that heuristic research involves "immersing oneself in the 'bathtub' of the phenomena." The researcher engages in intense inner seeking to discover the nature and meaning of the experience. They need to be fully present as they study the phenomenon and whatever comes into consciousness offers a path for further exploration. In their paper on music therapy clinical introspection in working with foster care youth, Michael Zanders et al. [91] described how heuristic inquiry transforms the researcher's personal experience and involves potential self-discovery.

Arts-Based Research

Authorial Reflexivity asks us to engage on deeper levels than just cognitive understanding. If we wish to explore and share our own experience because this is the knowledge we're able to access, then the arts offer enormously valuable tools. Arts-based researchers can engage in reflexive art-making using a variety of aesthetic forms [92] because different methods can generate diverse perspectives. We can explore our identity holistically, listen to ourselves within the noise of life, and identify and work with our own stories [93]. Arts-based research allows us to climb inside many different layers of experience, and reflexivity "arises when different elements or levels are played off against each other" [94, p. 249]. Tríona McCaffrey and Jane Edwards [95] explained that ABR sparks dialogue and provokes difficult questions. It can hold ambiguity and tension well. We're creating, interpreting, and reinterpreting without being constricted by narrative structures. In his paper on evaluation for arts-based research performance, Viega [96] highlighted how we can freely move around within pluralistic truths about a complex social phenomenon. Through arts-based methods we can explore experiences that are multiple, messy, and indefinite [97]. This is certainly not always a comfortable experience. Historian Rebecca Solnit [98] argued that becoming lost is an obligation in every worthwhile endeavour. Along the journey of art-based research, there can be moments where we feel completely lost. We can remember, though, that becoming lost and not knowing where we're going, are two different things.

In addition to being able to facilitate both nonverbal and verbal, embodied and cognitive, intuitive and considered forms of knowing and types of knowledge, ABR allows us—if we so choose—to remain *in* experience. Throughout data collection/creation, analysis/response, and presentation and dissemination of findings, we can stay inside a living, breathing *process* and invite readers to do so as well, without needing to step out, step back, analyse through verbal language, and reach a "final" conclusion (as if we've caught a butterfly and mounted it on a pinboard for objective display, classification and interpretation instead of remaining with it in its vitality and vibrancy as it keeps flying).

Viega described how he appreciates gaining a sense of the researcher's process. If we only see the product or read a simple explanation of why a researcher decided to include an art form in their study, then, he explained,

> I don't have a sense of or don't really know where you're at or your process of moving there. It just feels like you're kind of choosing an art form too easily, without the pain of creating, without taking sufficient effort. Everyone has talent and can create something, but to practice and refine and try to find something vulnerable and unique to present that feels particularly yours, your voice—that seems to me like a different type of effort. It takes trial and error, and it takes being uncomfortable. It takes vulnerability to present that.

Amanda Schenstead [90] wrote about the timelessness of arts-based research. She mentioned steps of arts-based reflexivity, including (1) initial reasoning (What am I telling myself about this issue I wish to explore? Why is this issue important to me?); (2) continued introspection (Where are the gaps in my reasoning? What am I not telling myself? Is there more?); (3) artistic response to introspection (How can I depict my insights and the gaps?); (4) reflection upon the artistic process (how do I feel about this now?); (5) another artistic response; (6) another reflection…and so on, until one reaches a point of evaluating the learnings one has reached and formulating new self-knowledge. Schenstead explained how experiencing her journey in multiple art forms helped her develop a more holistic picture of the phenomenon she was trying to describe.

Experiencing Engaging with Participants

Let's reflect on two examples of how researchers using Authorial Reflexivity might describe their engagement with participants. Claire Ghetti and colleagues [99] conducted an action research study on amplified cardiopulmonary recordings (ACPR) in music therapy bereavement care following suicide. The first author, Claire, described her roles as a music therapist and researcher who has worked with families at end-of-life but who doesn't have first-hand experience with ACPR. The second author, Brian, described himself as a music therapist with a humanistic orientation who developed and uses the ACPR intervention. Jeremy, the third author, presented himself as a musician and a father who tragically lost his son and was introduced to music therapy and ACPR by Brian as a way of helping him with his grieving process. By pooling their experiences and engaging in dialogue with each other, they could explore an example of what using heartbeat recordings could afford a bereaved parent.

In Devlin's [3] study she wrote about her clinical experience with Graham, a client who challenged her approach to music therapy. She noticed a significant gap between how she thought she was supposed to be with him and how he was experiencing her. As Devlin explored her perception of and relationship with Graham, she described how her understanding of him started to change through her reflexive process, as did the way she wanted to reflect on and write about her understanding of him through a richer narrative that could more fully express his complexity. She began trying to experience the process from Graham's perspective, but it didn't feel authentic to her to attempt to fully step into his perspective. Devlin wrote: "I came to realise that I can't actually be inside Graham because I am only inside myself. I can't fully know Graham's experience because all I know is my own. But I can know something about Graham's experience, and there is a great responsibility that comes with that" [3, p. 239]. She reached a point where she sought to simply connect with and describe her experience of him.

Exploring One's Experiences of a Phenomenon Through Creating, Collecting, and Analysing Data

Researchers engaging in Authorial Reflexivity may gather data from other sources (participants or literature, for example) and then emphasise their own meaning-making processes in terms of how they engage with that data. For example, Jennifer Bibb et al. [100] wrote about how using self-reflexivity when interpreting interview data entails observing ourselves in relation to the participant. In their research, they used their own experiences as registered music therapists in Australia to help them shape their understandings of the experiences of their fellow music therapists who contributed stories to their study.

Alternatively, researchers may produce autobiographical data. The choice to use this kind of data is often informed by the questions we're asking. When these relate to our own professional practice or personal experience, this clearly necessitates studying ourselves [101]. Cultural and disciplinary norms influence what we deem "tellable" in academic contexts [102], and this can lead us to self-censor. However, when we're generating data about our own lives, we need to authentically and disclose our process and our rationale. Our research might call us to confront topics we would actually prefer to avoid. In autobiographical research, the goal isn't to portray ourselves in a positive light—competent, organised, and in control—but to provide rich, comprehensive narratives that can embrace chaotic elements like self-doubt, mistakes, embarrassments, inconsistencies, or projections. Authentically examining our experiences can sometimes be an uncomfortable and even painful process. While we're seeking to be vulnerable, importantly we're also weighing up any potential harm that may arise from deep personal disclosures, including risks to mental health or professional reputation, and making wise decisions in this regard [103, 104].

Many types of researchers generate some autobiographical data. Action researchers frequently engage in self-reflection during the process of their study. Phenomenologists may craft narratives that are autobiographical [101]. In McCaffrey and Edwards' [105] study, mental health service users were invited to describe their experiences of music therapy through interviews. The authors noted their own thoughts and impressions while reading and analysing the transcripts. These were written in a reflexive journal and inserted in comment boxes in the interview transcript. Ethnographers compile field notes that record both participants' verbal and nonverbal behaviours, the context of these actions, as well as the researcher's own thoughts, feelings, perceptions, and insights [106].

Nandini Maharaj [106] developed a set of questions for researchers to explore their field notes:

- What insights do my notes reveal about my beliefs and values regarding myself, my relationships, and my views on knowledge, privilege, and power?
- How do I view my role in this scenario (as an observer/participant or insider/outsider)?
- How does my description align with my beliefs and values?
- In which sections of my notes do I show hesitation or uncertainty and what was influencing me in those moments?
- What kinds of words and language styles did I use?
- What details did I leave out of my notes, and why?
- In what ways did note-taking influence my understanding of the situation? How might my insights change if I had used video or audio recordings instead of field notes?
- How did my role as an observer impact those around me?

In research that includes autobiographical data, it can be helpful to start analysis early in the research process to limit us from accumulating excessive data and feeling overwhelmed by it [101]. Creating some temporal distance between experience and analysis can afford deeper insights, but immediate reflections could better capture the emotional intensity of an experience. that might otherwise fade. We may choose to alternate between immersion and distance.

When we're creating data about our own experiences, we're already "pre-saturated" in theoretical ideas, whether we like it or not. Our challenge as we analyse that data is to be able to think critically about the theoretical perspectives we're using and how to employ different perspectives. If we're documenting our personal experiences of facilitating a music therapy group, for example, the data would already be shaped by our assumptions about groups, our past experiences in groups and the theories we've learned about group dynamics and group behaviour. A helpful technique to play with can be to identify the level of analysis most obviously suitable to the topic we're studying, and then try out a theory that operates at a different level. In that example of group work, a theory like Tuckman's stages of group development [107] may be more immediately applicable, however, if we think with attachment theory, dynamic form, or perspectives such as feminism, or critical disability studies, we can generate new insights.

Through an arts-based research project, Viega [108] worked with teenagers in a residential programme who wrote songs. While listening to the songs they'd created, he responded through movement, singing, and imagery. He stayed open to feelings that emerged, identifying songs that provoked strong reactions for further exploration. After listening to one particular song, he felt driven to create a piece based on the emotions it evoked in him. He attended to the question of how music composition could reflect the experiences of these adolescents with adverse childhood experiences. Viega identified a creative space with access to instruments and room for movement that was also equipped for Hip Hop production. He created what he called remix compositions, cutting and pasting elements from original tracks. After completing these remixes, he listened to them in various contexts to reflect on their aesthetic content. While listening to one remix, he would choose which original song to analyse next, highlighting the cyclical nature of artistic research where data collection and analysis inform each other through aesthetic experiences. The deeper he explored his creativity, the more insights he gained, leading to a complex understanding of the subject.

In their arts-based duoethnography study, Thomas and Blanc [86] started off by discussing their interpretations of history in their respective professions and the perceived gaps. They then created individual artworks reflecting their feelings and the objectives they wanted to focus on in the project, followed by a sharing session. Next, they developed a "fairytale timeline" that incorporated both their professional and personal cultural histories. They analysed the data gathered in these phases through manual axial coding and by developing themes as well as through an analysis of their artwork using poetic inquiry. The outcome of this aesthetic response was an interactive map/timeline. Lastly, they synthesised their findings to present overarching themes.

Trustworthiness in a Study Employing Authorial Reflexivity

Researchers sometimes refer to theoretical saturation (e.g., those using grounded theory). At this point, new data and analysis are not generating additional ideas because the phenomenon has been thoroughly investigated and understood. (As Claire O'Callaghan and Fiona McDermott [109] acknowledged, though, this may not be possible when exploring multifaceted phenomena). Through Authorial Reflexivity, we're seeking a kind of internal saturation. Have I fully explored my perspectives, values, experiences, and assumptions and can I clearly articulate how I'm representing what I'm studying from this vantage point? We recognise here too that there's never an endpoint of self-knowing. In our interview, Michael Viega defined reflexivity as a kind of spiral of awareness. We begin with one area of consciousness and then allow new things to enter, continuously expanding our awareness of the complexity of what's happening. Complexity is always present; we're working to broaden our awareness of it. In a study using Authorial Reflexivity, the reader is invited to trust that the researcher has fully recognised how their account is situated, partial and one of multiple possible perspectives.

Music therapy researchers have acknowledged multiple realities [110–113], multiple viewpoints [95], and that meaning can be represented in multiple ways [97, 110]. Different researchers have different life histories and can thus interpret data in different, but not necessarily inferior or superior ways. The researcher's analysis entails linking certain segments of data and the categories they want to use to conceptualise those segments as opposed to finding "the" right conclusion [109]. Findings express partial truths that might, in turn, complement one another and create a more complex picture [112]. As we reflexively explore and present our own perspective, we're telling one of many possible stories. In my interview with Gro Trondalen, she explained, "…[W]e can always question what is true… It's my story. And I'm open to that critique. Yes, it's my story. But I'm not trying to be anything else—it is my story. I'm not trying to 'objectivise' anything saying: 'this is what it is for everybody'".

Engaging with an Audience

Nicky Haire and Raymond MacDonald [114] wrote that the presence of an audience can offer increased possibilities for surprise, inviting interaction between findings, improvisers, and witnesses. In their study on humour they invited readers/audience members to have their own experiences in relation to what they were sharing with them.

In our interview, Kerry Devlin reflected on how academic writing traditions have taught us to remove ourselves from our writing. She said,

> A lot of times I find research very impersonal and I understand that often the *intention* is to depersonalise and decontextualise, but I think the act of engaging in research means you're situated in it…I also think it's in some ways a parallel for the experience a lot of students have: feeling like they have to put on their "therapist hat" when they walk into a room; they have to be someone else. But actually, all people need from them is for them to just be themselves.

Presenting research that exposes our own views, positions, perspectives, and vulnerabilities can be difficult. Deciding how much to share requires thoughtful consideration. As we write ourselves into our texts we do so in liminal spaces between inner experience and cultural contexts, between professional identities and personal journeys, between roles as therapists, researchers and humans in the world. We attend to our assumptions and we challenge them. We grow our self-compassion as well as our self-questioning. We gaze deeply within ourselves so that we can relate better to others with more authenticity and less judgement. We tell our own stories and we hope that those stories resonate with and are helpful for others.

An Accessible Summary

When we use Authorial Reflexivity we acknowledge that our understanding of the world is always shaped by our individual perspectives and we embrace this as a valuable source of insight. The underlying premise is that truth isn't something "out there" waiting to be discovered, but consists of multiple stories yet to be constructed. Researchers engaging in Authorial Reflexivity are essentially saying: "I can only tell you how I see this. Despite my efforts to understand this topic and these participants' experiences, I cannot claim to have stepped inside their reality. I'm perceiving their experiences through the lens of my own, and that's what I'll share with you." This approach embraces the

(*continued*)

(**continued**)

fact that we'll never have the complete picture or final understanding of any phenomenon.

Several theoretical frameworks can underpin Authorial Reflexivity. Interpretivism maintains the idea of a common external reality, while acknowledging that individuals may interpret this reality differently based on their unique contexts. This leads to multiple smaller truths shaped by human subjectivities rather than a single universal Truth. Radical constructivism makes an even stronger claim, arguing that all knowledge is purely constructed and each person creates their own unique understanding based on personal experience. Field theory, drawn from Gestalt therapy, maintains that people are inseparable from their environments and this interplay becomes the focal point.

During Authorial Reflexivity, the researcher engages in rich self-exploration. They might examine different layers of self, including their ecological self (who they are in this place and activity), interpersonal self (how they engage socially), extended self (how memories and future anticipations shape them), private self (inner conscious experiences), and conceptual self (social roles and personality perceptions).

This approach values multiple ways of knowing beyond purely cognitive understanding. In embodied knowing, we experience and make sense of the world through our bodies, including felt senses that offer preverbal, bodily awareness of situations. Emotions are also essential to generating knowledge. Writing itself becomes a method of inquiry, a way of discovering insights rather than simply recording pre-existing ideas.

Research problems often emerge as researchers notice what really matters to them. Certain methodological strategies, like autoethnography, heuristic research, and arts-based research, offer rich frameworks for self-exploration. Researchers also mindfully recognise and explore their own responses when interacting with participants. This can become useful data. The trustworthiness of this kind of research rests on the recognition that the researcher's account is situated, partial, and one of multiple possible perspectives.

References

1. Denzin NK. Interpretive ethnography: ethnographic practices for the 21st century. Thousand Oaks, CA: Sage; 1997.
2. Trondalen G. Resource-oriented Bonny Method of Guided Imagery and Music (R-oGIM) as a creative health resource for musicians. Nord J Music Ther. 2016;25(1):5–31.
3. Devlin K. How do I see you and what does that mean for us? An autoethnographic study. Music Therapy Perspectives. 2018;36(2):234–42.
4. Hasselkus BR. In the eye of the beholder: the researcher in qualitative research. Occupat Ther J Resear. 1997;17(2):81–3.
5. Abrams B. Evidence-based music therapy practice: an integral understanding. J Music Ther. 2010;47(4):351–79.
6. Mullaney T, Rea C. Where research begins. Chicago: University of Chicago Press; 2022.
7. Scaffidi Abbate C, Boca S, Gendolla GH. Self-awareness, perspective-taking, and egocentrism. Self Identity. 2016;15(4):371–80.
8. Scaffidi Abbate C, Isgrò A, Wicklund RA, Boca S. A field experiment on perspective-taking, helping, and self-awareness. Basic Appl Soc Psychol. 2006;28(3):283–7.
9. Willis J. Foundations of qualitative research. Thousand Oaks, CA: Sage; 2007.
10. Every R. Incommensurability, relativism, methodology [Internet]. 1998 [cited 2005 Dec 3]. Available from: http://www.csad.coventry.ac.uk/IDN/neopraxis/psci.htm.
11. Von Glasersfeld E. Radical constructivism. London: Routledge; 2013.
12. Larochelle M. Key works in radical constructivism. Rotterdam: Sense Publishers; 2007.
13. Von Glasersfeld E. The radical constructivist view of science. Found Sci. 2001;6:31–43.
14. Mann D. Gestalt therapy: the basics. London: Routledge; 2024.
15. Staemmler F. A Babylonian confusion?: on the uses and meanings of the term "field". British Gestalt J. 2006;15(2):64–74.
16. Lewin K. Field theory. Springfield, IL: Charles C. Thomas Publisher; 1948.
17. Burnes B, Cooke B. Kurt Lewin's Field Theory: a review and re-evaluation. Int J Manag Rev. 2013;15(4):408–25.
18. Mann D. Gestalt therapy: 100 key points and techniques. London: Routledge; 2010.
19. Pieterse AL, Lee M, Ritmeester A, Collins NM. Towards a model of self-awareness development for counselling and psychotherapy training. Couns Psychol Q. 2013;26(2):190–207.
20. Hansen JT. Self-awareness revisited: reconsidering a core value of the counselling profession. J Couns Dev. 2009;87:186–93.

21. Eakin PJ. How our lives become stories. Ithaca, NY: Cornell University Press; 2019.
22. Campbell C. Romanticism, consumption, and introspection: some comments on professor Holbrook's paper. In: Belk RW, Dholakia N, Venkatesh A, editors. Consumption and marketing: macro dimensions. Cincinnati, OH: South-Western College Publishing; 1996. p. 96–103.
23. Bager-Charleson S. Relational research reflexivity. In: Goss S, Stevens C, editors. Making research matter. London: Routledge; 2016. p. 58–70.
24. Xue H, Desmet PM. Researcher introspection for experience-driven design research. Des Stud. 2019;63:37–64.
25. Holbrook MB. Consumer research: introspective essays on the study of consumption. Thousand Oaks, CA: Sage Publications; 1995.
26. Wallendorf M, Brucks M. Introspection in consumer research: implementation and implications. J Consum Res. 1993;20(3):339–59.
27. Chang H. Autoethnography as method. New York: Routledge; 2016.
28. Husserl E. The crisis of European sciences and transcendental phenomenology. Evanston, IL: Northwestern University Press; 1936.
29. van Manen M. Researching lived experience: human science for an action sensitive pedagogy. London, ON: Althouse Press; 1990.
30. Ashworth P. An approach to phenomenological psychology: the contingencies of the lifeworld. J Phenomenol Psychol. 2003;34(2):145–56.
31. Ashworth PD. Introduction to the place of phenomenological thinking in the history of psychology. In: Ashworth P, Chung MC, editors. Phenomenology and psychological science: historical and philosophical perspectives. New York: Springer; 2006.
32. Merleau-Ponty M. Phenomenology of perception. London: Routledge and Kegan Paul; 1962.
33. Fogel A. The psychophysiology of self-awareness: rediscovering the lost art of body sense. New York: WW Norton & Company; 2013.
34. Leigh J, Brown N. Embodied inquiry. London: Bloomsbury; 2021.
35. Gendlin E. Focusing. New York: Bantam Books; 1981.
36. Watson J. Knowing through the felt-sense: a gesture of openness to the other. Internation J Children Spiritual. 2013;18(1):118–30.
37. Coffey A. The ethnographic self. London: Sage; 1999.
38. Clarke C, Broussine M, Watts L. Researching with feeling: the emotional aspects of social and organizational research. London: Routledge; 2015.
39. Cvetkovich A. Depression is ordinary: public feelings and Saidiya Hartman's Lose Your Mother. Fem Theory. 2012;13(2):131–46.
40. Wilson S. Research is ceremony: indigenous research methods. Halifax, NS: Fernwood Publishing; 2008.

41. Hampton E. Memory comes before knowledge: research may improve if researchers remember their motives. Paper presented at: the First Biannual Indigenous Scholars' Conference; 1995 Mar 15–18; Edmonton, AB, Canada.
42. Hemmings C. Affective solidarity: feminist reflexivity and political transformation. Fem Theory. 2012;13(2):147–61.
43. Boncori I. Researching and writing differently. Bristol: Policy Press; 2023.
44. Kiriakos CM, Tienari J. Academic writing as love. Manag Learn. 2018;49(3):263–77.
45. Ahmed S. The cultural politics of emotion. New York: Routledge; 2004.
46. Richardson L. Writing: a method of inquiry. In: Denzin NK, Lincoln YS, editors. The SAGE handbook of qualitative research. 6th ed. Thousand Oaks, CA: Sage; 2024. p. 923–48.
47. O'Callaghan C. Qualitative data-mining through reflexive journal analysis: implications for music therapy practice development. J Soc Work Res Eval. 2005;6(2):217–29.
48. Richardson L. Writing: a method of inquiry. In: Denzin NK, Lincoln YS, editors. Handbook of qualitative research. 3rd ed. Thousand Oaks, CA: Sage; 2005. p. 959–78.
49. Mackinlay E, Madden K. Departing radically in academic writing. London: Routledge; 2024.
50. Bodry K, Schwantes M. Clinical applications of feminist music therapy: an overview of the literature. Nord J Music Ther. 2021;30(2):106–30.
51. Ahessy B. 'Boom Boom in the Zoom Zoom Room': online music therapy with children and adolescents with visual impairment. Br J Vis Impair. 2021;39(2):159–74.
52. Beer LE. From embedded to embodied: including music in arts-based music therapy research. Music Ther Perspect. 2016;34(1):33–40.
53. Barry P, O'Callaghan C, Wheeler G, Grocke D. Music therapy CD creation for initial pediatric radiation therapy: a mixed methods analysis. J Music Ther. 2010;47(3):233–63.
54. Furman R. Poetry as research: advancing scholarship and the development of poetry therapy as a profession. J Poet Ther. 2006;19(3):133–45.
55. Ulmer JB. Embodied writing: choreographic composition as methodology. Resear Dance Educat. 2015;16(1):33–50.
56. Venkatarangam S. Participants' experiences of a receptive music therapy intervention that incorporates raga: an interpretative phenomenological analysis. Arts Psychother. 2021;73:101762.
57. Carroll D. Portraiture and the role of researcher: reflections and questions/ La méthode de l'art du portrait et le rôle du chercheur: réflexions et questions. Canadian J Mus Ther. 2007;13(2):148–59.
58. Lawrence-Lightfoot S, Hoffman-Davis J. The art and science of portraiture. San Francisco, CA: Jossey-Bass; 1997.

59. McFerran K, Silverman M. A guide to designing research questions for beginning music therapy researchers. Silver Spring, MD: American Music Therapy Association; 2018.
60. Falola T. Decolonizing African knowledge: autoethnography and African epistemologies. Cambridge: Cambridge University Press; 2022.
61. Chang H, Ngunjiri FW, Hernandez KC. Collaborative autoethnography. Walnut Creek, CA: Left Coast Press; 2013.
62. Shaw CM. An autoethnographic journey in developing post-ableist music therapy. Voices: A World Forum for Music Therapy [Internet]. 2022 Mar [cited 2024 Jul 18];22(1). Available from: https://voices.no/index.php/voices/article/view/3334.
63. Hernandez T. "Where are you from?"-Navigating oppression, power, and privilege in music therapy spaces: a critical autoethnography on intersectional identities [doctoral dissertation]. Wellington: Open Access Te Herenga Waka-Victoria University of Wellington; 2023.
64. Freeman D. Use of reflexive thinking in music therapy to understand the therapeutic process; moments of clarity, self-criticism: an autoethnography. Qualitat Inqui Mus Ther. 2018;13(1):1–43.
65. Lipski G. Finding where I fit: an autoethnography on integrating ethnomusicology into music therapy [doctoral dissertation]. Montreal: Concordia University; 2014.
66. dos Santos A. Finding empathy through music therapy techniques in the midst of family trauma: an autoethnography. Voices: A World Forum for Music Therapy [Internet]. 2024 Jul [cited 2024 Jul 18];24(2). Available from: https://voices.no/index.php/voices/article/view/3688.
67. Gumble M. Embodied speech through song: a queer autoethnographic exploration of gender affirming voicework in music therapy [doctoral dissertation]. Slippery Rock, PA: Slippery Rock University of Pennsylvania; 2019.
68. Cooper-Stadler R. Capturing constructs of a music therapist's clinical intuition in music intervention for young children who live in urban poverty: an autoethnography [master's thesis]. Lawrence, KS: University of Kansas; 2020.
69. Santibanez LP. The use of guitar as self-care in music therapy internship: an arts-based autoethnographic exploration [doctoral dissertation]. 2022.
70. Lee KV. An autoethnography: music therapy after laser eye surgery. Qual Inq. 2010;16(4):244–8.
71. Echard A. Making sense of self: an autoethnographic study of identity formation for adolescents in music therapy. Music Ther Perspect. 2019;37(2):141–50.
72. Holman Jones S, Adams TE. Autoethnography and queer theory: making possibilities. In: Denzin NK, Giardina MG, editors. Qualitative inquiry and human rights. Walnut Creek, CA: Left Coast Press; 2010. p. 136–57.
73. Jones S, Harris A. Queering autoethnography. London: Routledge; 2019.

74. Crenshaw KW. Mapping the margins: intersectionality, identity politics, and violence against women of color. Stanford Law Rev. 1991;43(6):1241–99.
75. Collins PH. Intersectionality and epistemic injustice. In: Kidd IJ, Medina J, Pohlhaus G, editors. The Routledge handbook of epistemic injustice. London: Routledge; 2017. p. 115–24.
76. Chang H, Ngunjiri FW, Hernandez KC. Collaborative autoethnography. Walnut Creek, CA: Left Coast Press; 2012.
77. Kalmbach Phillips D, Harris G, Legard Larson M, Higgins K. Trying on—being in—becoming: four women's journey(s) in feminist poststructural theory. Qual Inq. 2009;15(9):1455–79.
78. Viega M, Druziako V, Millrod J, Hoberman A. Entering the ambient: a performative collaborative autoethnography of music therapists' improvising with digital music technologies. Voices: A World Forum for Music Therapy [Internet]. 2023 Mar [cited 2024 Jul 18];23(1). Available from: https://voices.no/index.php/voices/article/view/3462.
79. Sawyer R, Norris J. Duoethnography. Oxford: Oxford University Press; 2013.
80. Ellis C, Bochner A. Autoethnography, personal narrative, reflexivity: research as subject. In: Denzin N, Lincoln Y, editors. Handbook of qualitative research. 2nd ed. Thousand Oaks, CA: Sage; 2000. p. 733–68.
81. Koro-Ljungberg M, Yendol-Hoppey D, Smith JJ, Hayes SB. (E)pistemological awareness, instantiation of methods, and uninformed methodological ambiguity in qualitative research projects. Educ Res. 2009;38(9):687–99.
82. Norris JJ, Sawyer RD. Duoethnography: a polytheoretical approach to (re) storing, (re)storying the meanings that one gives. In: Leavy P, editor. The Oxford handbook of qualitative research. 2nd ed. Oxford: Oxford University Press; 2020. p. 397–423.
83. Thomas A, Sham FTY. "Hidden rules": a duo-ethnographical approach to explore the impact of culture on clinical practice. Aust J Music Ther. 2014;25:81–91.
84. Zhang X, Shi R, Hsu W. A collaborative autoethnographic exploration of experiences of three international music therapy interns during their clinical training [doctoral dissertation]. 2016.
85. Jerling P, Sánchez-Prieto CA, Rubio IS. Selecting the best music for the moment in a music and imagery session: how do we experience the choosing? A trioethnography. Voices: A World Forum for Music Therapy [Internet]. 2024 Mar [cited 2024 Jul 18];24(1). Available from: https://voices.no/index.php/voices/article/view/3595.
86. Thomas N, Blanc V. Break it then build again: an arts based duoethnographic pilot reconstructing music therapy and dance/movement therapy histories. Arts Psychother. 2021;73:101765.
87. Moustakas C. Heuristic research. Newbury Park, CA: Sage; 1990.

88. Bach L. Chapter 7: heuristic scholar: heuristic inquiry and the heuristic scholar. Counterpoints. 2002;183:91–102.
89. Brisola EBV, Cury VE. Researcher experience as an instrument of investigation of a phenomenon: an example of heuristic research. Estudos de Psicologia (Campinas). 2016;33(1):95–105.
90. Schenstead AR. The timelessness of arts-based research: looking back upon a heuristic self-study and the arts-based reflexivity data analysis method. Voices: A World Forum for Music Therapy [Internet]. 2012 Feb [cited 2024 Jul 18];12(1). Available from: https://voices.no/index.php/voices/article/view/589.
91. Zanders ML, Midach M, Waldemeier L, Barros B. A reflexive music therapy clinical introspection in working with foster care youth. Voices: A World Forum for Music Therapy [Internet]. 2018 Oct [cited 2024 Jul 18];18(4). Available from: https://voices.no/index.php/voices/article/view/2593.
92. Kay L. Research as bricolage: navigating in/between the creative arts disciplines. Music Ther Perspect. 2016;34(1):26–32.
93. Gombert DJ. Exploring identity: if your soul could speak, what would she say? Voices: A World Forum for Music Therapy [Internet]. 2017 Oct [cited 2024 Jul 18];17(3). Available from: https://voices.no/index.php/voices/article/view/947.
94. Alvesson M, Sköldberg K. Reflexive methodology: new vistas for qualitative research. Thousand Oaks, CA: Sage; 2000.
95. McCaffrey T, Edwards J. Meeting art with art: arts-based methods enhance researcher reflexivity in research with mental health service users. J Music Ther. 2015;52(4):515–32.
96. Viega M. Evaluation for arts-based research performance: audience perceptions of Rising from the Ashes. J Music Ther. 2022;59(1):62–86.
97. Gilbertson S. In visible hands: the matter and making of music therapy. J Music Ther. 2015;52(4):487–514.
98. Solnit R. A field guide to getting lost. Edinburgh: Cannongate; 2017.
99. Ghetti CM, Schreck B, Bennett J. Heartbeat recordings in music therapy bereavement care following suicide: action research single case study of amplified cardiopulmonary recordings for continuity of care. Action Research. 2023;14767503231 20799.
100. Bibb J, Howden A, McFerran KS. Exploring the experiences of professional practice for Australian based registered music therapists. Aust J Music Ther. 2021;32(2):79–98.
101. Tenni C, Smyth A, Boucher C. The researcher as autobiographer: analysing data written about oneself. Qual Rep. 2003;8(1):1–12.
102. Chang H. Autoethnography as method. Walnut Creek, CA: Left Coast Press; 2008.

103. Edwards J. Ethical autoethnography: is it possible? Int J Qual Meth. 2021 [cited 2024 Jul 18];20:1609406921995306. Available from: https://doi.org/10.1177/1609406921995306.
104. Chatham-Carpenter A. "Do thyself no harm": protecting ourselves as autoethnographers. J Res Pract. 2010 [cited 2013 Mar 1];6(1). Available from: http://jrp.icaap.org/index.php/jrp/article/view/213/183.
105. McCaffrey T, Edwards J. "Music therapy helped me get back doing": perspectives of music therapy participants in mental health services. J Music Ther. 2016;53(2):121–48.
106. Maharaj N. Using field notes to facilitate critical reflection. Reflective Pract. 2016;17(2):114–24.
107. Tuckman BW, Jensen MAC. Stages of small-group development revisited. Group Facilitat. 2010;10:43–8.
108. Viega M. Science as art: axiology as a central component in methodology and evaluation of arts-based research (ABR). Music Ther Perspect. 2016;34(1):4–13.
109. O'Callaghan C, McDermott F. Music therapy's relevance in a cancer hospital researched through a constructivist lens. J Music Ther. 2004;41(2):151–85.
110. O'Callaghan C, McDermott F. Discourse analysis reframes oncologic music therapy research findings. Arts Psychother. 2007;34(5):398–408.
111. Kennelly JD, Baker FA, Daveson BA. Professional supervision as storied experience: narrative analysis findings for Australian-based registered music therapists. J Music Ther. 2017;54(1):80–107.
112. Stensæth K. Music therapy and interactive musical media in the future: reflections on the subject-object interaction. Nord J Music Ther. 2018;27(4):312–27.
113. Ghetti CM, Vederhus BJ, Gaden TS, Brenner AK, Bieleninik Ł, Kvestad I, et al. Longitudinal study of music therapy's effectiveness for premature infants and their caregivers (LongSTEP): feasibility study with a Norwegian cohort. J Music Ther. 2021;58(2):201–40.
114. Haire N, MacDonald R. Thinking through improvisation: how arts-based reflexivity can offer new knowing about music therapists' experiences of humour in music therapy. Voices: A World Forum for Music Therapy [Internet]. 2021 Jun [cited 2024 Jul 18];21(2). Available from: https://voices.no/index.php/voices/article/view/3156.

CHAPTER 6

Empathic Reflexivity

One way we form meaning as researchers is through closely getting to know our participants. Qualitative research, in particular, is rooted in the desire to empathically understand others [1]. Researchers may seek to offer the experience of a "triangulated empathic bond" [2, p. 221]: the researcher draws insights empathically from participants and presents these to readers so that they can also respond with empathy.

Empathy, as Signe Stige et al. [3] defined it, is a human ability that enables us to actively pursue and understand others' perspectives, requiring us to step back from our own viewpoint. Common conceptualisations of empathy distinguish between affective empathy and cognitive empathy. Affective empathy entails purposefully sharing in another person's feelings (whilst being able to distinguish the feeling as belonging to the other person). Cognitive empathy involves perceiving the meaning of the emotional experience for the other person. These two aspects can be integrated into a process of empathy that I've termed "insightful empathy," which can be understood as "purposefully sharing and understanding another's emotions" [4, p. 26]. In this chapter, we'll be exploring empathy as it relates

---

Deliberately acknowledging and exploring our active participation in creating and shaping knowledge in our study *as we work to insightfully attune to our participants* and responding to these insights *by making interactional adjustments.*

A. dos Santos, *Reflexive Research in Music Therapy*,
https://doi.org/10.1007/978-3-032-02033-8_6

to our roles as researchers. Even as you anticipate stepping into a research project, you may wish to think about who you expect to empathise with in your study. Why? How? Where might empathy be difficult? How do these expectations potentially complicate or enrich the process you're about to embark on?

We do need to recognise upfront that we can't simply "climb into" another person's experience. An ethical position involves accepting that any account is necessarily partial and provisional [5]. Our empathic insight remains an approximation of another person's experience, even as it's continually refined through our ongoing interactions. As we engage in Empathic Reflexivity, we think carefully about our active meaning-making role, while still centring the participants' experiences as we understand them.

An Empathic Stance

We need to adopt a particular stance when engaging empathically with another person, which has certain components. Firstly, we need self-awareness to distinguish our feelings from those of others and recognise our personal perspectives that may cloud our perception of them. Secondly, we need the willingness to offer sustained, focused attention and genuinely tune in to the other person—something that naturally fluctuates regardless of our professional identity and skills. Thirdly, we need the personal capacity to empathise and, fourthly, the courage to be open to what may emerge, non-judgmentally receiving what participants share [4]. Writing from the perspective of phenomenology, Linda Finlay [6] described how researchers believe that participants' expressions represent their truth within their context of understanding. Through "empathic dwelling," we strive to immerse ourselves in our participants' narratives. Debbie Carroll [7] emphasised that we need to create space for others to express themselves and be open to change in the process. In their study with children and adolescents in child welfare, for example, Viggo Krüger and Brynjulf Stige [8] argued that we need to ask children and adolescents what they experience and think, and we need to trust each individual's experiences and competencies.

Time and Proximity

If I'm seeking to get to know participants' views and experiences well, have I designed a study that allows for enough time to genuinely do this? In a study by Kari Batt-Rawden et al. [9] on the role and significance of music in the everyday life of people with long-term illnesses, they conducted eight interviews with each participant over a period of one year, focussing on past musical experiences, musical metaphors, musical narratives, and the practices participants used to create and maintain meaningful worlds. In my interview with Efrat Roginsky, she discussed reflexivity in research and in her clinical practice, saying,

> [W]hen I work with people without language, reflexivity is really the main part of the process. I need time to be there, I need time to experience, and I think I need time to let the people with me experience and process. So maybe reflexivity is the essence of such communication and therapy with and without music. And I think reflexivity can be used as a way of being. Working through music therapy with these people helps me remember, you know, the slow processes of slow processing. It's also that I give myself to learning, being, learning slowness, learning reflexivity.

Philosopher Bonnie Talbert [10] argued that the best way to understand another person and their mental state is through dynamic, real-time, face-to-face exchange of information. Having a shared encounter—where we're simultaneously seeing, hearing, and even smelling the same things—enables joint attention, making it more likely for both individuals to be on the same page [11]. In the EPICURE acronym developed by Brynjulf Stige et al. [12] for evaluating research quality, "E" stands for engagement—the ongoing engagement of the researcher with the studied phenomenon.

As Nicky Haire and Raymond MacDonald [13] noted, we come to know through an encounter with the other. Interactions are participatory, dynamic, and fluid [10]. In her paper on Resource-oriented Bonny Method of Guided Imagery and Music (R-oGIM) as a creative health resource for musicians, Gro Trondalen [14] explained that the only way we can study another person is to experience their behaviour in an interpersonal context because it's active engagement that gives us the first-hand experiences and empathy we need to understand the phenomena from the inside. Interaction, not contemplation, lies at the heart of knowing another person [10]. In music therapy research, sometimes we interact with participants through a dual role if we're facilitating a music therapy process that we are also researching. In other studies, we remain purely in the role of researcher.

Building Rapport in Research Relationships with Singular Roles

Rapport in research has been defined as a harmonious relationship between researcher and participant and as "affiliation and empathy" [15, p. 489]. It involves trust and facilitates a freer exchange of information. Essentially, it means "getting along with each other" [16].

In music therapy research, we may be inviting participants to share matters close to their heart—their struggles, journeys, relationships, emotions, difficult experiences, and healing processes. If the researcher is a relative stranger, expressing this content could feel strange or difficult for them. We usually express emotions to others to convey vulnerabilities and needs, demonstrate trust, communicate about our welfare and relationships, demonstrate social referencing, and receive validation through others' empathic responses [17]. In research terms, this raises questions: Does the participant want to convey their vulnerabilities? Do they wish to receive support from us? Is it our role to give support? What is the quality of our relationship and how will this be expressed through emotions that are shared and withheld? How may the participants' perceptions of us, e.g., as similar and/or different, impact their and our emotional responses? How can we be researchers who are trustworthy?

The relationship trajectory between researcher and participants typically involves significant moments that signal turning points towards closer connection. Margaet Pitts and Michelle Miller-Day [18] identified several phases that research relationships could progress through. We follow different relational paths with different participants, in different study contexts and within different research paradigms. In the initial phase, other-orientation, the researcher focuses on helping participants feel comfortable. In the second phase, self-in-relation-to-other, both parties express a desire to develop a potential partnership. In the third phase, self-and-other linking, the researcher and participants recognise each other as whole beings beyond their research roles. The fourth phase, interpersonal connection, involves mutual respect and friendly reciprocity. In the final phase, partnership, high levels of self-disclosure may occur and personal friendships or collaborative relationships can develop that extend beyond the research study. Not all researchers reach this final phase with participants; in fact, most remain in the first phase.

Building rapport could be critiqued as a strategy for developing "fake friendship", which is unethical, particularly when researchers use techniques like self-disclosure or reciprocity to create an atmosphere of mutuality for purposes of eliciting more personal information. As reflexive researchers, we need to carefully consider questions like: How much rapport is sufficient? Is it ethical to build a sense of closeness and trust with participants simply for the purpose of drawing out information from them? How can we recognise and respect participants' resistance to our attempts at rapport? [19] An ethics dilemma for researchers lies in recognising participants' zones of privacy and determining when and how much to probe, ensuring a meaningful research relationship while respecting their well-being and privacy [20, 21].

Building rapport requires particular sensitivity when working cross-culturally, especially given that culture is dynamic and constantly evolving. Cross-cultural interactions can bring richness and multi-textured understanding and they can also evoke misunderstandings and miscommunications. Culture is not the only consideration. In Daryl Lindo's [22] study on music therapy training in the United Kingdom for ethnic minority communities, he explained how his race likely influenced interviews, potentially making participants feel more comfortable disclosing their experiences because they saw the researcher as potentially having a shared understanding. Yasmine Iliya and Brian Harris [23] noted how a therapist's gender and sexual orientation can influence participants' comfort levels, even if not explicitly discussed.

Under-rapport can leave participants feeling unsafe when discussing personal experiences with a researcher who they haven't had previous encounters with. Conversely, over-rapport might lead participants to share more than they later feel comfortable with, even raising potential for re-traumatisation. Intense sharing by participants can also impact the researcher's emotional health. Balanced rapport, marked by clear roles, sincerity, and emotional intelligence, helps protect both parties' well-being [19]. This requires what Marilys Guillemin and Lynn Gillam [24, p. 157] call "ethical mindfulness": recognising ethics significant moments, valuing feelings of discomfort as clues to carefully consider, articulating what is ethically significant, maintaining reflexivity about our influence, and having the courage to question established research practices. Taking the time to establish trust well is especially important not only with participants but potentially also with their family members, caregivers, colleagues, or other stakeholders [25].

Navigating Dual Role Relationships

In many music therapy studies, the researcher holds a dual role in their relationship with the participant. They're not merely encountering the participant for the short duration of an interview, for example, but are also engaging with them as a music therapist throughout a process or project. Health research frequently addresses questions derived from clinical practice, and when clinicians are involved in research, there are several benefits, including increased relevance of research questions, access to clinical settings, insider perspectives, and greater participant trust in the researchers [26]. Music therapy researchers have emphasised how having multiple roles can enable deep engagement with the topic and familiarity that invites deeper discussions [8, 27], sharper insights [21], enhanced empathy [28], and greater rapport [27, 29]. Participants may feel more relaxed [30] and comfortable [21]. As Stephanie Thompson et al. [21] noted, being central to every aspect of the clinical and research process enables researchers to interpret what they've witnessed, with findings co-constructed between clinician/researcher and participants.

The acceptability of holding dual roles is influenced by the power imbalance between professional and participant. When power differentials are higher, therapy duration longer, and termination indefinite, the potential for harm increases [31]. Researchers have developed various strategies to navigate these complexities (as they shift roles [32]). One way of tackling the power differential is through informed consent: (1) explaining all relevant aspects of what will and could happen during the research; (2) ensuring participants comprehend this information; (3) confirming that participants can make a rational judgement; and (4) guaranteeing that participation is voluntary and free from coercion or undue influence. While this seems clear, real-life situations can complicate things. For example, although participants are informed at the start of the process about the study's purpose and the intended use of the revealed materials, they may forget. As a therapy process proceeds, participants may not hold in mind how much of their lives they're sharing that will be used in the research [32]. As researchers, however, we're aware of the level of personal information being disclosed, and typically, the responsibility to protect the participant rests with us. Although ethics committees and research protocols offer protection, ultimately, each therapist-researcher needs a high level of ethical reflexivity to remain aware of and sensitive to ethics issues.

Alternating between a closer role and a more distant analytic role could be helpful [30, 33]. However, it can be challenging to disentangle ourselves from the therapeutic relationship to examine data more critically [34]. Hans Solli and Randi Rolvsjord [30] highlighted how reflexivity notes, and clinical as well as research supervision can assist us as we continuously review our positioning, drawing on rich insights through closeness and critical thinking through distance.

There are some exploratory questions that we can engage with as reflexive researchers who are thinking about the impact of dual relationships and how to manage them well: [32, 35]

- Is entering into a research relationship in addition to the therapeutic one (or a therapeutic one in addition to a research relationship) necessary, or should I avoid it?
- Can a dual relationship potentially cause harm to the participant/client?
- Would the additional relationship be beneficial? For whom?
- Is there a risk that adding a research relationship could disrupt the therapeutic relationship?
- Might I be using trust to further my own ends at the expense of the participants?
- What signs are there that a patient-participant might feel coerced or obliged?
- Can I stand back and evaluate this matter with self-awareness? How will I know if I'm "too close to see"?
- What credible consultations will help me think through this critically (e.g., people who are experts in the therapeutic modality as well as ethical matters)?
- Have I adequately documented the decision-making process? Do the documents reflect a patient-oriented decision-making process?

(*continued*)

(**continued**)

- What are the best ways of obtaining informed consent regarding the dual relationship (especially in light of power relations)? (E.g., how much time am I giving the participant to make this decision? Am I implementing processes of continuous consent?) [36]
- Does knowledge of the client support the establishment of a dual relationship (given that more information about a client is helpful in determining whether the choice to enter into a dual relationship is a wise one)?
- Are there diagnostic issues that matter when considering this dual relationship?
- Does my theoretical orientation matter when considering this dual relationship in this research study? How?

Knowing Another Through Thinking About Their Experiences and Perspectives

One of our core tasks as empathic researchers is to understand participants' experiences and perspectives as they understand them as much as possible, rather than assuming meaning from our own point of view. For example, in Rebecca Fairchild and Katrina McFerran's [36] study on collaborative group songwriting with children experiencing homelessness and family violence, they described how important it was that their findings were grounded in the children's experiences and ideas instead of representing adult interpretations of the children's views. However, a golden thread throughout this book is that we can never purely represent another's experience without this being influenced in some way by our own. How do we then think about the process of understanding another's experiences when we're using Empathic Reflexivity?

In music therapy literature, the notion of perspective-taking is used in two ways. Firstly, it can be thought of as a process through which we formulate an understanding of another person, which has an impact on the way we engage with them [37]. For example, as a music therapist, I may choose to use a psychodynamic perspective to understand a service user's situation. As a researcher, I may be engaging my own sociocultural perspectives when developing my research questions. This notion of perspective-taking is particularly helpful to explore when engaging in Lens Reflexivity. However, when engaging in Empathic Reflexivity, we're focusing largely on a second conceptualisation of perspective-taking: trying to understand another person's state of mind and perceiving a situation from their point of view [4, 38].

There are many (sometimes competing) theories about how humans accomplish this. In philosophy, whether we can know other people's mental and emotional states is called the problem of other minds [39]. Export theories suggest that we first understand our own inner experiences and then use this to infer others' experiences [40, 41]. This rests on the shared manifold hypothesis, where interpersonal relationships are understood to depend on a shared space created by the assumption that others are like us [42].

Theory of Mind (ToM) refers to the ability to attribute beliefs, desires, intentions, and knowledge to oneself and others [43]. Alternative terms for ToM are "mind-reading" [44] and "mentalising" [45]. Abrahams and Rohleder [46, p. 150] describe mentalising as "the ability to view yourself from the outside and others from the inside." First-person mentalising involves attributing mental states to oneself, while third-person mentalising involves attributing them to others [47]. Two primary alternative explanations to ToM are theory theory and simulation theory. Advocates of theory theory argue that humans use generalisations to connect observations of others' actions with particular mental states (for instance, we might think that someone who comes to a group music therapy session for the first time may feel somewhat anxious); we associate mental states with specific behaviours (e.g., we may believe that a happy person is likely to smile); and we relate certain mental states to one another (we generally think that a person experiencing pain will want to seek relief) [47]. Simulation theory (ST) [48] suggests that we predict others' behaviours by mentally placing ourselves in their situation, using our own experiences as a model.

Direct social perception (DSP) theorists argue that we can sometimes perceive others' mental states directly [49, 50]. Expressive behaviour itself can reveal mental states: an infant's cry conveys distress; a child reaching for the drum signals that they desire to play it [51, 52]. Rather than inferring intention, DSP suggests we perceive intention within the action itself.

Cognitive empathy involves understanding another's state of mind from their perspective [51]. While general perspective-taking encompasses thoughts, emotions, and intentions, empathic perspective-taking focuses on another's emotional state [53]. For music therapists, gaining insight into another's perspectives can occur through musicking (either with participants or as we reflect afterwards). Laura Beer [54], for example, described incorporating music into research by improvising compositions based on participants' impressions, which deepened her reflexive engagement.

Some scholars suggest that understanding another's experience is more challenging without having faced a similar situation yourself. For instance, a study conducted by Loren Nordgren et al. [55] showed that participants who hadn't suffered social exclusion tended to underestimate the social distress encountered by those who had. A person's understanding of someone else's experiences improves when they "relive" their own similar experience, provided this reflection remains focused on the other person [56]. Music therapy researchers such as Helen Short [57], Suzanne Sorel [58], and Jin Hyung Lee [59], purposely used their own shared experiences to gain insights into their participants' situations. Drawing on personal experiences to understand another's works best when we have a nuanced self-concept and can identify both similarities and differences between ourselves and the other person [60]. We must bear in mind, though, that we tend to overestimate our ability to understand other people's thoughts, feelings, or desires, potentially resorting to stereotyping when we perceive another to be very different from ourselves or projecting when we think they are very similar [4].

When we're seeking to understand our participants' experiences, we can ask ourselves questions such as:

- How is this person different from me in the circumstances of their life and how might the experience they describe make sense within the context of that life?
- How is this person similar to me? How are their experiences similar to my own?
- What am I revealing or hiding about my own motivations and orientation towards the experience we're exploring and how does that limit or enable what is said?

(*continued*)

(**continued**)

- Does it seem that what I have knowingly and/or unknowingly disclosed about myself is influencing the participant's willingness to trust me and to perceive that I will be able to grasp what this experience means for them? In what ways can I grasp it? In what ways can't I?
- To what degree am I genuinely empathising with my participants compared to merely engaging in a misguided form of projection, projective identification, or countertransference?
- What it would be like if the experiences that this person is describing happened to me, or to someone close to me? How is that impacting my meaning-making here? [61]

Instead of perspective-taking, perspective-getting can be a more effective way to understand another person's views and emotions. This involves directly asking them to share their thoughts, beliefs, attitudes, and feeling [38]. Typically, the most trustworthy source of information is the individual in question [61, 62] and while self-reports can sometimes be unreliable, they're still the strongest predictors of behaviour [63, 64]. Enhancing interpersonal understanding is usually most effectively achieved by becoming a better questioner and listener.

In music therapy research, we may be working with people who communicate without speech. We might use strategies such as being alert to vitality effects, attunement through musical expressions, and awareness of embodied communicative gestures. This can introduce greater interpretive subjectivity as nonverbal communication can be more ambiguous and requires a high degree of emotional consciousness and sensitivity towards the reactions of the other person. However, we're still engaged in a process of perspective-getting here, rather than merely perspective-taking by using nonverbal information. In our interview, Efrat Roginsky described her work with people who are restricted in their expressive range (e.g., people with locked-in syndrome). She described a stance of generosity towards noticing, receiving, and making meaning.

Knowing Another by Sharing in Their Feelings

As mentioned in the introduction, affective empathy involves consciously sharing another's emotions while recognising that these feelings belong to them. In music therapy literature, this has been described as "resonating" [65, 66], "creating emotional connection" [67], "tuning in" [68], and "being on the same wavelength" [69]. Accuracy in empathy is measured both in terms of content (discerning the specific emotions) and valence (perceiving their pleasantness or unpleasantness) [70]. A holistic approach to tuning in to another's emotions includes bodily sensations, feelings, and exploring lived experiences [71].

Affective empathy entails purposefully "stepping into" (and being able to "step out of") another person's emotional experience, which is different from emotional contagion where we unconsciously "catch" another person's emotions. In emotional contagion, we tend to automatically mimic and synchronise the other person's facial expressions, vocal quality, postures, and movements and therefore converge emotionally [72]. If we want to transform an experience from emotional contagion to empathy we need enough self-awareness to know that the feeling belongs to the other person (we can help ourselves here by even slightly de-linking our synchronised embodied actions and expressions), the ability to shift perspectives between our own and the other person, and the ability to self-regulate. These are important skills for researchers to have as we seek to understand others' experiences as clearly as possible. Emotional granularity [73]—having a nuanced vocabulary for emotions—can also enhance our reflexivity.

As we're attempting to empathise with participants' emotions, it may be helpful to ask ourselves questions such as these:

- How am I receiving the participant's emotional expressions?
- How is my body responding as I am tuning into their emotions (e.g., what sensations arising? Am I replicating their bodily expressions; am I tensing like they are?)
- How are the emotions I'm experiencing as I empathise offering insights that are useful as data?
- How are my displays of affective empathy received and interpreted by participants?
- Is the empathy I'm engaging in with participants alerting me to any harm that this research process may be causing and what should I do about that?

Empathy is not always easy. Researchers, like everyone else, may struggle to be empathic due to low mood, distress, power imbalances, moral judgements, or in-group biases. Empathy can decrease when we believe suffering is beneficial (e.g., due to a medical procedure), or when one's personal resilience results in others' struggles seeming less justified. Chronic exposure to suffering can also lead to emotional detachment as a coping strategy [74]. By starting from the position of humbly acknowledging that empathy can be challenging, we open up opportunities for honest reflexivity and for our empathy to grow.

Listening

Daily life presents many barriers to empathic listening. Sometimes we're concentrating on what we want to say next instead of really paying attention to what the other person is communicating. Our agenda may be to win an argument. Historical grudges can filter what we hear, as can fatigue, boredom, distractions, urgency, hunger, or a headache. In research encounters, we might assume that these obstacles aren't in play because this is a structured, intentional situation of information gathering. However, especially as novice interviewers, we may still feel pressure to think of the next question rather than listening actively. We might be distracted. Our agendas may guide conversations strictly towards gathering desired data. We may filter participants' words and expressions through the literature we've read. Humbly recognising how all these potential obstacles can hinder empathic listening is the first step to addressing this, so that we can listen from a place of stillness and connect with participants more deeply.

In the literature, a range of adjectives are used to distinguish types of listening. Deep listening has five main components: (1) the desire to truly hear the other, (2) care that honours what the other expresses and invests more in them than in ourselves, (3) being aware of and ameliorating power differentials, (4) acknowledging difference (quietening our inner perspectives and embracing alternative language, viewpoints, and approaches because if we assume commonalities and identification in the context of differences we could be at risk of reproducing structures of oppression [75]), and (5) courage (because we may be disturbed by what we hear, disagree with what is said, fail to listen well and need to try again) [76, 77]. Deep listening requires the willingness to have your mind changed.

Active listening, as conceptualised by Rogers [78], requires deep emotional engagement, non-judgement, thoughtful responsiveness, creativity, sensitivity, and empathy [79]. Attentive listening or "attentive being-with" [80, p. 77] entails an attitude of "letting-be-ness." This form of listening requires us to slow down and immerse ourselves in the presence of the other person (reflecting back, asking more about their experience, giving space and validating). It includes listening in silence and listening to silence, because it is there that something deeper may also emerge. Music therapists are particularly skilled at listening to silence [81].

Ansdell [82] highlighted three primary components of listening in Creative Music Therapy, which are also useful for researchers exploring musicking processes. We can focus on the purely musical aspect as musicians; perceive the emotional and physical characteristics of participants through music; and assess the quality of the relational dynamics in the music. De Backer [83] expanded this list to include embodied listening, as we connect with participants through our bodily experiences. Bruscia [84] outlined empathic, complementary, and reactive listening positions, each offering a different interpretive stance. These insights highlight how listening involves not just hearing, but also sensing, interpreting, and responding within a broader communicative ecology.

In Guro Klyve and Randi Rolvsjord's [29] study on children's experiences of music therapy in mental health care, they wrote that they listened to the children through what they said, how they said it, and what they did, the songs they played, how they played instruments, how they improvised their drawings and how they chose not to engage—attuning to their experiences of being at the hospital and participating in sessions.

Empathic Relationships in a Research Team

Thinking about and engaging in empathy is not only about our relationships with participants. When we work in research teams, building constructive relationships can greatly enhance our research (and make the process more enjoyable and generative for everyone). As we build empathic research teams (that still respect professional boundaries in healthy ways) we can consider starting meetings with brief check-ins where team members can share their current thinking about the research and any challenges they're experiencing. When giving feedback, we can approach this through a lens of "wondering" ("I'm wondering what led you to interpret this data point this way?" or "I'm curious about how you see this connecting to our research questions?") as opposed to using criticism. We can establish clear processes for handling disagreements about interpretation or analysis (just as we would set norms with a therapy group). Our willingness to hold multiple valid interpretations when appropriate can be an invaluable resource. A teamwork may wish to keep a shared reflexive journal where members can document their evolving thoughts and feelings about the research process. In team meetings we can purposefully make space to acknowledge and discuss power dynamics and different roles within the team. An empathic team is not one that agrees all the time—far from it! It means working to understand each other's perspectives while engaging in rigorous academic dialogue with mutual respect. We bring our skills as therapists as we show kindness and compassion within our research teams.

Drawing on Empathic Reflexivity Throughout the Stages of Research

Engaging with Related Literature to Learn About Participants' Experiences

As we read literature to contextualise our studies, there are debates around whether this helps us understand the phenomenon and the participants better or whether it clouds our judgement in unhelpful ways upfront (as can be found in some perspectives on grounded theory [85, 86].) It's through reflexivity that we make this decision with intentionality and critically reflect on the benefits and drawbacks of each approach. Kerry Devlin's [87] study exemplified how literature can challenge assumptions. Engaging with writings by autistic self-advocates led her to reconsider behaviours she had previously framed as "problems." This reading expanded her understanding, shaping a more nuanced, participant-centred approach. In this case, rather than clouding judgement, using literature reflexively could deepen empathy and insight into participants' lived realities.

Research Questions that Invite Empathic Knowing

Let's consider some examples of objectives and research questions within the studies that seemed to resonate, in my opinion, with Empathic Reflexivity (as at least one of their reflexive approaches). In Klyve and Rolvsjord's [29] study of narratives of children's experiences of music therapy in mental health care, they asked: (1) How do children experience music therapy in mental health care at the hospital? And (2) How do they express these experiences? Solli and Rolvsjord [30] asked: (1) what is it like for inpatients with psychosis to participate in music therapy?; and (2) how do participants with psychosis experience music therapy in relation to their mental health and current life challenges? Julie Krøier [88] et al. aimed to explore how music therapists experience nonverbal interactions with persons with dementia living in nursing homes. In their narrative inquiry of identity constructions in a rock band of ex-inmates, Lars Tuastad and Brynjulf Stige [89] asked: (1) How do Me and THE BAND'its use narratives to construct their identities? And (2) How do they use rock music as a resource in this process? Katarina Lindblad [90, p. 428] studied communication patterns in a music listening group with older men by asking: "How do older men interact and communicate with each other, with a female group leader and 'with' the music in a music listening group?"

Approaches and Designs that Afford Deep Knowing

In research that engages deeply with participants' experiences, we employ methods that enable us to tune into the nuances of what it may feel like to be in the participant's position. Approaches like constructivist grounded theory, interpretive phenomenology, arts-based research, and narrative inquiry have been used in music therapy studies to afford this kind of deep engagement.

Constructivist grounded theory, as seen in Moshe Bensimon's [91] study about music therapists working with children in war zones, is rooted in an inductive approach, generating theory directly from participants' experiences and emphasising empathy in both data collection and analysis [92–94]. Theory evolves through the researcher's interaction with participants. In relation to grounded theory, when studying the experiences of people who are distressed, Kathy Charmaz [95] cautioned researchers against rushing participants to express their lived experience. Sharing memories of suffering might take time, especially if trust in the listener has not yet been established. As researchers, we should also avoid imposing a narrative framework on participants' experiences too quickly because this can obscure rather than clarify their meanings. From the participant's viewpoint, the unfiltered experience of suffering may not align with narrative logic or coherent storytelling.

Stephen Venkatarangam [96], in a study of receptive music therapy using raga, explained how interpretive phenomenology involves both the researcher and participant entering a dialogue to understand the participant's lived experience. In Krøier and colleagues' [88] research on nonverbal interactions between music therapists and persons with dementia, they described interpretive phenomenology as being characterised by an attitude of openness to whatever is significant for the understanding of an explored, often complex phenomenon.

Arts-based research offers rich and versatile methods of exploring participants' experiences [54], which traditional methods may not so easily reveal [97]. As music therapists, we're intimately acquainted with getting to know another person deeply through arts-based methods, particularly musicking. Through the arts "we find 'living presence' that calls to the beholder: Welcome to my world. When we attend to this, we reach out to this living presence, and they to us, and we enter a dialogue about life" [98, p. 33]. Arts-based research operates within an "aesthetic intersubjective paradigm" [99], where the beauty and relational depth of the arts contribute to empathy and reflexivity [100]. While ABR can build critical consciousness, its strongest asset lies in fostering empathy [101]. ABR promotes "re-seeing" and "re-hearing" [102], inviting us to be attentive, curious, and engaged, while avoiding quick conclusions.

If we want to know someone deeply, we can invite them to tell us their story. Narrative inquiry offers a valuable way to understand and engage with participants' experiences. Tuastad and Stige [89] (2015) emphasised how, through narratives, we can explore not just the events of a person's life, but the meanings they attach to those events. We're also invited to consider how the telling of a story shapes both the storyteller and the listener. The act of storytelling itself becomes a process of interpretation and reflection [101]. Science seeks to establish truth, while narrative's role is to give meaning to experiences [103].

Gary Kenyon [104] wrote a paper on telling and listening to stories with older people in end-of-life care. It's not situated in music therapy, but it's pertinent to our current conversation. He wrote that story listening is an art form. Story listeners can also serve as storytellers by willingly sharing their own experiences, which opens up dialogue and prevents them from merely imposing their own themes onto others. During end-of-life care, it's crucial for the story listener to be present with genuine openness. Each biographical encounter is unique and the story of a dying individual may evolve from week to week, day to day, or even hour to hour. It requires skill to continually refine the narrative. Kenyon [104, p. 32] wrote that "people's life stories are possibly their most intimate possessions."

Close Knowing Through Collecting and Making Data

We can think of research methods as "empathy tools." In a paper by Pratte et al. [105, p. 1] on empathy tools in design contexts, they're defined as "experiences designed to evoke empathetic responses by placing the user in another's lived and felt experience." These kinds of tools can simulate what it's like to have a certain experience or to be in a body that moves differently. These empathy tools are categorised by agency, perspective, and sensations. In terms of agency, a tool could offer freedom to the user to explore an experience or strategically limit agency so the user experiences the challenges and frustrations of the reference population. For example, technologies like the GERonTologic simulator allow users to experience age-related challenges from a first-person perspective [106]. Empathy tools can also offer the second-person perspective. An example is the live-action interactive VR experience titled *Injustice*, created by Jaehee Cho et al. [107] Users witness and can influence a scene where an African American character faces injustice. In terms of sensations, empathy tools can stimulate physical sensations in the wearer, like the wear.mascha by Janne Beuthel et al. [108], which is a wearable device designed to replicate the experience of a migraine.

If we think of data collection and analysis methods as empathy tools, we can ask ourselves the following reflexive questions:

- Is the agency that a certain data collection method offers me (e.g., the flexibility of the interview questions I can choose to ask, and the themes I can shape) enabling opportunities for richer insights into these participants' lived experiences? How can I best use this agency? How can I use a method that offers even more agency?
- Is the lack of agency I'm experiencing when using a certain method a reflection of the participants' lived experiences (e.g.,

(*continued*)

(continued)

their difficulty interacting within a verbal interview context and my struggle to understand their meaning), and does this give me helpful insights? (Or have I been trying to simply minimise these restrictions without fully reflecting on how they're offering empathic opportunities?)
- Do the methods I'm using offer first-person perspectives (e.g., through empathic attunement in clinical improvisation within musicking with a participant) or second-person perspectives (witnessing their experiences in an interview or as they create an image)? Which perspective am I seeking and how is the tool I'm using affording this? Do I need to change the method I'm using to align with my goal in this regard?
- What sensations are arising empathically in an interaction with a participant? Can sensations arising through countertransference be helpful to reflect on (especially if there is a dual relationship between participant/client and therapist/researcher)? What sensations are arising in extended ethnographic encounters as daily experiences are shared (involving, for example, tiredness)?

Responsive and Flexible Adapting

In (particularly qualitative) research that employs Empathic Reflexivity, we flexibly adapt to how participants wish to express themselves and the unique contexts in which we interact. Haire and MacDonald [13] highlighted the importance of adapting methods to participants' needs and taking a playful approach. Lindblad [90] described how the design of group work in their study was exploratory and unfolding. Participants' illnesses resulted in interview challenges in Hans Solli's [109] study, so he decided to include both interview quotes and his own narratives. Fairchild and McFerran [36] revised their approach when they found that the children participating in their study struggled with verbal engagement, which made a song-sharing activity less effective for answering their research question.

Interviews

Carolyn Arnason [110] described dialogue in qualitative interviews as involving an open and genuine conversation to discover facets of a particular topic. Interviewing is not just a research method, it's a social relationship crafted and shaped by researcher and participant, their personalities, interactions and feelings towards each other [19].

In a study by Jeanette Kennelly et al. [111] on professional supervision as a storied experience, they used Rubin and Rubin's [112] Responsive Interviewing Model, in which interviews are designed and facilitated to invite vivid, nuanced, and rich descriptions. This approach emphasises the importance of making findings feel real to those who haven't heard the conversation, and embraces multiple shades of nuanced meaning rather than binary perspectives. In Haire and MacDonald's [13] study, they used video clips to stimulate discussion about humour in music therapy with persons living with dementia. The meeting transcended a typical research interview, becoming what they termed an "interview-encounter". Tuastad and Stige [89, p. 262] noted how humour and mutual respect created a "conciliatory culture" in their interviews, whilst Solli and Rolvsjord [30] adopted a flexible, nondirective approach to enable participants to express experiences in ways that suited their personal narrative style. Thompson and McFerran [113] provided interview questions to participants beforehand. This was helpful because the interviews were conducted in their home environment where they could have been distracted and interrupted.

Considering relationship dynamics is particularly important when working with vulnerable participants. For example, Zara Thompson et al. [21] explored ways to make interviews more accessible for people living with dementia, emphasising the importance of familiar environments, timing for optimal alertness, and flexible questioning techniques. They found that caregivers could support participation by interpreting nonverbal expressions and providing additional context. These authors also discussed the use of music in interviews (e.g., to prompt memories, stimulate communication, increase comfort, and build rapport). When interviewing children, Klyve and Rolvsjord [29] highlighted the importance of adapting questions to individual capacities and competencies, recognising that children's expressions extend beyond verbal communication. Given the children's challenges with attachment and social interaction, the inclusion of alternative forms of expression, such as music playing or drawing, offered richer and potentially more authentic data.

Group Discussions

Focus groups have faced criticism for failing to provide researchers with deep, detailed insight into participants' experiences [114]. To address these limitations, we can use active listening, emotional awareness [115], and creative facilitation methods [116]. Tríona McCaffrey et al. [117] used focus groups to explore the role and impact of group songwriting in recovery-oriented mental health services. They were careful to encourage quieter members to share their thoughts so that all voices were heard. As the songwriting itself was a method of data collection, the focus groups were led by a qualified music therapist.

Dimitra Dimitrakopoulou and Petros Theodorou [118] introduced "Affective Facilitation" to invite people to share their lived experiences in focus groups. Individual differences can still be recognised within the collaborative conversation. After a check-in, the process begins with brainstorming, where a graphic facilitator documents participants' contributions and allows spontaneous idea-building. The facilitator manages the time carefully to ensure that everyone has the chance to share. The next phase involves discussing emotions associated with concepts being brainstormed, followed by sharing personal stories that are visually depicted in individual "bubbles" with other group members' comments noted around the bubbles. The session concludes with an open discussion about connecting past experiences to present relevance and future actions, followed by a check-out ritual for reflection and feedback on the process. In this technique, facilitators should be open, present, and self-aware. They're aiming to understand the stories that people share without interpreting them, by using active listening and fostering empathy. The principle of horizontalisation is used so that no story element is prioritised over others. Group members are encouraged to explore open-ended questions with curiosity instead of seeking agreement or final conclusions.

Arts-Based Data Creation

We discussed earlier how the design of an arts-based research study can invite empathic ways of knowing and connecting, especially in that we can share experiences that may be inaccessible through words alone. We find examples in music therapy literature where arts-based data collection methods were used specifically for this purpose [13, 88]. In her study with Asian music therapy students studying in the USA, Laura Beer [54] discussed how improvisation afforded participants opportunities to express themselves and gain new insights into their experiences. Grace Thompson and Katrina McFerran [113, p. 22] described music making with mothers in their study as offering "a natural opportunity for each person to gently share their expertise." For Fairchild and McFerran [36], arts-based methods such as play, art, drama and music, allowed children to communicate their experiences in a way that felt authentic and accessible. In their study on music listening and health promotion, Batt-Rawden et al. [9] used music CDs as interactive tools, allowing participants to connect music with life experiences, such as coping with illness.

Staying "Close" During Analysis

The intentional use of empathy can potentially strengthen analysis across different methodologies, but there's not a lot of literature on how to leverage empathy as a resource during (particularly qualitative) data analysis [3]. Analysis can be a deeply subjective and relational process that mirrors our experiences of meaning-making in therapeutic relationships. As Kerry Devlin pointed out in our interview,

> In academia, reflexivity has to fit within the system that we're comfortable with: it's looking at your bias as a researcher. It's this objective application of what I think most clinicians would describe as a very subjective, intersubjective process of reflection and a very relational, personal process. We think of research as this one kind of thing and we think of clinical practice as this other kind of thing and so we're siloing them when that's actually not helpful because if we're trying to research clinical practice the process should parallel in some way what's happening in the therapy room.

Often, as we begin data analysis, we take a step back from the closer interaction we had with participants—unless our process of analysis is also a collaborative one. In Giorgos Tsiris' [119] study on music therapy and spirituality, for example, the participants weren't provided with a working definition of spirituality. They offered their own understandings of what spirituality meant, which were then organised into themes. In our conversation, Efrat Roginsky explained her processes of working collaboratively with parents of young people who communicate without speech:

> The research was with parents of people and young adults, children and young adults without language, all kinds of diagnoses. I couldn't ask the people themselves. We had a mutual reflection on the analysis. I gave good space for the mutual reflection. So, the parents themselves work with their

> children, live with their children, communicate with their children but they don't have the theory, they don't have the terminology. So, it took us until the last session with most participants to reach some kind of mutual terminology. We're talking about emerging themes. Here they can emerge, they have enough time, there is enough time for reflection, for mutuality, for processing and things do emerge.

Even if we step out of a collaborative interaction with participants to analyse data alone as the researcher, we can still explore ways of remaining empathically close to the data. As Linda Finlay [6] argued, we can read a text by opening our heart, intuition and imagination, being attuned empathetically, listening attentively and responding reflexively. Although transcripts lack the emotional and contextual nuances present in the actual exchanges we had with participants, high-quality verbatim versions can help provide depth.

Empathy enhances qualitative analysis of transcripts in various ways. Firstly, we need to make time and room for prolonged engagement with data. We can't rush empathic data analysis and we can't simply be in "sorting mode." Empathy requires curiosity, openness and non-judgement, mindfulness, and active engagement with the text. Secondly, to grasp what deeply matters to others, it's crucial that we consider both their current and historical contexts, as well as the motivations behind their actions. Using the audio or video recordings alongside the written transcripts during the initial analysis phase can also enrich our empathetic capacity because we'll be more aware of details like speech rhythm, repetitions, pauses, silences, tone, and voice quality, which help us to make sense of the content. Thirdly, we need a clear sense of the distinction between ourselves and our participants and the ability to purposefully centre them and their perspectives, knowing these may be different from our own. We want to avoid blurring the distinction between us through projection or emotional contagion. Fourthly, we can pay attention to our visceral experiences and bodily sensations. Since we actively use ourselves as instruments in qualitative analysis, we're maintaining a dual focus: engaging with the data while being mindful of how it affects us. Our bodies offer us valuable information. Fifthly, we can harness our imagination and creativity. Stories or texts grounded in specific examples resonate with us differently than vague, technical descriptions [3].

In their narrative inquiry of identity constructions in a rock band of ex-inmates, Tuastad and Stige [89, p. 258] described how they focused on deciphering the narratives of their participants, aiming "to locate themes within the voices of each narrative in the interviews, rather than to locate distinct themes across all interviews." In Klyve and Rolvsjord's [29] study of children's experiences in music therapy, they emphasised the importance of flexibility when analysing interviews with children. They used a narrative approach because it allowed them to pay attention not only to what the children said but also to what they did. Lindblad [90, p. 428] used content analysis of communication patterns in a music listening group with older men with the aim of taking the role of the other: "to understand the participants from the point of view of the men themselves." She held explorative questions in mind such as: "What is happening here? What strikes me?"

Using interpretive phenomenological analysis (IPA), Venkatarangam [96] described how researcher and participant engage in a dialogue where both parties attempt to understand the participant's accounting of their experience. Through IPA we immerse ourselves in the fullness of the participant's lived experience while considering how these aspects shape their behaviour and interactions. The participant is seen as the expert on their experience [120, 121], and the researcher's task is to interpret the participant's experience from their perspective. Central to IPA is the concept of the hermeneutic circle, which is a process that invites iterative, dynamic engagement with data as we seek to understand the parts in relation to the whole and the whole in relation to its parts. Interpretation in IPA is like detective work: we identify potential meanings and critically assess them against our own developing understandings. In their study with women with breast cancer, Stephanie Thompson et al. [122] remained continually engaged in reciprocal interpretation with their participants, entering into ever-expanding circles of understanding to reveal, examine, and revise meanings. Jonathan Smith et al. [121] also highlighted the importance of the "double hermeneutic," which refers to the researcher trying to make sense of the participant's efforts to make sense of their experiences. This means that we're empathising with the participant while also maintaining a critical stance and probing for additional meanings [120]. Smith [123] introduced the concept of the "gem" as an interpretative tool in IPA research. We can use an insightful remark or excerpt from an interview to anchor meaning. Gems can be shining, suggestive, or secret. Shining gems are clearly significant, while suggestive gems require deeper engagement to uncover their full meaning, and secret gems are subtle and easily overlooked.

The arts can take us straight into visceral, emotional, and empathic engagement. Haire and MacDonald [13, p. 1] wrote about "thinking through improvisation," drawing on Finlay's [6] reflexive approach to phenomenological analysis. In their study, this involved empathising with data, lingering over selected passages, then stepping back and interrogating data using lifeworld-oriented questions. Krøier et al. [88] explained how musical improvisation allows music therapists to reflect on their knowing-in-action when researching nonverbal interactions, supporting verbal reflection on their practice when words alone feel insufficient to capture the complexity of their experiences. McCaffrey [124] reflected on participants' creative materials from multiple perspectives: as a group participant, a music therapist, and as a qualitative researcher. By composing music in response to participants' artwork, she could hold and reveal her reactions to the materials, acknowledging that her own feelings were integral to how she made meaning of others' feelings.

Of course, empathy alone doesn't guarantee high-quality analysis and findings. Our empathy allows us to get closer to others' experiences, yet it can never provide direct access to their perspectives. Although we can work intentionally to centre our participants' perspectives and try to gain as rich an understanding of their experiences as possible, our perceptions will invariably be influenced by our situatedness and personal life story. We can also try to mitigate the risks of our power and privilege as researchers but these won't be completely resolved. We have to pair empathy with humility and tentativeness while we recognise the ongoing difficulties in transcending our own frames.

Using Empathy in Supervision

Supporting students in their journey of Empathic Reflexivity requires empathy on the part of the supervisor too. Students and supervisors can encounter phases of uncertainty in the research process and this can be uncomfortable and stressful. If managed well, though, this can offer opportunities for self-development and learning. Students' uncertainty often stems from self-doubt, feelings of overwhelm, and inexperience, leading to behaviours like procrastination, a need for reassurance, or masking uncertainty to appear confident. An empathic supervisor who can contain these feelings by genuinely listening, holding space, and collaboratively exploring ways to move forward can guide a student constructively [125,

126]. Maintaining confidentiality is also important for encouraging students to engage in honest reflexivity [5].

In a study with counselling and psychotherapy doctoral students in the UK, Sofie Bager-Charleson et al. [127] found that supervisors' empathy and research knowledge were rated as equally important by students, with empathy rated even higher by supervisors. Their 3C model for research supervision highlights clarity (exploring needs, clear communication, imparting skills, giving helpful feedback, supporting writing); containment (meeting students on a relational level, giving reassurance, exploring together, discussing reflexivity, working through anxiety, and promoting networking); and compassion (preparing the student for the journey ahead providing support throughout the process, helping students remain ethically sensitive and to care for participants and themselves).

Unfortunately, the university context is not always (perhaps not often?) one that prioritises well-being and relational care. In a South African context, Chris Callaghan [128] hypothesised that supervision grounded in caring values would be associated with greater achievement. Instead, he found that postgraduate throughput was more strongly associated with values of achievement and prioritising the needs of the self. In response (and in a Canadian context), Carolin Kreber [129] argued that care and autonomy can and should be understood as interconnected. She suggested that true caregiving fosters a student's independence and growth. Students grow by being encouraged to think independently, take risks, and make decisions, making the thesis journey not only technical but emancipatory.

Inviting the Reader/Audience into an Empathic Relationship Too

The imagined presence of future readers can shape our process even from the planning phase [102]. As we think through how best to present our findings, we're shifting from empathically understanding participants to inviting readers into an empathic relationship. External empathetic validity refers to readers' or audiences' connection to the study as we encourage them to become "connected knowers" [130, p. 280]. Audiences/readers are invited to step beyond their own perspectives, gaining insight into both the participants' and researchers' viewpoints.

Many researchers now seek to invite their readers to truly "hear" their participants. Balancing the voices of both the participants and the researcher can be difficult, though. We may choose to include not only participants' words but also paralinguistic elements like pauses, lapses, and reformulations in our text. In Tuastad and Stige's [89, p. 253] narrative inquiry of identity constructions in a rock band of ex-inmates, they presented a vignette, which "invites you into the life story of Kjell and his fellow musicians." Anthony Meadows and Katherine Wimpenny [131] used video to complement written narratives, welcoming viewers into the interpretive process and enhancing the research's emotional depth. Participatory and arts-based mediums like plays and forums designed by the participants themselves can vividly foreground their voices [132]. Beer [54] noted that when creative arts are incorporated, data become part of an interactive experience, enabling readers to feel participants' experiences emotionally as well as intellectually. In arts-based inquiry, the audience can deeply engage in the meaning-making process alongside the participants and researchers [102].

Trustworthiness in a Study Employing Empathic Reflexivity

In a study using Empathic Reflexivity, the researcher is working to show the reader how they got to know the participants as well as possible while critically evaluating that process. This chapter has detailed the many facets of this process. Empathy is not always automatically a "good thing," though. When empathy is tied to a notion of representation as correspondence ("I have accurately represented your experience in my study"), it may obscure the fact that the researcher can never fully become the participant, nor can the written account ever replicate the lived experience [133]. Feminist researchers, such as Patti Lather [130], have critiqued empathy, voice, and authenticity as potentially imperialist. If we employ empathy for the purpose of collecting reliable data, this can mask the differences between researcher and participant, silencing the "Other" [1] and serving our interests instead of the participant's best interests [134].

Importantly, then, empathy needs to be counterbalanced with an acknowledgement of difference [130]. Excellent qualitative research celebrates complexity, while poor research oversimplifies and stereotypes [135]. When we use empathy thoughtfully, it allows us to compassionately, respectfully, and humbly engage with others as uniquely different people but also as fellow human beings.

An Accessible Summary

Researchers engaging in Empathic Reflexivity carefully examine how they are drawing insights empathically from participants and presenting these to readers so they too can respond with empathy. Self-awareness is needed to distinguish their own feelings from those of others, and researchers need genuine willingness to offer sustained, focused attention as they genuinely tune into participants' experiences. To do this well, they also need sufficient personal capacity to empathise and the courage to remain open to what could emerge as they receive participants' contributions non-judgmentally.

Building meaningful research relationships is central, whether through a singular researcher role or in a dual therapist-researcher position. Time and proximity matter enormously. We can't meet participants briefly or at a distance and expect deep empathic understanding.

Cognitive empathy involves understanding another's state of mind from their perspective, whilst affective empathy entails purposefully sharing another's emotions whilst recognising these feelings belong to them. This differs significantly from emotional contagion, where researchers unconsciously "catch" others' emotions. There are also other theoretical perspectives that can inform our understanding of what it means to try to perceive another's experience, such as theory of mind, simulation theory, direct social perception, and "perspective-getting" (directly asking participants to share their thoughts, beliefs, attitudes, and feelings rather than merely inferring these through perspective-taking). However, the fundamental challenge remains: we can never fully and truly "climb into" another person's experience. We do the best we can, while staying humble about our conclusions.

Throughout all research stages, from engaging with literature to collecting and analysing data, empathic reflexivity calls us to responsively and flexibly adapt to how participants wish to express themselves. Research methods become empathy tools that can simulate experiences, offer different perspectives, and generate various sensations that help researchers understand participants' lived realities. During data analysis, researchers using Empathic Reflexivity remain closely attuned to participants' experiences. Analysis can become a deeply subjective

(*continued*)

(continued)

and relational process, while researchers still maintain clear distinctions between themselves and participants and purposefully centre the participants' perspectives.

Excellent qualitative research celebrates complexity rather than oversimplifying experiences. To demonstrate trustworthiness, researchers work to show readers how they came to know participants as fully as possible, while critically evaluating that process.

References

1. Gair S. Feeling their stories: contemplating empathy, insider/outsider positionings, and enriching qualitative research. Qual Health Res. 2012;22(1):134–43.
2. Keen S. A theory of narrative empathy. Narrative. 2006;14(3):207–36.
3. Stige SH, Oddli HW, Hjeltnes A, Watson J, Stige B. The researcher as instrument-how our capacity for empathy supports qualitative analysis of transcripts. Qual Res Psychol. 2024;1–21.
4. dos Santos A. Empathy pathways: a view from music therapy. London: Palgrave Macmillan; 2022.
5. Elliott H, Ryan J, Hollway W. Research encounters, reflexivity and supervision. Int J Soc Res Methodol. 2012;15(5):433–44.
6. Finlay L. Phenomenology for therapists: researching the lived world [Internet]. Chichester: J. Wiley; 2011 [cited 2024 Jul 18]. Available from: https://doi.org/10.1002/9781119975144.
7. Carroll D. Portraiture and the role of researcher: reflections and questions/ La méthode de l'art du portrait et le rôle du chercheur: réflexions et questions. Canadian Journal of Music Therapy. 2007;13(2):148–59.
8. Krüger V, Stige B. Between rights and realities–music as a structuring resource in child welfare everyday life: a qualitative study. Nord J Music Ther. 2015;24(2):99–122.
9. Batt-Rawden KB, DeNora T, Ruud E. Music listening and empowerment in health promotion: a study of the role and significance of music in everyday life of the long-term ill. Nord J Music Ther. 2005;14(2):120–36.
10. Talbert BM. Knowing other people: a second-person framework. Ratio. 2015;28(2):190–206.
11. Peacocke C. Joint attention: its nature, reflexivity, and relation to common knowledge. In: Eilan N, Hoerl C, McCormack T, Roessler J, editors. Joint

attention: communication and other minds issues in philosophy and psychology. Oxford: Oxford University Press; 2005. p. 298–324.
12. Stige B, Malterud K, Midtgarden T. Toward an agenda for evaluation of qualitative research. Qual Health Res. 2009;19(10):1504–16.
13. Haire N, MacDonald R. Understanding how humour enables contact in music therapy relationships with persons living with dementia: a phenomenological arts-based reflexive study. Arts Psychother. 2021;74:101784.
14. Trondalen G. Resource-oriented Bonny Method of Guided Imagery and Music (R-oGIM) as a creative health resource for musicians. Nord J Music Ther. 2016;25(1):5–31.
15. Prior MT. Accomplishing "rapport" in qualitative research interviews: empathic moments in interaction. Applied Linguistics Review. 2018;9(4):487–511.
16. Seidman I. Interviewing as qualitative research. A guide for researchers in education and the social sciences. New York: Teachers College Press; 2019.
17. Clark MS, Lemay EP. When emotion expression will (and will not) enhance listening and responsiveness. Curr Opin Psychol. 2024;55:101695.
18. Pitts MJ, Miller-Day M. Upward turning points and positive rapport-development across time in researcher—participant relationships. Qual Res. 2007;7(2):177–201.
19. Schmid E, Garrels V, Skåland B. The continuum of rapport: ethical tensions in qualitative interviews with vulnerable participants. Qual Res. 2024;21:1468794123122460.
20. Freeman S, Skinner K, Middleton L, Xiong B, Fang ML. Engaging hard-to-reach, hidden, and seldom-heard populations in research. In: Knowledge, innovation, and impact: a guide for the engaged health researcher. Toronto: University of Toronto Press; 2021. p. 81–91.
21. Thompson Z, Baker FA, Clark IN, Tamplin J. Making qualitative interviews in music therapy research more accessible for participants living with dementia–reflections on development and implementation of interview guidelines. Int J Qual Methods. 2021;20:16094069211047066.
22. Lindo D. Examining the accessibility of MA Music Therapy training in the United Kingdom for ethnic minority communities. British J Music Therapy. 2023;37(1):5–16.
23. Iliya YA, Harris BT. Singing an imaginal dialogue: a qualitative examination of a bereavement intervention with creative arts therapists. Nord J Music Ther. 2016;25(3):248–72.
24. Guillemin M, Gillam L. Ethical mindfulness: narrative analysis and everyday ethics in health care. In: Rothman BK, Armstrong EM, Tiger R, editors. Bioethical issues, sociological perspectives. Bingley: Emerald Group Publishing Limited; 2007. p. 157–78.

25. Gresham R. Trusting relationships: a key for cross-cultural engagement. J High Educ Policy Manag. 2012;34(5):491–501.
26. McNair R, Taft A, Hegarty K. Using reflexivity to enhance in-depth interviewing skills for the clinician researcher. BMC Med Res Methodol. 2008;8:73.
27. Ghetti CM, Vederhus BJ, Gaden TS, Brenner AK, Bieleninik Ł, Kvestad I, et al. Longitudinal study of music therapy's effectiveness for premature infants and their caregivers (LongSTEP): feasibility study with a Norwegian cohort. J Music Ther. 2021;58(2):201–40.
28. Bruscia K. The process of doing qualitative research. Part I: introduction. In: Wheeler B, editor. Music therapy research: quantitative and qualitative perspectives. Gilsum (NH). Barcelona Publishers; 1995. p. 389–400.
29. Klyve GP, Rolvsjord R. Moments of fun: narratives of children's experiences of music therapy in mental health care. Nord J Music Ther. 2023;32(2):100–20.
30. Solli HP, Rolvsjord R. "The opposite of treatment": a qualitative study of how patients diagnosed with psychosis experience music therapy. Nord J Music Ther. 2015;24(1):67–92.
31. Gottlieb MC. Avoiding exploitive dual relationships: a decision-making model. Psychother Theory Res Pract Train. 1993;30(1):41–8.
32. Hay-Smith EJC, Brown M, Anderson L, Treharne GJ. Once a clinician, always a clinician: a systematic review to develop a typology of clinician-researcher dual-role experiences in health research with patient-participants. BMC Med Res Methodol. 2016;16:95.
33. Rickson D. Researching one's own clinical practice: managing multiple roles in an action research project. Voices: A World Forum for Music Therapy [Internet]. 2009 Mar [cited 2024 Jul 18];9(1). Available from: https://voices.no/index.php/voices/article/view/33.
34. dos Santos A. Empathy and aggression in group music therapy with teenagers: a descriptive phenomenological study. Music Ther Perspect. 2019;37(1):14–27.
35. Younggren JN, Gottlieb MC. Managing risk when contemplating multiple relationships. Prof Psychol Res Pract. 2004;35(3):255–60.
36. Fairchild R, McFerran KS. "Music is everything": using collaborative group songwriting as an arts-based method with children experiencing homelessness and family violence. Nord J Music Ther. 2019;28(2):88–107.
37. Devlin K. Perspectives on perspective: a critical appraisal of perspective-taking in music therapy education and clinical practice [PhD thesis]. [Aalborg]: Aalborg University; 2024.
38. Eyal T, Steffel M, Epley N. Perspective mistaking: accurately understanding the mind of another requires getting perspective, not taking perspective. J Pers Soc Psychol. 2018;114(4):547–71.
39. Avramides A. Other minds. London: Routledge; 2001.

40. Shoemaker S. The first-person perspective and other essays. Cambridge: Cambridge University Press; 1996.
41. Zahavi D. Subjectivity and selfhood: investigating the first-person perspective. Cambridge, MA: MIT Press; 2005.
42. Gallese V. The roots of empathy: the shared manifold hypothesis and the neural basis of intersubjectivity. Psychopathology. 2003;36(4):171–80.
43. Gallagher H, Frith C. Functioning imaging of 'theory of mind'. Trends Cogn Sci. 2003;7(2):77–83.
44. Apperly I. Mindreaders: the cognitive basis of "theory of mind". Hove: Psychology Press; 2011.
45. Saxe R, Carey S, Kanwisher N. Understanding other minds: linking developmental psychology and functional neuroimaging. Annu Rev Psychol. 2004;55:87–124.
46. Abrahams D, Rohleder P. A clinical guide to psychodynamic psychotherapy. London: Routledge; 2021.
47. Goldman A. Theory of mind. In: Margolis E, Samuels R, Stich S, editors. The Oxford handbook of philosophy and cognitive science. Oxford: Oxford University Press; 2012. p. 1–25.
48. Gordon RM. Folk psychology as simulation. Mind Lang. 1986;1(2):158–71.
49. Reddy V. How infants know minds. Cambridge (MA): Harvard University Press; 2008.
50. Zahavi D, Gallagher S. The (in)visibility of others: a reply to Herschbach. Philos Explor. 2008;11(3):237–44.
51. Spaulding S. On direct social perception. Conscious Cogn. 2015;36:472–82.
52. Colle L, Becchio C, Bara BG. The non-problem of the other minds: a neurodevelopmental perspective on shared intentionality. Hum Dev. 2008;51(5–6):336–48.
53. Zurek PP, Scheithauer H. Towards a more precise conceptualization of empathy: an integrative review of literature on definitions, associated functions, and developmental trajectories. Int J Dev Sci. 2017;11(3–4):57–68.
54. Beer LE. From embedded to embodied: including music in arts-based music therapy research. Music Ther Perspect. 2016;34(1):33–40.
55. Nordgren L, Banas K, MacDonald G. Empathy gaps for social pain: why people underestimate the pain of social suffering. J Pers Soc Psychol. 2011;100(1):120–8.
56. Ratcliffe M. Phenomenology as a form of empathy. Inquiry. 2012;55(5):473–95.
57. Short H. It feels like Armageddon: identification with a female personality-disordered offender at a time of cultural, political and personal attack. Nord J Music Ther. 2017;26(3):272–85.

58. Sorel S. Presenting Carly and Elliot: exploring roles and relationships in a mother-son dyad in Nordoff-Robbins music therapy. Qualitative Inquiries in Music Therapy. 2010;5:1–30.
59. Lee JH. A qualitative inquiry of the lived experiences of music therapists who have survived cancer who are working with medical and hospice patients. Front Psychol. 2016;7:1840.
60. Redmond M. Social decentering: a theory of other-orientation encompassing empathy and perspective taking. Berlin: De Gruyter; 2018.
61. Damen D, Pollmann MM, Grassow TL. The benefits and obstacles to perspective getting. Frontiers Communication. 2021;6:611187.
62. Zhou H, Majka EA, Epley N. Inferring perspective versus getting perspective: underestimating the value of being in another person's shoes. Psychol Sci. 2017;28(4):482–93.
63. Greenwald AG, Poehlman TA, Uhlmann EL, Banaji MR. Understanding and using the Implicit Association Test: III. Meta-analysis of predictive validity. J Pers Soc Psychol. 2009;97(1):17–41.
64. Oswald FL, Mitchell G, Blanton H, Jaccard J, Tetlock PE. Predicting ethnic and racial discrimination: a meta-analysis of IAT criterion studies. J Pers Soc Psychol. 2013;105(2):171–92.
65. Abbott EA. Subjective observation in music therapy: a study of student practicum logs. Music Ther Perspect. 2018;36(1):117–26.
66. Dileo C. Ethical thinking in music therapy. 2nd ed. Philadelphia (PA): Jeffrey Books; 2021.
67. Valentino R. Attitudes towards cross-cultural empathy in music therapy. Music Ther Perspect. 2006;24:108–14.
68. Kwan M. Music therapists' experiences with adults in pain: implications for clinical practice. Qualitative Inquiries in Music Therapy. 2010;5:43–85.
69. Robarts J. Music therapy with sexually abused children. Clinical Child Psychology and Psychiatry. 2006;11(2):249–69.
70. Ickes W. Empathic accuracy: its links to clinical, cognitive, developmental, social, and physiological psychology. In: Decety J, Ickes W, editors. The social neuroscience of empathy. Cambridge (MA): The MIT Press; 2009. p. 57–70.
71. Walter AM. Embodying ineffable concepts: empathic intimacy as tool for insight. In: Stodulka T, Dinkelaker S, Thajib F, editors. Affective dimensions of fieldwork and ethnography. Cham: Springer; 2019. p. 143–56.
72. Rempala DM. Cognitive strategies for controlling emotional contagion. J Appl Soc Psychol. 2013;43(7):1528–37.
73. Feldman BL. How emotions are made. Boston: Houghton Mifflin Harcourt; 2017.
74. dos Santos A. Finding empathy through music therapy techniques in the mist of family trauma: an autoethnography. Voices: A World Forum for Music

Therapy [Internet]. 2024 Jul [cited 2024 Jul 18];24(2). Available from: https://voices.no/index.php/voices/article/view/3688.
75. Bondi L. Empathy and identification: conceptual resources for feminist fieldwork. ACME: An International E-Journal for Critical Geographies. 2003;2(1):64–76.
76. Greenhalgh-Spencer H. Deep listening as bridge-building in school–community partnerships. Educ Theory. 2023;72:793–811.
77. Trimboli O. How to listen: discover the hidden key to better communication. London: Macmillan; 2022.
78. Rogers CR. Perceptual reorganization in client-centered therapy. In: Blake RR, Ramsey GV, editors. Perception: an approach to personality. New York: Ronald Press; 1951. p. 307–27.
79. Kluger AN, Mizrahi M. Defining listening: can we get rid of the adjectives? Curr Opin Psychol. 2023;52:101639.
80. Todres L. Embodied enquiry: phenomenological touchstones for research, psychotherapy and spirituality. Basingstoke: Springer; 2007.
81. Sutton J. The pause that follows. Nord J Music Ther. 2002;11(1):27–38.
82. Ansdell G. Music for life. London: Jessica Kingsley; 1995.
83. De Backer J. Music and psychosis: a research report detailing the transition from sensorial play to musical form by psychotic patients. Nord J Music Ther. 2008;17(2):89–104.
84. Bruscia KE. A qualitative approach to analyzing client improvisations. Music Ther Perspect. 2001;19(1):7–21.
85. Hickey G. The use ofliterature in grounded theory. NT Res. 1997;2(5):371–8.
86. Ramalho R, Adams P, Huggard P, Hoare K. Literature review and constructivist grounded theory methodology. Forum Qualitative Sozialforschung/ Forum: Qualitative Social Research [Internet]. 2015 Aug [cited 2024 Jul 18];16(3). Available from: https://www.qualitative-research.net/index.php/fqs/article/view/2313.
87. Devlin K. How do I see you and what does that mean for us? An autoethnographic study. Music Therapy Perspectives. 2018;36(2):234–42.
88. Krøier JK, Stige B, Ridder HM. Non-verbal interactions between music therapists and persons with dementia. A qualitative phenomenological and arts-based inquiry. Music Ther Perspect. 2021;39(2):162–71.
89. Tuastad L, Stige B. The revenge of Me and THE BAND'its: a narrative inquiry of identity constructions in a rock band of ex-inmates. Nord J Music Ther. 2015;24(3):252–75.
90. Lindblad K. "No, I guess it's kind of sensitive"- Communication patterns in a music listening group with older men. Nord J Music Ther. 2021;30(5):424–39.

91. Bensimon M. Perceptions of music therapists regarding their work with children living under continuous war threat: experiential reframing of trauma through songs. Nord J Music Ther. 2020;29(4):300–16.
92. Charmaz K. Grounded theory in the 21st century: applications for advancing social justice studies. In: Denzin N, Lincoln Y, editors. The Sage handbook of qualitative research. 3rd ed. Thousand Oaks, CA: Sage; 2005. p. 507–37.
93. Charmaz K. The power of constructivist grounded theory for critical inquiry. Qual Inq. 2017;23(1):34–45.
94. Charmaz K. Special invited paper: continuities, contradictions, and critical inquiry in grounded theory. Int J Qual Methods. 2017;16:1–8.
95. Charmaz K. Stories and silences: disclosures and self in chronic illness. Qual Inq. 2002;8(3):302–28.
96. Venkatarangam S. Participants' experiences of a receptive music therapy intervention that incorporates raga: an interpretative phenomenological analysis. Arts Psychother. 2021;73:101762.
97. Greenwood J. Arts-based research: weaving magic and meaning. Internat J Edu Arts. 2012;13(1):1–20.
98. Stout CJ. The art of empathy: teaching students to care. Art Education. 1999;52(2):21–34.
99. Chilton G, Gerber N, Scotti V. Towards an aesthetic intersubjective paradigm for arts based research: an art therapy perspective. UNESCO Observatory Multidisciplinary Journal in the Arts. 2015;5(1):1–27.
100. McIntyre M. Ethics and aesthetics: the goodness of arts-informed research. In: Cole AL, Neilsen L, Knowles JG, Luciani TC, editors. Provoked by art: theorizing arts-informed research. Halifax, NS: Backalong Books & Centre for Arts-informed Research; 2004. p. 251–61.
101. Leavy P. Method meets art. 3rd ed. New York: Guilford Press; 2020.
102. Bresler L. Toward connectedness: aesthetically based research. Stud Art Educ. 2006;48(1):52–69.
103. Bleakley A. Stories as data, data as stories: making sense of narrative inquiry in clinical education. Med Educ. 2005;39(5):534–40.
104. Kenyon G. Telling and listening to stories: creating a wisdom environment for older people. Generations. 2003;27(3):30–3.
105. Pratte S, Tang A, Oehlberg L. Evoking empathy: a framework for describing empathy tools. In: Proceedings of the Fifteenth International Conference on Tangible, Embedded, and Embodied Interaction; 2021 Feb; Salzburg, Austria. New York: ACM; 2021. p. 1–15.
106. Fernández-Gutiérrez M, Bas-Sarmiento P, del Pino-Chinchilla H, Poza-Méndez M, Marín-Paz AJ. Effectiveness of a multimodal intervention and the simulation flow to improve empathy and attitudes towards older adults in nursing students: a crossover randomised controlled trial. Nurse Educ Pract. 2022;64:103430.

107. Cho J, Won Y, Kothari A, Fawaz S, Ding Z, Cheng X. Injustice: interactive live action virtual reality experience. In: Proceedings of the 2016 Annual Symposium on Computer-Human Interaction in Play Companion Extended Abstracts; 2016 Oct; Austin, TX, USA. New York: ACM; 2016. p. 33–7.
108. Beuthel JM, Wilde D, Wear X. Developing wearables that embody felt experience. In: Proceedings of the 2017 Conference on Designing Interactive Systems; 2017; Edinburgh, United Kingdom. New York: ACM; 2017. p. 915–27.
109. Solli HP. Battling illness with wellness: a qualitative case study of a young rapper's experiences with music therapy. Nord J Music Ther. 2015;24(3):204–31.
110. Arnason C. Music therapists' listening perspectives in improvisational music therapy: a qualitative interview study. Nord J Music Ther. 2003;12(2):124–38.
111. Kennelly JD, Baker FA, Daveson BA. Professional supervision as storied experience: narrative analysis findings for Australian-based registered music therapists. J Music Ther. 2017;54(1):80–107.
112. Rubin HJ, Rubin IS. Why we do what we do: philosophy of qualitative interviewing. In: Qualitative interviewing: the art of hearing data. Thousand Oaks, CA: Sage; 2005. p. 19–38.
113. Thompson G, McFerran KS. "We've got a special connection": qualitative analysis of descriptions of change in the parent–child relationship by mothers of young children with autism spectrum disorder. Nord J Music Ther. 2015;24(1):3–26.
114. Hopkins PE. Thinking critically and creatively about focus groups. Area. 2007;39(4):528–35.
115. Coetzee JK, Kotze PC. Optimizing the epistemological potential of focus groups in research on a contested issue. Qual Sociol Rev. 2014;10(2):30–41.
116. dos Santos A, Wagner C. Musical elicitation methods: insights from a study with becoming-adolescents referred to group music therapy for aggression. Int J Qual Methods. 2018;17(1):1609406918797427.
117. McCaffrey T, Higgins P, Monahan C, Moloney S, Nelligan S, Clancy A, et al. Exploring the role and impact of group songwriting with multiple stakeholders in recovery-oriented mental health services. Nord J Music Ther. 2021;30(1):41–60.
118. Dimitrakopoulou D, Theodorou P. Affective facilitation: a framework for surfacing lived experiences and harnessing creativity in focus group research. Int J Qual Methods. 2022;21:16094069221133225.
119. Tsiris G. Music therapy and spirituality: an international survey of music therapists' perceptions. Nord J Music Ther. 2017;26(4):293–319.
120. Eatough V, Smith J. Interpretive phenomenological analysis. In: Willig C, Stainton Rogers W, editors. The Sage handbook of qualitative research in psychology. 2nd ed. London: Sage; 2017. p. 193–211.

121. Smith JA, Flowers P, Larkin M. Interpretative phenomenological analysis: theory, method and research. London: Sage; 2009.
122. Thompson S, Grocke D, Dileo C. The use of group descriptive phenomenology within a mixed methods study to understand the experience of music therapy for women with breast cancer. Nord J Music Ther. 2017;26(4):320–37.
123. Smith JA. 'We could be diving for pearls': the value of the gem in experiential qualitative psychology. Qualitative Methods in Psychology Bulletin. 2011;12:6–15.
124. McCaffrey T, Edwards J. Meeting art with art: arts-based methods enhance researcher reflexivity in research with mental health service users. J Music Ther. 2015;52(4):515–32.
125. Albertyn R, Bennett K. Containing and harnessing uncertainty during postgraduate research supervision. High Educ Res Dev. 2021;40(4):661–75.
126. Lee A, Murray R. Supervising writing: helping postgraduate students develop as researchers. Innov Educ Teach Int. 2015;52(5):558–70.
127. Bager-Charleson S. Relational research reflexivity. In: Goss S, Stevens C, editors. Making research matter. London: Routledge; 2016. p. 58–70.
128. Callaghan C. Do benevolent and altruistic supervisors have higher postgraduate supervision throughput? The contributions of individual motivational values to South African postgraduate supervision throughput. South African J Higher Education. 2020;34(6):27–51.
129. Kreber C. On a pedagogy of authentic care in postgraduate research supervision. Stud High Educ. 2023;48(12):1796–808.
130. Lather P. Against empathy, voice and authenticity. In: Jackson A, Mazzei L, editors. Voice in qualitative inquiry. London: Routledge; 2009. p. 17–26.
131. Meadows A, Wimpenny K. Core themes in music therapy clinical improvisation: an arts-informed qualitative research synthesis. J Music Ther. 2017;54(2):161–95.
132. Lincoln YS, Lynham SA, Guba EG. Paradigmatic controversies, contradictions, and emerging confluences, revisited. In: Denzin NK, Lincoln YS, editors. The Sage handbook of qualitative research. 4th ed. Thousand Oaks, CA: Sage; 2011. p. 97–128.
133. Watson C. The impossible vanity: uses and abuses of empathy in qualitative inquiry. Qual Res. 2009;9(1):105–17.
134. Shuman A. Entitlement and empathy in personal narrative. Narrat Inq. 2006;16(1):148–55.
135. Watts J. Emotion, empathy and exit: reflections on doing ethnographic qualitative research on sensitive topics. Medical Sociology Online. 2008;3(2):3–14.

CHAPTER 7

Restorative Reflexivity

If our reflexive strategy entails restraining biases, values and assumptions (as we sought to do through Sentinel Reflexivity in Chap. 3), it could be argued that this limits our ability to purposefully support and generate perspectives and actions that could bring about positive social change. It may involve standing back rather than taking a stand. Even if we're reflecting on our own influence in a study (as we did through Lens Reflexivity in Chap. 4), and our own perspectives (especially if we're writing from a privileged position), as we discussed in relation to Authorial Reflexivity in Chap. 5, it could be argued that this may not do enough to trouble power relations that are embedded in the research process and in social life. What we study and how we study it always supports or challenges certain values and interests in society [1]. Research functions as a microcosm through which oppressive relationships in society at large are reproduced [2]—unless we consciously seek to do otherwise. If we get too absorbed in our own subjective processes, reflexivity, in its worst form, can serve to reproduce oppressive structures instead of transforming them [3].

Deliberately acknowledging and exploring our active participation in creating and shaping knowledge in our study *as we seek to promote greater social justice* and responding *by continuously critiquing power relations and acting in the best service of others' flourishing.*

A. dos Santos, *Reflexive Research in Music Therapy*,
https://doi.org/10.1007/978-3-032-02033-8_7

Constructively, reflexivity can be about not just restraining our influence or examining our inevitable influence, but embracing the *potential* of our influence—alongside our participants' influence—to contribute to positive social transformation. Reflexivity's emancipatory potential lies in facilitating a "politics of the possible" [4, p. 1519]. Through reflexivity, researchers can move beyond merely investigating the world to actively shaping how people perceive and inhabit it.

Music therapy researchers who we'll encounter in this chapter tend to state their perspectives explicitly, using these directly as part of their agenda to conduct research that can further social justice. They are arguing for truth/truths. ("There is a better way to see this". "It is good/right to give space for the voices of particular people to be heard or to be heard more loudly so their/our truth can be recognised.") I have called this approach Restorative Reflexivity to align with a stance that values human flourishing and restoring innate wholeness, "letting people be," and accompanying them as they determine their futures, as opposed to using damage-centred lenses that highlight deficiencies and impose interventions from a place of power and control [5]. As Bagele Chilisa [6] reminded us, the research we undertake holds the potential to work towards solutions. Researchers can act as both a provocateur and a transformative healer guided by the principles of accountability, respect, reciprocity, and the rights of those with whom we conduct research.

Critically Articulating Relational Positioning

In Restorative Reflexivity, it's essential that we critically examine our own positioning. When we discuss positioning, it's in relation to the topic we're studying in a specific project and the people who are involved. In my interview with Natasha Thomas, she explained,

> I think of reflectivity as constantly coming back to the question of "what is my relationship to this thing and how is that impacting the choices I'm making?" You're not just looking down at your feet and seeing the grass that you're standing on. You actually have to look up and see where you are in relation to other things and get to know that place.

A technique for exploring positioning could be to create a map of your intersecting categories of identity, including personal experiences, social factors, and organisational experiences. You could, for example, circle those that bring you advantage while underlining those that bring you disadvantage. If your study includes human participants, you may wish to create another map exploring how your participants might be represented, as well as looking at the relationships between these two maps and the implications of those relationships. As we create these kinds of images, it's important not to see positions as fixed or as stereotypes.

When Researchers are Part of Marginalised Groups

Some studies focus on making room for, highlighting, and amplifying the voices of those who tend to be silenced. This may take the form of a study in which the researcher identifies as part of a minoritised group [7–9]. For example, in Natasha Thomas and Valerie Blanc's [10, p. 1] duoethnography, Thomas described herself as

> a Black Queer Femme, a chronically ill academic and board-certified music therapist (MT-BC), living and working in the Midwest region of the United States. You will not find many people who look like me in my profession. Yet I am one of billions of Black and/or Indigenous People of Color (BIPOC) from cultures where the use of music as a healing modality is a foundational aspect of their collective history and current practices.

The term "Own Voices" burst onto the literary scene in 2015, coined by Corinne Duyvis. It refers to books written by and about people from the same marginalised community. The term has since been recognised in many spaces, including academia [11]. This approach could be argued to align with standpoint theory, which suggests that certain things are understood most effectively from the standpoints of those who are less privileged, powerful, or entitled [12]. The theory is grounded in the understanding that many claims put forward as knowledge are socially situated, and people who are socially subordinated have a better chance of accessing a viewpoint that serves their interests.

Standpoint theory has received some criticism for potentially reinforcing the binary divisions and power structures it claims to challenge, as well as for its potential for essentialism. Identity is now also seen as much more fluid than standpoint theory originally accounted for. In response, scholars have reconceptualised standpoint theory as "standpoint thinking," emphasising flexibility and diverse lived experiences [13]. Additionally, more action-oriented approaches advocating for collective activism have gained traction. Intersectionality emerged as another theoretical framework, offering a more sophisticated understanding of overlapping identities and systems of oppression [13, 14]. Disadvantaged identities experienced simultaneously result in significant degrees of disadvantage [15]. Indigenous Standpoint Theory has also developed, centring Indigenous ways of knowing within colonial contexts [16, 17].

When Researchers Write from More Dominant Positionalities

In some music therapy studies, researchers from more dominant positions strive to present fair and just views of phenomena while acknowledging their privileged stance [18, 19]. This approach requires researchers to dismantle potentially hegemonic positions as much as possible and recognise how certain ways of knowing suppress others [20]. These researchers try to be attuned to how their language relates to social justice concerns [21], and consider how privilege, power, and social status influence their research decisions [22]. These studies often pose questions that highlight injustices, such as Lars Tuastad and colleagues' [23] exploration of stigmatisation. Ideally, such research is conducted collaboratively with individuals who have directly experienced the studied phenomena.

As an example of how authors writing from more dominant positions articulate their positioning, Michael Viega [24, p. 69] described himself as "a white, cis-male, nondisabled, neurotypical person," acknowledging his societal privileges and positioning himself as an "aspiring ally and accomplice." Kailey Campbell [25, p., e5] reflected on her position as "a white clinician, in a profession dominated by white clinicians, writing about Hip Hop."

Researchers engaging in (what I've termed) Restorative Reflexivity while occupying more dominant positions typically provide clear justification for their epistemological approach. Katrina McFerran et al. [26] opted for a post-ableist framework that prioritises contextually generated embodied knowledge, while Viega [24] employed an ecological approach that recognises the sociocultural, biopolitical, community, and environmental contexts influencing definitions of health, evidence, and therapeutic relationships. Maren Metell and Brynjulf Stige [27] used critical theory-informed approaches that intersect with community music therapy, critical special education, and disability studies.

I would argue that if we're conducting research as part of a dominant group while seeking to be allies, we need to be alert to the viewpoint that we're somehow immune to the ways that "other people" may respond to injustice. Alison Bailey [28, p. 62] explored what she called "privilege-evasive epistemic pushback," which is a form of wilful ignorance prevalent among members of dominant groups when confronted with the lived experiences and structural injustices faced daily by marginalised groups. This phenomenon is broadly an expression of resistance to understanding that typically arises in discussions involving topics that challenge our own epistemic comfort zones. As Michael Viega noted in our interview,

> When you're writing an article for publication—even when you refer to yourself as an aspiring ally—I'm trying to be and I might not have it all figured out yet. I'm always going to be changing...my ideas of language and where I'm positioned. So a lot of my writing is messy.

Viega conceptualises reflexivity as "a human necessity." He explained that this process can be enhanced through various practices, including therapy, creative activities, supervision, journalling and, increasing cultural awareness.

Here are some questions for reflection if you wish to examine your own openness and willingness to be challenged:

- What specific topics or perspectives make me uncomfortable, defensive, or dismissive when raised by participants from marginalised groups?
- In what ways might my research methodologies or analytical frameworks subtly reinforce dominant perspectives while appearing neutral or objective?
- How do I respond emotionally and intellectually when my assumptions or approaches are challenged by those with different lived experiences?
- What strategies can I develop to recognise my own resistance when it emerges during research encounters?
- How can I distinguish between legitimate methodological concerns and defence mechanisms that protect my privileged perspectives?
- In what ways might my social position influence how participants from marginalised groups share (or withhold) their experiences with me?
- How can I ensure that my efforts towards social justice research go beyond intellectual acknowledgement to substantive action and change in my research practice?

Anti-Oppressive Research and Research as Activism

Research can cause harm. Studies conducted in the social sciences and humanities (for example) have reinforced one-dimensional portrayals of marginalised communities as "depleted, ruined, and hopeless" [29, p. 409]. Studies have perpetuated inaccurate stereotypes and adopted pathologising lenses [30]. There are instances where the word "transformation" has been used in deceptive ways: focussing on promises of newness and novelty, while failing to take account of the problematic ground of the present [31]. For research to be transformational, it's been argued that the topic *and* the process of research need to align with this intention [32, 33].

Anti-oppressive research (AOR) emerged as a critical approach to addressing the systemic subordination of specific social groups and promoting social change. It developed from various activist traditions, including feminist research, disability-led participatory research, decolonising methodologies, and user-led mental health research [34]. Some aspects of music therapy practice have been highlighted as having the potential to promote and embody activism [35–38], but others have been critiqued for focusing on individual "problems" instead of acknowledging and addressing systemic oppression [39, 40]. Susan Hadley [41] claimed that music therapy is entrenched in pervasive oppressive forces, calling for vigilance in exposing these. Alejandra Lindan [39] interviewed Sue Baines, Cynthia Bruce, and Carolyn Kenny to identify practices that can help music therapists resist oppression. They highlighted the importance of legitimising lived experience as knowledge, reframing inspiration and tragedy narratives, and encouraging collective engagement. We need to trouble our foundations, attend to systemic conditions rather than "fixing" individuals, and create more spaces to have challenging conversations about social justice.

Anti-oppressive research is an epistomology approach rather than a specific methodology [32]. Knowledge creation is inherently political and AOR seeks to confront oppression at all stages of inquiry, supporting people's actions to achieve freedom from oppression [2, 42]. Sue Baines and Jane Edwards [43] argued that anti-oppressive practices should be integrated throughout all the research stages. A core principle of AOR is its focus on shifting power dynamics within the research process. In my interview with Natasha Thomas, she spoke of "treating power dynamics with tremendous care." While the term "anti-oppressive research" defines itself in relation to what it's opposed to, we can also frame this in a positive sense as "liberatory" or "transformative" research.

Some authors refer to the type of reflexivity that's required in this research as "critical reflexivity" [44]. In music therapy studies, critical reflexivity is an approach that entails critical reflection [27], functions in the service of ethical practice and activism [18], involves managing power relations [45], and includes considering privilege [43]. Researchers may find themselves questioning long-held assumptions and practices, which can be uncomfortable but often lead to more nuanced and ethically sound research [46].

Epistemic Injustice

Epistemic injustice, a concept explored by Gayatri Spivak [47] and further developed by Miranda Fricker, refers to the systematic silencing of marginalised groups and undermining individuals in their capacity as knowers. Fricker [48] identified two forms: testimonial injustice and hermeneutical injustice. Recognising people as knowers enables their participation in conversations and social meaning-making. Testimonial injustice happens when we give less credibility to what a person says based on our prejudices about them (e.g., their skin colour, gender, social background, sexual orientation, accent, style of expression, and so on). Testimonial injustice is being inflicted here because the communicator's status as a knower is being undermined [49]. Being and being seen as a knower is a fundamental aspect of personhood. To be wronged as a knower is to be wronged in terms of one's human value [48, 50].

Kristie Dotson [49] further distinguished between two types of testimonial oppression: testimonial quieting, where audiences fail to recognise speakers as knowers, and testimonial smothering, where speakers self-censor, perceiving their audience as unwilling or unable to receive their testimony appropriately. The impact of testimonial injustice can be profound, potentially diminishing recipients' confidence in their intellectual capabilities and, in some cases, leading them to embody the prejudicial stereotypes working against them.

The second type of epistemic injustice, hermeneutical injustice, can follow from testimonial injustice. When certain people's testimonies are not heard or taken seriously, their knowledge is not added to the pool of hermeneutic resources—the collective stock of meanings, concepts, and understandings available for making experiences intelligible. This can lead to "hermeneutical marginalisation", where less powerful groups have fewer resources to draw on to make sense of their own experiences [48]. Through control over hermeneutical resources, meanings that express the perspective of the powerful are normatively enforced. Epistemic appropriation also occurs, where marginalised epistemic resources gain popularity in other spaces without their origins being acknowledged [51].

Jose Medina [52] described epistemic injustices as social pathologies of recognition. Two main deficiencies can occur (although they're often intertwined). When there's a quantitative recognition deficit, a person may not be seen or heard at all, or they may be insufficiently acknowledged with few opportunities to communicate and be recognised. What is needed here is more recognition. Misrecognition relates to *how* one is recognised, which may be inappropriate. What is necessary here is a shift in the mode of recognition. Importantly, the role of epistemic agency shouldn't be overlooked. People find ways to use epistemic resources to participate in knowledge production and to revise those resources. Also, forms of knowledge belonging to a minoritised group are still there, even if those who are more powerful are wilfully refusing to recognise them [49].

In research contexts, one way of trying to combat epistemic injustice is by involving people with lived experience to ensure that the views of those at the centre of an issue are heard and can inform decision-making. This isn't without its critique, though. The process of selecting "appropriate" participants may exclude those deemed "too unwell," "too unstable," or "unskilled," potentially forming an elite subset of a marginalised group. There's also a risk of epistemic exploitation, where marginalised people are expected to educate dominant groups about their oppression [53]. It's also problematic when research requires participants to revisit their experiences of harmful systems when meaningful change seems unlikely.

Including people with lived experience in one's study doesn't guarantee epistemic justice or the transformative potential of the research. We need to carefully consider whether the knowledge generated through our research actually serves those with the investigated lived experience meaningfully. When social change is not central to research aims, incorporating lived experience might actually perpetuate oppression. (I may benefit from publishing a study as a researcher, whilst the participants do not, yet again positioning us in an exploitative relationship.) Understanding who benefits from knowledge production becomes as crucial as the knowledge itself. Avraham Kluger and Moran Mizrahi [54, p. 4] defined listening as "the degree to which a person devotes themselves to co-explore the Other with and for the other." In research with human participants/co-researchers we're seeking to listen. However, if our goal is to listen in order to gather data that benefits our professional development rather than in a way that is *for* the person and communities we're engaging with, are we really listening?

Fostering Epistemic Justice

If we want to advance epistemic justice, we need epistemic courage, which is fuelled by inquisitiveness, open-mindedness, and intellectual humility [55]. These qualities motivate us to pay attention, engage seriously with others' perspectives, continue to seek a wide range of stories, and question our assumptions. If we see ourselves as anti-oppressive researchers (having "arrived" at this better way of doing research), we need to ensure that we aren't closing ourselves off from constant constructive critique [56]. Achieving epistemic justice requires ongoing effort, dedication, and a deep interest in truth [55]. Anti-oppressive research is certainly not just an intellectual exercise. It involves more than studying the topic of oppression; it's about improving the lives of participants and also creating knowledge that can be used by others to work against oppression in society.

"Giving" Participants a Voice

A researcher's openness and good intentions don't guarantee that the voices of participants have been represented faithfully. Ethics concerns can arise when researchers from dominant groups attempt to represent marginalised participants. Also, the notion of "giving" others a voice is also problematic as it affirms the researcher's power to bestow opportunities to speak (on people who already have the right to speak). Even if researchers elect to include extensive verbatim quotations [57, 58], they're still organising and presenting their manuscript by making choices about whose voices should be heard, how much of a participant's comments should be included, and which statements to exclude. They're also framing their participants' expressions in particular ways.

Gail Crimmins [59, p. 4] asked: Is it appropriate for an academic researcher in a majority group with relatively more power to use this power "to elicit and research an Other's story; and if it is appropriate—how do we do this in such a way that doesn't advance the dominance of the non-Other and the silencing of Others?" The researcher may be seen to function as bestowing credibility and legitimacy on the marginalised person/s or phenomenon—and developing their academic career by doing so [60, 61]. More recent attempts to democratise research practice, such as through co-produced activist research, involve giving participants a voice, a vote, and a veto [34].

Michael Zanders et al. [21] explained how it's challenging to write about people's experiences in music therapy, while still honouring their experiences as co-participants and co-creators of the process. In a paper on music therapists' and traditional healers' (THs) perceptions of each other's work, my fellow author and I cautiously acknowledged that our power and privilege to present our findings in an academic context could potentially harm the traditional healers who participated because their knowledge could be misrepresented or appropriated, despite the utmost care we exercised to attempt to prevent this [62].

In our interview, Viggo Krüger highlighted a tension in research:

> We can write up our small-scale qualitative research studies and they are published and people read them. And that's good. But the question then is, do we need to scale up the research and move into more RCTs and bigger quantitative research studies to make an impact? And that move from our small-scale studies where we interview and we actually give the voices of the young children a space to the big RCTs will then be lost...The struggle of still believing that the voices of the children have a very big impact and that conflict with implementing big research projects where money and politics and researchers' own careers and stuff come into place. There you have the struggle right there.

Epistemic Justice and Illness Research

Mental and physical illness renders individuals particularly susceptible to epistemic injustice [63]. People are vulnerable to testimonial injustice when they're viewed as being cognitively unreliable or emotionally unstable. Ill persons are vulnerable to hermeneutical injustice because aspects of the illness experience may be difficult to understand and communicate due to gaps in collective hermeneutical resources. The subjective experiences of mental health service users frequently receive insufficient attention in music therapy research. Solli and Rolvsjord [64] discussed how critical voices have claimed that this lack of first-person accounts has led to silencing a whole group of people who are then subject to others' perspectives. Tríona McCaffrey [65] and McCaffrey et al. [66] also emphasised the importance of service users' voices in recovery contexts.

An ill person experiences testimonial and hermeneutic *justice* when their testimonies are recognised, sought out, taken seriously, seen as relevant, and included within epistemic considerations. As Havi Carel and Ian Kidd [63, p. 532] explained, an epistemically just clinician may be conveying something like this (but with more accessible terminology), "'The fact that I don't understand you isn't your fault, but mine; even your best efforts to make yourself understood are failing, not because of their inarticulacy, but because I am untrained in the appreciation of the sort of articulacy you are using, and this hermeneutical context does not provide me with those resources'." The quest for knowledge can be a shared enterprise as patients and healthcare practitioners bring different types of knowledge to their relationship.

Carel and Kidd [63] explained that phenomenology can offer valuable tools for addressing epistemic injustice because it seeks to identify structures that underpin people's experiences and takes individual experiences seriously. However, Marianne Klinke and Anthony Fernandez [67] noted that phenomenological interviewing alone may be insufficient in research with people who struggle to describe their experiences, making a case for including observation in research. This needs to be engaged in carefully, though, because we need to resist prematurely imposing meaning on ambiguous experiences (as it's the researcher who has the power here to word the experiences). In music therapy research, where observation of musicking is common, we need to carefully navigate power dynamics in interpretation [68, 69].

Epistemic Justice and Disability

Maren Metell [70] highlighted how research has violated disabled people's experiences, been irrelevant to their needs, and failed to improve their quality of life and material circumstances. Since the 1970s, disability activists have argued that research does not serve them; it contributes to their oppression.

Epistemic injustice in relation to intellectual disabilities presents unique challenges, particularly where cognitive impairments restrict symbolic communication [71]. The diverse nature of intellectual disabilities further complicates this issue. People with intellectual disability diagnoses encompass a broad spectrum of capabilities and experiences. Mike Oliver [72] introduced "emancipatory disability research" to empower disabled individuals through research. He advocated for researchers to relinquish control to participants. This aligns with the title of James Charlton's [73] book "Nothing about us without us". Emma Stone and Mark Priestley [74] outlined key principles for emancipatory disability research, including adopting the social model of disability, rejecting claims of objectivity, and ensuring accountability to disabled communities.

In research by Katrina McFerran et al. [26] on social inclusion for people with disabilities through online music gatherings, they wrote about the importance of seeing and honouring diverse experiences in their research group. Those with lived experience in the disability community were in the majority in their study.

Epistemic Justice and Neurodiversity

Autism advocate Jim Sinclair [75] highlighted how autistic individuals might communicate in ways others fail to recognise, resulting in unjust credibility deficits. Ming Yuan Low et al. [76] critiqued the lack of representation of autistic voices in autism research, including in music therapy. Their IPA study purposefully offered a voice for autistic participants. It's crucial to respect and include the perspectives of autistic individuals to accurately portray their experiences and prevent the spread of misinformation and discrimination about autism. While some studies have focused on the viewpoints of autistic participants and autistic music therapists have shared their first-hand experiences, there's still a challenge in the broader field of music therapy to reconcile the medical model and the neurodiversity affirmative model in understanding music therapy and autism.

Epistemic Justice in Research with Children

Children frequently experience testimonial injustice through the attribution of diminished epistemic credibility [77]. While children (especially those who are very young) lack competency and knowledge about a range of things, they are also likely to have access to information that adults don't. It's essential to bear in mind that children's ability to testify develops relationally. Supportive adults create conditions for children's voices to be heard and for them to develop an identity as a reliable testifier, as well as self-confidence, self-esteem, and self-regard. The notion that scholarly research about children's lives should occur *by* and *with* children is supported by Article 12 of the United Nations Convention on the Rights of the Child (UNCRC) [78].

Research with children exists along a spectrum of involvement, from tokenism (making only a symbolic effort to include children's voices), to consultation (asking for children's views), collaboration (including active, ongoing partnership), and child-led/controlled research (which is driven by children) [79]. An increasing number of contemporary researchers are engaging in co-design, youth participatory action research [80], and working with children-as-researchers [81].

In music therapy, Guro Klyve and Randi Rolvsjord [82] emphasised the importance of epistemic justice in research with children. They advocated for paying closer attention to verbal, nonverbal, and multimodal communication. Viggo Krüger and Brynjulf Stige [83] stressed the necessity of respecting children's competencies. Rebecca Fairchild et al. [84] described how they included children's voices in their study on homelessness and family violence. The children's perspectives were central to their project. They highlighted adult researchers' responsibility to protect children while ensuring their voices are heard, developing creative methods like songwriting for research participation. Through collaborative songwriting, Fairchild and Malakai Mraz [22], showed how children can co-author academic work. In their doctoral research, Hanna Hakomäki's [85] also invited a former child music therapy client to be a co-researcher, valuing the child as a capable knowledge producer.

Ellie Scrine and Katrina McFerran [86] wrote that in participatory research with youth, adults need to be committed to scrupulous reflexivity. Young people may experience AOP in complicated ways (e.g., a non-conventional, non-hierarchical approach to group facilitation may be uncomfortable—impeding their capacity to participate). Critics of child-led research question children's capacity for rigorous research, cautioning against essentialising or homogenising children's perspectives. There are questions about which children get to participate and whether child researchers are expected to represent all children [87]. The evidence for long-term empowerment effects is still limited, and only a small number of children typically benefit. Most child-led research still occurs within adult-dominated frameworks. Advocates of this approach respond by questioning whether research that isn't participatory can be considered ethical [79]. With appropriate support and training, children can carry out high-quality research if we use different evaluation criteria [87].

Hakomäki [85] drew on a range of authors to generate a list of essential ethical questions that need to be considered when involving children in research. These include exploring who benefits, how choices regarding participation are made, risk, whether refusal to participate is genuinely experienced as an option, how confidentiality and anonymity are managed, whether research methods are fully understood by all concerned, how voices are represented in the findings, how feedback is shared, and what the impact of the research is.

Epistemic Justice and Music Therapy Researchers
In their editorial entitled, "Who you mean 'we?'," Natasha Thomas and Marisol Norris [88, p. 5] critiqued the marginalisation of voices within music therapy, positioning themselves as "outsiders within," as they navigate "the complexity of sociopolitical systems of control." Preferred "outsiders" are elevated for their "exceptionality," but their epistemological authority is denied, and the knowledge of more marginalised individuals remains unrecognised. Sangeeta Swamy and Adenike Webb [9] also wrote an editorial about learning from the lived experiences of minoritised music therapists. They highlighted how academic imperialism promotes exclusion and lack of accessibility, resource disparities and privileging written over oral traditions, all of which can disproportionately affect minoritised scholars. They recognised how sharing about one's experiences as a minoritised member of the profession can vulnerably open one to scrutiny, which can perpetuate harm. Thomas and Blanc [10] called for decolonising the arts therapies by reclaiming and integrating marginalised healing practices, as well as drawing on critical race theory and healing justice perspectives.

Planning and Conducting Studies Using Restorative Reflexively

In the studies I analysed that used what I'm calling Restorative Reflexivity, the authors employed a range of methodological strategies when designing and conducting their studies. To varying degrees, their aims and research questions reflected their reflexive concerns (and their examination of how and why they asked these questions), as well as the way they drew on literature to contextualise their studies, their methodological choices, relationships with participants, analysis and presentation of findings.

The Power to Ask Questions and Set Aims

Naming the issue that will be investigated is an exercise of power. Research questions open certain doors and close others; they turn our ears to some people's voices and away from others. They determine what gets included and excluded. Researchers exercising Restorative Reflexivity deeply and carefully reflect on who initiates and shapes the questions, what is being asked, what assumptions underpin the questions, why a certain question is being asked, what related questions are not being asked, whose interests are prioritised, and the implications of asking these questions. They also critically explore their relationship(s) with the topic they're studying. Developing research questions with an anti-oppressive commitment takes the form of continuous cycles of reflecting, collaborating, and questioning [32]. It's still very rare for music therapy studies to be guided by research questions that have been developed collaboratively with participants instead of decided by the researchers [89].

In terms of research aims, firstly, some music therapy researchers have sought to amplify participants' perspectives. We discussed a moment ago how some researchers aim, for example, to highlight children's voices [82, 84]. Efrat Roginsky and Cochavit Elefant [90] looked at how parents' experiences enrich knowledge about communication with children with cerebral palsies and multiple disabilities, how parents appropriate music with their children and how they describe the meanings of music in the lives of their children and families. McCaffrey [65] created room for adults' experiences in mental health care to be heard.

Secondly, resource-oriented approaches have been used to frame music therapy research objectives. For example, Gro Trondalen [91] aimed to explore the Bonny Method of Guided Imagery and Music as a health resource for musicians and adolescents' experiences in community-based music therapy assessments. Aitchison and McFerran's [92] goal was to study how adolescents experience resource-oriented music therapy assessment (ROMTA) in a community-based mental health day programme.

Thirdly, studies seek to critique existing perspectives, such as Thomas and Blanc's [10] process of deconstructing the histories they'd been taught in their arts therapies training and practice. Karin Mössler et al. [93] elected to use a relational lens, critiquing individualistic, pathologising viewpoints in research with autistic participants to explore which circumstances can support or disrupt attunement dynamics and what resources and social skills an autistic child brings into therapy.

Conceptual Framing and Reviewing Literature

Anti-oppressive researchers critically examine existing knowledge to understand its construction, authorship, intended benefits, and relationship with their values. They may also draw on knowledge beyond academic publications [32]. Metell and Stige [27] highlighted how critical theory advocates for reflective and discerning engagement with literature and theory, urging researchers to consider the impact of the knowledge they draw on when formulating their studies.

Framing Concepts, Terms, Phenomena, and Approaches

Researchers using Restorative Reflexivity critically reflect on the concepts that function as the building blocks of their study. Even when music therapists seek to amplify diverse voices, their interpretations may be informed by professional and social discourses imbued with hegemonic elements that subjugate alternative perspectives [94]. McCaffrey & Edwards [95] highlighted how all ideas and knowledge models can be reinterpreted, although social norms and dominant discourses often resist these changes. Engaging with research participants about conceptual frameworks may reveal contradictions and stimulate discussions about differing interpretations [32].

Researchers have also critically examined how variations in human experiences and functioning are framed and what such framing does. Rickson [96], for example,

argued that communities define "normality" based on dominant characteristics, marginalising those who differ. Anna Helle-Valle et al. [18] critiqued the dominant medical framework for attention deficit hyperactivity disorder (ADHD), instead advocating for seeing children's restlessness as part of normal development rather than as a neurological deficit. They also challenge the framing of dysfunction as an individual problem. Roginsky and Elefant [90] critiqued the term "cerebral palsy," advocating rather for the use of "cerebral palsies" to encourage individualised approaches to diverse experiences and ways of being. In Hans Solli's [97, p. 205] qualitative case study of a young rapper's experiences with music therapy, he explained their preference for more socially just approaches to understanding behaviours of persons experiencing psychosis: "When people with first-hand experiences of mental health problems are asked, they offer alternative ways of understanding."

Music and musicking are also carefully considered. For example, Helle-Valle et al. [18] argued for the value of understanding musicking as an activity that makes possible participation in the widest sense and music therapy as supporting participation in a resource-oriented way that embraces ecological perspectives. McSorley [98] highlighted the potential harm of musical choices and lyrics in music therapy, such as reinforcing gendered stereotypes and marginalising diverse identities. Calling for greater attention to reflexivity in trauma research, McFerran et al. [99] emphasised the value in approaches that don't treat music as an objective variable, but rather as a context-bound resource that affords possibilities and can enact social critique. Also, Viega et al. [100] explored how music technologies can resist dominant narratives in therapeutic contexts.

Researchers reflect critically on understandings of the therapeutic processes. For example, Scrine [40] argued that music therapists create psychological safety not only by influencing the autonomic nervous system, but by addressing power dynamics that may perpetuate harm within therapeutic spaces. Mössler et al. [93] critiqued the traditional view of attunement as a therapist-driven phenomenon, proposing instead that attunement is a co-constituted process shaped by context. In their paper on collaborative songwriting, Fairchild and McFerran [101] promoted resource-oriented and community music therapy approaches, celebrating participants' strengths and active roles in their own lives. A number of researchers emphasised a recovery approach within mental health care. For example, Solli and Rolvsjord [64] highlighted how mental health recovery is deeply personal and distinct from clinical recovery, which often focuses on symptom remission.

Engaging with Literature

In addition to critically examining conceptual building blocks, researchers employing Restorative Reflexivity think carefully about the published studies they draw on to contextualise their research, what needs to be critiqued within this body of literature, and how they are using (and/or resisting) this knowledge.

Researchers emphasise the importance of acknowledging the situatedness and identities of authors who they reference. For example, Helle-Valle et al. [18] chose to present previous case studies in their literature review based on geographical region in order to highlight contextual situatedness. McSorley [98] discussed the importance of addressing sexism and cisgenderism in music therapy spaces, cautioning that studies often centre dominant (i.e., white, cis, nondisabled) experiences of womanhood. In her review of the literature within a study on music therapists' beliefs, education, and uses of Hip Hop in clinical practice, Campbell [25] explained how most articles about Hip Hop in music therapy focus on the (often white) therapist's reflections on their work, rather than centring the experiences of the service users whose culture is being explored.

In Comte's [19] critical interpretive synthesis of literature concerning music therapy with refugees, she found that authors often emphasised a cultural divide between themselves as members of a Western cultural group and the individuals they worked with who are refugees, presenting them as a homogeneous group primarily defined by trauma. This generalisation led to prioritising their shared refugee status over their distinct cultural identities. Scrine [40] explained how they chose to centre critiques of the dominant trauma paradigm, led in particular by decolonial and critical race scholars and clinicians, particularly research conducted by First Nation scholars, Black scholars, and scholars of colour, on issues impacting their own communities.

Regarding music therapy approaches, McFerran et al. [26] observed that critical perspectives in literature are increasingly questioning the persistence of outdated expert models. However, in their paper on the impact of international student placements on music therapy practice and professional identity, Bolger and Murphy [102] noted that many related papers still focus on music therapists' experiences and do not include the experiences of local participants.

Researchers also critique the methodology of the studies they review. Helle-Vale et al. [18] noted that mainstream ADHD research often relies on quantitative approaches that overlook the role of social constructs. A narrow focus on outcomes also risks ignoring the rich insights of individuals [65].

Approaches and Designs

Inclusive research can take many forms, such as action, participatory research, emancipatory, user-led research, community research, and Indigenous research. Instead of research *on* people, inclusive research is research *with*, *by* or sometimes *for* people [103]. You may be conducting a study in order to impact policy decisions, in which case a design that incorporates statistical analysis and generates valid and reliable conclusions to speak your audience's language may be what is required, while still being cognisant that the procedures involved are in alignment with anti-oppressive research values, ethics, and practices. When we conduct participatory studies, we may be adopting creative approaches as we co-design research questions with participants, fostering more equitable relationships and shared ownership of the process. The plan for this kind of study may not fit into a conventional mould. We also need to think about the quality criteria that should be used to evaluate these studies, such as who gets to decide what these criteria are?

Action Research

Reason and Bradbury [104] described action research as a participatory and democratic process that develops practical knowledge for addressing meaningful human concerns. It blends action and reflection, theory and practice. The aim is to understand the change that may be needed through the eyes of those involved—who are seen as the experts on their own lives and contexts—and to collaborate in a way that can bring about greater individual and community well-being [105]. Daphne Rickson [106] characterised action research as a critical method that seeks to improve outcomes and self-understanding. It prompts practitioners to critique their work while exploring how history, culture, and discourse shape individuals and contexts. Rickson also highlighted the importance of shared ownership of research. Schwantes and Rivera [107] explained how action research can create opportunities for reflexivity and social critique. In their action research, Stuart-Röhm et al. [108] co-developed a caregiver singing model for dementia care, ensuring relevance to the context and carefully addressing intersecting power relations.

Participatory Action Research

Participatory action research (PAR) can be a valuable way of addressing epistemic injustice [109]. This approach is particularly designed to listen to and value marginalised people's voices [1, 14]. Participants are typically seen as co-researchers. Elephant [110] characterised PAR as a communicative methodology where collective reflection plays a critical role in identifying problems and solutions. Practical actions are explored and evaluated as springboards for ongoing, collective reflection. Like action research, PAR has a cyclical shape, involving rounds of assessment, planning, action, evaluation, and reflection, which enables participants to engage deeply in the research process, and learn from their experiences. In many ways, this structure also mirrors the therapeutic process.

Kerry Devlin et al. [111] discussed the ethical implications of co-authoring research with music therapy stakeholders. While this approach can pose ethics challenges (such as thinking through the best ways to manage consent, boundaries, safety and decision-making), the benefits can be substantial as we learn more about the role of music therapy in people's lives while embodying values of justice, equity, and power sharing. Randi Rolvsjord [112] described collaboration in music therapy as a dialogic process based on mutuality, equality, and active participation. Collaboration also includes the shared responsibility for and negotiation of the purpose and direction of the therapy process. This can entail highly complex negotiation processes. Even when these are difficult, engaging in these negotiations is where the value of collaboration in music therapy can be found [113]. This intentional and committed approach to collaboration helps us avoid tokenism and including only those voices that are "easy" to include. There are many forms and layers of possible collaborations in research (a very helpful guide for this can be found in the book *Collaborative qualitative research* by Mulvihill and Swaminathan [114]).

In her study on the relevance of disability perspectives in music therapy practice with children and young people who have intellectual disability, Rickson [96] explained how PAR is a form of experimentation that relies on reflexivity and active risk-taking. Participants took charge of the project by engaging in beat making, music production, and video editing, collaboratively analysing results with the primary researcher and discussing project outcomes. This approach aligned with the community music therapy principles outlined in the "PREPARE" framework by Stige and Aarø [115]. Scrine and McFerran [86] described a project where music therapy was used as an anti-oppressive practice for young people in high school to explore gender and power in nuanced ways. The lead author spent eight months in the school running the music therapy programme, observing, learning, and building on the participants' perspectives.

We can't assume that using participatory action research automatically means that our study has adequately addressed power relations and potential oppressive practices. There are many complex issues. The form that participation may take may still be guided by the researcher's ideas of what participation is. A PhD student conducting PAR then obtains a degree, while the other community member co-researchers do not. In light of the earlier discussion on recognition: in what ways are co-researchers actually being recognised as such in practice? In Indigenous research contexts, while PAR has been proposed as a solution to working more ethically with

Indigenous people, it doesn't fully prevent the risk that Indigenous ways of knowing may be marginalised by the scientific community and Indigenous methods may still therefore be better routes to take in this regard [116].

As Pott and Brown [29] explained, researchers navigate constraints such as time, resources, and institutional frameworks like ethics review boards that may be rooted in positivist understandings and expectations. Often one may be required to propose questions upfront when writing a research proposal to obtain approval from an ethics review board—as opposed to engaging in a process where the questions are genuinely developed by community members, for example. It can be difficult to conduct fully inclusive research within the confines of a postgraduate degree as there may not be enough time to allow the process to reach an ending that participants see as appropriate for their process rather than the researcher's requirements. As a result, you may elect to design a study that is informed by participatory practices while still holding some boundaries (e.g., a set timeline) to manage expectations and ensure safety, care, and ethical closure. Some of the contexts in which we work also have more rigid organisational structures, firm gatekeeping and problematic power dynamics that limit a fully participatory process. This can set up ethical tensions between the researcher's values and inclusive intentions, and the context's restrictions. For example, a school principal may decide that the staff no longer have time to continue participating in the study you've been facilitating, even though the teachers personally wish to go on, and the children who have been taking part are disappointed. You know that their therapeutic process is incomplete, but the power has been taken out of your hands to continue. Being alert to these potential dilemmas through gaining a thorough understanding of the context as possible is important from the start of designing a study so that we can co-design proactively.

Arts-Based Research

It's imperative to maximise our ways of seeing [117] if we want to increase possibilities for action. The arts lend themselves to collaboration and participants having more control over the research process. Arts-based methods welcome imagination, creating diverse counter-narratives, and challenging binary thinking (self/other; empowered/disempowered; researcher/subject), which can be inherent in more conventional research practices. Arts-based research can handle ambivalence, mystery, and disequilibrium [118, 119].

In their paper that focused on collaborative songwriting with children, Fairchild and McFerran [101, p. 93], highlighted how arts-based methods allowed "children, even those who are less talkative, developmentally impaired or otherwise marginalised, the opportunity to fully participate and contribute through creative modes of communication without the need to rely on verbal or written accounts." Arts-based methods with youth can help make their experiences visible and nurture change and transformation [120]. Some authors have proposed that the arts can also support an Indigenous research agenda by encouraging participant engagement, relationship building, community action, Indigenous knowledge creation, and capacity building [121].

Duoethnography and Collaborative Autoethnography

In Chap. 5, where we explored Authorial Reflexivity, we examined how researchers have drawn on collaborative approaches to autoethnography as they explored their own stories and reflected on their experiences together. These studies sometimes also use Restorative Reflexivity. For example, in Natasha Thomas and Valerie Blanc's [10] duoethnography, combined with arts-based methods, they tackled three critical questions. What emerges when a dance/movement therapist (Valerie) and a music therapist (Natasha) creatively collaborate to deconstruct their professional histories?; How does this collaborative deconstruction enhance their critical thinking about the histories of their fields and their roles?; And how can this process foster culturally affirming practices in creative arts therapies education, particularly concerning technology and interdisciplinary collaboration? Thomas and Blanc [10, p. 1] described how they used "a critical lens rooted in healing justice and influenced by decolonial theory" to "name and begin to deconstruct the complicated histories of both clinical fields, attempting to embody and amplify the healing practices of movement and music that came long before the 'founders' of dance/movement or music therapy as clinical fields." In Viega and colleagues' [100] performative collaborative autoethnography of music therapists' improvising with digital music technologies, they explained their approach as transformative because it could challenge assumptions about the nature of knowledge creation in research, including how data is generated, analysed, and shared.

Constructivist Grounded Theory
In Baines and Edwards' [122] study on music therapy as an anti-oppressive practice in long-term and psychiatric residential care, they described constructivist grounded theory (CGT) [123, 124] as a flexible methodology shaped by anti-oppressive practices. This offers opportunities for participants with cognitive and communicative disorders to contribute to research because it acknowledges diverse perspectives. Researchers using CGT adopt a reflexive stance regarding their backgrounds, values, actions, relationships with participants, and representations of them, and they carefully situate their research within historical and social contexts. The researcher resists imposing a pre-existing theoretical frame from the outset. Data collection and analysis are conducted simultaneously, which helps generate theories that are grounded in participants' experiences [125].

Participants/Co-Researchers

Describing People
When planning and conducting a study with human participants, or that explores literature referring to humans, the language we use to describe people actively plays a role in constructing them (bearing in mind that people also resist other's descriptions of them and actively construct themselves too). Our language also constructs our relationships with others, as well as serves a role in constructing ourselves (how I describe someone else tells you a lot about how I see myself). If we invite participants to describe themselves, what questions do we ask and how do those invite particular framing? For example, as trauma-informed perspectives have encouraged questions like "What happened to you?" as opposed to "What's wrong with you?", this is now shifting further to prioritise asking "What matters to you?" [5, 126]

When we're describing participants in our papers, how might we name the person offering music therapy and the person making use of those services? [127, 128] Randi Rolvsjord [129] highlighted how "clients" and "therapists" are described as dichotomous within mental health care. The binary frames clients in relation to pathology, weakness, and passivity, while the therapist is framed in terms of expertise, strength, and action. Grace Thompson [130] underscored researchers' responsibility in their language choices, as terms such as "suffering from a certain condition" tend to reduce participants rather than highlight the complexities of their subjective experiences. Some authors focus on describing participants' symptoms or use terms such as "high/low functioning," rather than explaining participants' multifaceted characteristics, features, or strengths. Overemphasising individual features can also come at the expense of recognising the impact of systemic and structural issues. Thompson encouraged authors rather to engage reflexively with language, challenging ableism and being more transparent about their language choices.

Here are some examples of how music therapy researchers thought carefully about how to describe participants and the implications of these decisions. Zanders et al. [21] critiqued the use of the term "at-risk," highlighting its potential to be stigmatising. Fairchild and Mraz [22] also challenged the portrayal of children solely through the lens of risk, arguing that such challenges represent only a part of their stories. In the study by McFerran et al. [26] exploring online music gatherings for people with disabilities, the authors took a non-pathologising approach. Instead of regarding people with disabilities as a vulnerable group, they used a strengths-based lens. Their use of the term "disabled" referred to dynamic interactions between a person with a health condition(s) and personal and environmental factors. Also, rather than concentrating on participants' type or level of disability, they focussed on how music functioned for people at different stages in life.

Kate Aitchison and Katrina McFerran [92] didn't use diagnostic labels or descriptions of struggle to describe participants attending a community-based mental health day programme. They referred to them rather in relation to their interests and activities. Hans Solli and Randi Rolvsjord [64] emphasised the importance of recognising individuals experiencing psychosis as active agents in their therapeutic journeys. As Elly Scrine [40] wrote, one of most notable distinctions that differentiated music therapy and other creative arts therapies from verbal therapies is that individuals are seen as "active participants," rather than "subjects" or "objects."

Fairchild et al. [84] chose the terminology, "children experiencing homelessness" in their study. There have been increasing conversations about the language that should be used in this space. Where "homeless" was commonly previously used as an adjective (often evoking stigma), there's been a shift towards terms like "unhoused" or "houseless" [131]. An individual may not live in a house but may view the place they are currently staying (a tent, vehicle, a shelter) to be their home, at least for now. However, it's still crucial to consult stakeholders about their preferred terminology, because language preferences vary significantly and we should be guided ethically by how participants want to describe themselves [132].

Recruiting Participants/Co-Researchers

Anti-oppressive researchers tend to use the goals of community building, empowerment, and understanding over representativeness or validity to inform how they encounter and work alongside participants. Sampling is rarely random. Ideally, the process involves a community of participants or insider researchers rather than entailing an outsider researcher extending invitations [32].

Relationships with Participants/Co-Researchers

Before seeking to understand someone else's experiences, it's important that we've critically reflected on our own personal history, embodied experiences, and positions of power and/or marginalisation. This is a kind of "difference-attuned witnessing" [133, p. 345] that honours the space between oneself and the other. By doing this we avoid approaches to difference like collapsing (asserting that "everyone is the same"), appropriating (wishing to become like the other), eliminating (believing that difference is problematic), or overcoming (through assuming that difference is insignificant). Indigenous and Black feminist writers have stressed the importance of attentive listening with all our senses. In this context, listening transcends merely hearing (and includes d/Deaf individuals). It incorporates seeing, perceiving and feeling to create a relational, embodied witnessing of the other. Lee Maracle [134, p. 21] stated, "My listening is sentient, a total body experience. I trust my body to imbibe the words, to swallow them, commit to them, take the words on a journey through my body and then discipline my response to them." Indigenous scholar Willie Ermine [135] referred to this kind of encounter as creating an ethical space—a realm of possibilities where ethical engagement or co-witnessing can occur, acknowledging and honouring difference.

If we aim to embrace and incorporate Other(ed) knowledge systems, we have to genuinely respect participants' cultures and create honouring and compassionate environments for research [136]. There also needs to be a shift in focus from individual integrity—which is the foundation of Western ethical standards—to collective responsibility [30]. Ermine et al. [137] noted that in Indigenous cultures, it's unacceptable for a researcher to pose any question to an Indigenous individual just because they can.

Simply asking can be seen as disrespectful and inappropriate. There are often established protocols that must be followed by anyone, Indigenous or otherwise, prior to seeking information. There are procedural, spiritual, or cultural reasons that might restrict access to the information and these need to be respected.

In their research on the experiences of young autistic adults in Nordoff-Robbins music therapy, Ming Yuan Low et al. [76] highlighted that neurotypical researchers often face double empathy issues when working with autistic participants. There are differences in communication and comprehension styles between autistic and neurotypical individuals [138] and, as a result, misunderstandings can occur during interviews and data analysis. Through interpretative phenomenological analysis (IPA), their study recognised autistic participants as experts on their own experiences. The neurotypical lead researcher sought to engage with the autistic participants in a reflexive manner, including seeking guidance from his dissertation committee and continuously critically reviewing his understanding of autistic experiences, ensuring the participants' voices were prioritised throughout the research. At the start of the process, they took specific actions to improve comfort and accessibility for potential participants, involving their parents or music therapists in introducing the study to ensure voluntary participation.

Anti-oppressive research needs well-honed ethical awareness. In music therapy literature we see a range of considerations mentioned. For example, Klyve and Rolvsjord [82] argued that what is needed in research with children are tailored consent processes with distinct information for children and parents/guardians, and safety and protection. Lars Tuastad et al. [23] described how involving service users in research carries numerous benefits, especially relating to marginalised groups being heard, but that there are also ethical challenges and dilemmas here, particularly related to complex potential questions of power imbalances. Power relations have been highlighted in studies using interviews, and focus groups, where unarticulated assumptions and norms may be at play. Kjetil Hjørnevik et al. [45] emphasised the importance of careful scrutiny towards dual relationships. A number of researchers advocate positioning participants as co-researchers to honour their expertise and treat them as colleagues in the research process [24, 43, 96, 101, 111].

Insider-Outsider Status
Our insider/outsider status in relation to the community we're conducting research with is a central factor in how our positionality impacts the study because it informs how our participants perceive us and how we perceive them [139]. Outsiders navigate unfamiliar contexts, while insiders have a history of shared experiences with the participants [140, 141]. If we're an insider researcher, we hold epistemic privilege. The community may accept us more easily and we could gain deeper access and, therefore, richer data. However, as an insider, we could fall into the trap of assuming that we're similar to (or even the same as) the participants and miss uniqueness and differences within the group. We might make assumptions [142] or project our personal experiences onto the participants. We may need to balance enjoying and making the most of the benefits that insider status can bring, while ensuring that we keep working to "make the familiar strange" [139, p. 1303] so that we can see with fresh eyes. If we're operating as outsiders, we may struggle to build connections and rapport, and to grasp cultural nuances [32]. Our expectations may be challenged [143]. Participants could be less inclined to engage openly with us (or to engage at all). However, the distance could potentially enable us to notice patterns that insiders might miss [141].

Researchers often occupy a mixed role: some of their characteristics and experiences may overlap with participants while others diverge. Insider/outsider identities can also shift throughout the research process [140, 141]. A researcher might think they're an insider, only to find that participants see them as outsiders. Some feminist researchers have argued for more flexible boundaries between researchers and participants so that research relationships can be more authentic and diverse. The idea of an "inbetweener" researcher has started to gain traction. The most realistic position is probably to acknowledge that we're never fully an insider or outsider, and the best strategy is to manage this reflexively and transparently, ethically balancing these shifting positions [139].

Data Collection

We can think about data as cultural artefacts. The practices of collecting and making data are always subjective and context-specific and any data is only a partial truth [144]. Data can also be seen as a dialogue between different people's experiences (e.g., participants and researchers) [145, p. 272]. When gathering data as researchers engaging in Restorative

Reflexivity, we're using deep and active listening as well as critical and "political listening," which Karen Potts and Leslie Brown [32, p. 272] explained as listening "not for what we expected to hear or for what fits with what we already think, but for assumptions made both by ourselves as listeners and by speakers while attending to the dance of power." Anti-oppressive researchers embrace diverse interpretations and multiple truths. They're also responsive, attentive and flexible [95], open to changing their focus and strategies as they learn and build relationships.

Interviews and Focus Groups

Researchers may seek to create the most mutual dialogue possible within an interview or focus group space, but it can be hard to eliminate problematic power imbalances [146]. The structure of these methods is often intrinsically hierarchical [147], and factors like socioeconomic status, education, gender, and ethnicity still play a role in the room. Even if an interviewer works intentionally to adopt a less dominant role, this may not change the interviewee's perception of their authority.

If we take a more nuanced view though, we can consider that both parties (or all parties in the case of a focus group) are exerting influence and that power dynamics are constantly shifting as participants decide what they want to reveal and withhold, what categories of questions are up for discussion, how open or closed the questions are (and hence how much room there is to change the focus and direction of the conversation), and participants' expression of desire to discontinue the conversation and how these are responded to. In all these ways, there can be ongoing negotiations of power [146]. Rapport can be used as a way to reduce power or as a manipulative tool to wield power. There are also occasions when the researcher could become vulnerable in an interview encounter [148]. They may experience fear, anxiety or insecurity if they are in unfamiliar territory, if participants are unpredictable, if they feel powerless to help, or exposed in situations beyond their control or in the face of harrowing stories.

Researchers in other fields have argued for ways of engaging in interviewing as collaborative storytelling [149]. Techniques like sharing circles have been included as more relevant and respectful communication tools that honour Indigenous peoples, especially those within First Nations cultures [150]. "Chats" and meals have also been used in ethnographic studies to create safer spaces for participants to lead the process of sharing ideas and suggestions [151]. Some authors have written about the importance of giving choices to participants between individual interviews and focus groups to honour what feels safest to them and to be responsive to participants in terms of their cultural expectations of how group conversations should proceed and when the facilitator should "stay out of the way" [152]. In music therapy, Low et al. [76] also offered participants choices. They could take part through in-person interviews, phone/video interviews, text message interviews, and music improvisation. Participants could also review their most recent music therapy session videos to help them describe their experiences.

In their study with mothers of young autistic children, Grace Thompson and Katrina McFerran [153] discussed how power dynamics are particularly in play when interviewees are asked to reveal their private thoughts. These authors reflected on how the mothers in their study might have felt pressure to give socially acceptable answers. However, they could choose what aspects of their experiences to share. Their existing relationship with the interviewer was warm and collaborative (the first author was also the music therapist). The authors also avoided asking the mothers to evaluate the therapist so they would not experience pressure to provide a pleasing answer.

In their study on attunement dynamics between an autistic child and a non-autistic music therapist, Mössler et al. [93] interviewed the therapist and conducted focus groups with

parents of autistic children and colleagues from different professions. Since the interview would be inviting participants to share personal experiences, they decided to only ask parents to participate who were already familiar with at least one of the interviewers. Tuastad et al. [23] employed the User Interviewing User (UIU) approach, which is a method in which people with experiences as service users interview other participants. This can engender greater trust, honesty, equality, and the freedom to give critical answers.

Arts Processes

In my interview with Natasha Thomas, she said, "I really do think that art yields things that can't be accessed any other way, that can only be accessed by being in the creativity and letting yourself be moved." As music therapists, we intimately know how the arts are able to create, convey, and challenge meaning. We discussed arts-based research earlier in the section on different research approaches. However, the arts can be used within a range of study types. While arts-based research tends to use these methods throughout the research process, arts-informed research enables a more flexible integration of artistic resources at specific points [154]. The arts can facilitate expression when people communicate without words or when verbal communication is difficult, allowing participants to share their experiences more fully [155]. Arts-based methods can welcome diverse emotional responses and encourage participants to challenge norms [156–159], enhance participants' agency [160] and empowerment [161], interrupt epistemic injustice [162], amplify marginalised people's voices, foster social connectedness, and create knowledge that is more accessible and relatable [163].

Data Ownership

The term "data" originates from the Latin word for "gift," suggesting that participants provide their insights as gifts, which must be treated with due regard [32]. This aligns well with many of the values of anti-oppressive research. However, if reflexivity entails researchers deliberately acknowledging and exploring how they are active role players in creating and shaping knowledge in their studies and how they might respond or be transformed in return, then the data generated within our studies is created collaboratively, to a greater or lesser degree. Who then owns this data? If a researcher wishes to respect the knowledge of a certain group and they are part of that group, conducting the research together, then there may be less tension involved in addressing this question. Alternatively, if a researcher is not part of the group they're researching and wishes to respect data ownership, how do they balance this while also working reflexively? We might choose to share our emerging interpretations openly while inviting community members to respond, challenge, or build upon these so that we sustain a dialogical approach in which our reflexivity is part of a shared conversation rather than a private analytical process. Negotiated ownership agreements could also be established at the start of a research project that specify how different forms of knowledge will be attributed, stored, shared, and published. We'd also need to engage in rigorous transparency about our positionality as we clearly identify which insights have emerged from our own perspectives and which ones more closely reflect community understandings. We may decide to have regular check-ins where community members can evaluate whether our reflexive practices are respectful and beneficial.

In the history of research, much data has been gathered about Indigenous peoples and nations, but most of this data has not respected or centred Indigenous worldviews, nor has it served Indigenous interests [164, 165]. Indigenous data sovereignty supports the right of Indigenous peoples to manage the collection, ownership, and use of their data. In health research, the privacy of participants is typically a researcher's dominant concern and this shapes discussions around data ownership and data sharing. The idea of stewardship is conceptually different from ownership. It refers to the data holders' duty to protect and share data wisely and ethically. The negotiation of this stewardship can be complex and multiple parties may be involved [166]. When we see research data as co-constituted knowledge then this also makes data stewardship even more complicated. There are no easy answers, but a researcher using Restorative Reflexivity intentionally grapples with these matters using ethical reasoning, integrity, and contextual sensitivity while prioritising participants' wishes in the pursuit of greater social justice.

Data Analysis

Reflexive researchers consider meaning-making to be an ongoing process; it's not a discrete phase of research [32]. As we more formally step into the data analysis phase of a study, we bear in mind that interpretive processes have already been vividly active from the outset of the study. During data analysis, we're exploring a range of reflexive questions relating to power dynamics: who has the privilege to create meaning?; how appropriate are our analytic tools?; and who are the beneficiaries of the findings that we're working towards?

Researchers may choose to saturate themselves in the data to gain the most thorough understanding or they may find that distancing themselves during the analysis can facilitate deeper reflection and critical consideration of their relationship with the data and the implications of their analysis. We may collaboratively engage with participant-researchers and other stakeholders. Participants may be experts on the subject matter, while a researcher may have expertise in specific analytical techniques (bearing in mind that these will guide the meanings derived from the data in particular ways) [32].

Music therapy researchers have worked to authentically hear and represent participants' voices during data analysis in various ways. Some share themes they've developed with participants to elicit feedback from them

[62]. In a study by McFerran et al. [26], in which they reflected on their use of online music gatherings to support social inclusion for people with disabilities, they emphasised the need to question whether the themes they developed aligned with the language used by participants. In their study on narratives of children's experiences of music therapy in mental health care, Klyve and Rolvsjord [82] described how analysis process involved thorough exploration of written data, returning to audio material, and blending the voices of the children and researchers in a narrative dialogue.

Sometimes the process of analysis may not be about most faithfully representing participants' views, but critiquing certain perspectives. For example, Claire O'Callaghan and Fiona McDermott [94] used discourse analysis to reframe oncologic music therapy research findings. They described how discourse analysis can be used to enhance reflexive inquiry into one's own clinical gaze (professional assumptions and understandings), which can eclipse other ways of knowing. Music therapists increasingly acknowledge the coexistence of multiple realities and that music therapy meaning can't be captured within one overarching theory, therefore embracing interpretive research methods. A discourse analysis can examine how ideas are produced. Although ironically, "the 'expert's' discourse analysis also in turn contributes to an evolving, potentially hegemonic, discourse" [92, p. 406].

Collaboration in Research Teamwork and Through Supervision

The value of working in a team has been highlighted in a number of music therapy studies, with emphases placed on regular team discussions [108] and critical feedback [24, 45]. In our interview, Natasha Thomas reflected on her duoethnography with co-author, saying,

> I was grateful for the trust and…pre-existing care that Val and I had for each other already…I think it was like going into a really deep wood, a hiking trip with somebody you really trust…There was a lot of Val acting as witness for me and there were moments where I might have been challenging Val…[P]art of the deal with her being in the project as the white dominant person, and me being in the project as the racial and gender, sexual minority, all of those layers…I feel like there were places where she named that…[S]o yeah, we did challenge each other.

Tuastad et al. [23] also highlighted the value of team meetings in music therapy research as they discussed their collaborative process. A music therapist/researcher, service user representative, and music therapy student worked together and strived for reflexivity throughout the study. They discussed and reflected on their assumptions and preunderstandings, challenges of distance and proximity, insider/outsider status, ethical dilemmas, power imbalances, theory use, roles, and their influence on the research field. McFerran et al. [26] described how being positioned in a multidisciplinary group enabled reflexive and critical dialogues that generated new perspectives.

The mentor/protégé relationship provides insights into power dynamics, particularly within universities [167]. The process of supervision may look different in some ways if a researcher is writing from within a minoritised group versus if they're exploring their more privileged position. (These could also overlap in relation to intersecting axes of greater and lesser privilege.) Researchers operating from positions of greater privilege may find that supervision can assist them (when supervisors have done their own work in these areas) in becoming aware of their privilege, and making mindful decisions as Viega [168] described in relation to his research on Hip Hop.

Kathomi Gatwiri et al. [169] pointed out that mentoring racially minoritised academics necessitates a deep understanding of racial dynamics, specifically how race affects structures and hierarchies within academia. This awareness is crucial for navigating processes like peer reviews, promotions, funding, and evaluations. Numerous studies highlight the importance of mentorship for academic success, notably for minoritised academics who encounter unique challenges, underrepresentation, and discrimination [170]. Research conducted in the USA indicated that graduate students and faculty of colour experience less fair and effective mentoring at all levels, suggesting that mentoring experiences differ significantly for those in socially privileged groups versus those from marginalised groups [171]. While research supervision with a person who can relate to your experiences may be profoundly helpful, diversity can also add a rich dimension to the supervision relationship, especially when misunderstandings can be dealt with in constructive ways [172–174].

More participatory approaches to postgraduate supervision (as opposed to conventional forms of expert-novice interaction) are developing, such as participatory action learning. This can create a relational environment that encourages dialogue, equalises power dynamics, and promotes collaborative knowledge creation. It's a model that enables postgraduate candidates to see themselves as self-directed lifelong learners and leaders in collaborative action [175].

Trustworthiness in a Study Employing Restorative Reflexivity

When using Restorative Reflexivity, trustworthiness means that we're demonstrating how the study has lived up to its social justice commitments. Importantly, who are we asking to trust us? Only the readers or also the participants/co-researchers? People who've expressed their views and wish for these to be presented faithfully, or who seek the space to present their own views? People who rightly wish to be afforded due recognition for contributing their insights? Groups who might be hoping that by participating in the research some change may come about? Music therapy research has started to take these questions seriously but, I would argue, we still have more work to do.

As we seek to assess the quality of our study in terms of trustworthiness when we're on a quest to explore and argue for a better, more socially just view of what we're examining, there are some questions we can work with:

- Have the research process and findings actively challenged oppressive power structures rather than reinforcing them?
- Does the knowledge produced serve the interests of marginalised communities?
- Does the study contribute to meaningful change? How?
- Have I/we engaged with power dynamics reflexively and worked to minimise harm while maximising benefit to the communities involved?
- Have I/we respected the epistemic agency of those most affected by the issues being studied?
- Have the interpretations created space for counter-narratives that can disrupt dominant discourses?

(*continued*)

(**continued**)

- Have the methodological choices reflected a commitment to ethically engaging with participants as knowledge co-creators rather than subjects of study?
- Has the research process itself modelled the social justice principles it advocates for?
- Do the findings represent a collaborative effort to imagine and articulate more just alternatives to current realities?
- Have I, as the researcher, critically examined my own complicity in systems of privilege while being part of working towards generating transformative insights?
- Have I/we shown accountability towards the communities who are directly impacted by the research topic by ensuring that they have meaningful input into how the knowledge was/will be created, interpreted, shared, and used?

Presenting Findings

In research with human participants, people share their stories, researchers (re)tell those stories, and readers interpret them. Meaning-making involves all three role-players. How we present our findings influences how they are received [1, 32]. Who we are speaking to shapes what we say. Every language choice involves selection, distortion, and amplification.

Formal texts written in academic language can limit access because they're exclusionary. Kerry Devlin highlighted this in our interview (with reference to her collaboratively written paper *Making mistakes together* [111]):

> A lot of times I find research very impersonal and I understand that often the *intention* is to depersonalise and decontextualise. But I think the act of engaging in research means you're situated in it. Just to use one example from my own experience [drawing from what] disabled folks do—writing really accessibly, using regular words, defining words when they're used if it's not a word that's common conversational language. This project I'm working on right now is challenging me to write in a similar way. It's even made me feel self-conscious, thinking: is this too casual? I'm writing in such plain text. Will this, is this even publishable? But you know, all of these things are expected in order to get something published so people can read

> it. It has to be in a certain format. But I've really grappled with, you know, why don't we have more plain text? I had to write to journals and say, would you publish this? How would this be hosted? Is it just going to be an appendix that nobody will read? Is there a way to make it really prominent so that people will also experience the plain text version of the article? Because I think that's a really important parallel for making research accessible to anybody who wants to engage in it…It's challenged a lot of the assumptions that I have about what is good writing, what is clear writing, what is meaningful writing.

In our field of music therapy, where nonverbal elements like music play a crucial role, conveying findings through written language may be even more limiting [176]. Klyve and Rolvsjord [82] chose to present their findings through four narratives that encapsulated their participating children's experiences of music therapy in mental health settings. These narratives illustrated a diverse array of experiences articulated through various modalities, including drawing, words, music, silence, movement, and gestures. They also consulted a poet to enhance the aesthetic quality of their narratives, selecting four out of seven narratives to showcase the rich nuances and variations in content. They still acknowledged that their interpretations were filtered through their perspectives as music therapists and adults. Some anti-oppressive researchers across different fields explore alternative dissemination methods like community workshops and musical or theatre presentations. The power of anti-oppressive research is that it can transform the observer into a participant who becomes moved to realise that this could be their story too [177]. Decisions we make about presenting findings link to critical questions about how we hope people will engage with them, who will benefit, and what impact we hope the research will have [32].

An Accessible Summary

Research functions as a microcosm through which oppressive relationships in society can be reproduced or challenged. Restorative Reflexivity is a transformative research approach that consciously recognises the role researchers play in creating and shaping knowledge, while also working to advance social justice. This strategy is called "Restorative Reflexivity" to align with approaches that embrace innate wholeness and flourishing, and that seek to accompany people as they determine their futures instead of using damage-focused perspectives that emphasise weaknesses and call for action from a place of authority or control.

When we engage in Restorative Reflexivity, we need to critically examine our positioning in relation to the research topic and the people involved in our studies. We are positioned not only in relation to our demographic characteristics, but also within a complex web of personal experiences, social factors, and organisational contexts that mould how we understand and approach our work.

Restorative Reflexivity works against epistemic injustice, which refers to the systematic silencing of marginalised groups and undermining of individuals in their capacity as knowers. Rather, we can emphasise the importance of recognising people as knowers and ensuring their perspectives are heard and valued. Instead of conducting research "on" people, Restorative Reflexivity emphasises research "with" and "by" communities. This might involve participatory action research, where participants are positioned as co-researchers, or arts-based methods that welcome diverse forms of expression and challenge traditional power dynamics. The goal is to create more equitable relationships and shared ownership of the research process, though researchers need to be careful not to assume that simply using participatory methods automatically addresses power imbalances.

How researchers describe participants, frame concepts, and present findings all play active roles in constructing reality and relationships. Instead of using deficit-based language that reduces people to their diagnoses or problems, Restorative Reflexivity encourages strengths-based approaches that recognise the full complexity of human experience. This extends to considerations of data ownership and stewardship.

(*continued*)

(**continued**)

When research is co-created, who benefits from and controls knowledge becomes a complex ethical consideration.

Evaluating the quality of this research includes assessing whether one can trust that the research has actively challenged oppressive structures, served the interests of marginalised communities, and contributed to meaningful change. Did the research process model the social justice principles it advocates for? Have interpretations created space for counter-narratives? Did the work demonstrate accountability to the communities most affected by the research topic? Ultimately, Restorative Reflexivity represents a commitment to research as a form of activism that can contribute to more just and equitable societies. It recognises that all research is political and chooses to use that reality constructively, working alongside participants as they imagine and express alternatives to current realities.

References

1. Stige B. Do we need general criteria for the evaluation of qualitative research articles, and if we do, how could such criteria be formulated? Nord J Music Ther. 2002;11(1):65–71.
2. Strier R. Anti-oppressive research in social work: a preliminary definition. Br J Soc Work. 2007;37(5):857–71.
3. Idahosa GEO, Bradbury V. Challenging the way we know the world: overcoming paralysis and utilising discomfort through critical reflexive thought. Acta Acad. 2020;52(1):31–53.
4. McCabe JL, Holmes D. Reflexivity, critical qualitative research and emancipation: a Foucauldian perspective. J Adv Nurs. 2009;65(7):1518–26.
5. Leonard H, dos Santos A. Aesthetics in music therapy: supporting the creative impulse to flourish. In: Handbook of Music therapy. 2nd ed. New York: Guilford Press; 2025. p. 19–33.
6. Chilisa B. Indigenous research methodologies. Thousand Oaks: Sage Publications; 2019.
7. Davies H. 'Autism is a way of being': an 'insider perspective' on neurodiversity, music therapy and social justice. Br J Music Ther. 2022;36(1):16–26.
8. Leonard H. A problematic conflation of justice and equality: the case for equity in music therapy. Music Ther Perspect. 2020;38(2):102–11.

9. Swamy S, Webb A. Voices of change: learning from the lived experiences of minoritized music therapists. Music Ther Perspect. 2022;40(2):121–4. https://doi.org/10.1093/mtp/miac027
10. Thomas N, Blanc V. Break it then build again: an arts based duoethnographic pilot reconstructing music therapy and dance/movement therapy histories. Arts Psychother. 2021;73:101765.
11. Arnold JM, Sableski MK. Where are you from? Building bridges over walls with #ownvoices literature. J Child Lit. 2020;46(2):19–26.
12. Tanesini A. Standpoint then and now. In: Fricker M, Graham PJ, Henderson D, Pedersen NJL, editors. The Routledge handbook of social epistemology. New York: Routledge; 2020.
13. Paradies Y. Whither standpoint theory in a post-truth world? Cosmop Civ Soc. 2018;10(2):119–29.
14. Wheeler J, Shaw J, Howard J. Politics and practices of inclusion: intersectional participatory action research. Community Dev J. 2020;55(1):45–63.
15. Forbay TR, Mnguni PP. Labyrinth moments: evidencing reflexivity in intersectional research using constructivist grounded theory. S Afr J High Educ. 2024;38(4):46–61.
16. Cox GR, FireMoon P, Anastario MP, Ricker A, Escarcega-Growing Thunder R, Baldwin JA, et al. Indigenous standpoint theory as a theoretical framework for decolonizing social science health research with American Indian communities. AlterNative. 2021;17(4):460–8.
17. Nakata M. Disciplining the savages: savaging the disciplines. Canberra: Aboriginal Studies Press; 2007.
18. Helle-Valle A, Binder PE, Anderssen N, Stige B. Is restlessness best understood as a process? Reflecting on four boys' restlessness during music therapy in kindergarten. Int J Qual Stud Health Well-being. 2017;12(sup1):1298266.
19. Comte R. Neo-colonialism in music therapy: a critical interpretive synthesis of the literature concerning music therapy practice with refugees. Voices. 2016;16(3).
20. McFerran KS, Shoemark H. How musical engagement promotes well-being in education contexts: the case of a young man with profound and multiple disabilities. Int J Qual Stud Health Well-being. 2013;8(1):20570.
21. Zanders ML, Midach M, Waldemeier L, Barros B. A reflexive music therapy clinical introspection in working with foster care youth. Voices. 2018;18(4).
22. Fairchild R, Mraz M. "Everything changed when I got those drums": a collaborative case reflection. Voices. 2018;18(1).
23. Tuastad L, Johansen B, Østerholt AL, Nielsen I, McIvor DSH. Being a person who plays in a band rather than being a person with a mental illness playing in a band: a qualitative study of stigma in the context of music therapy in mental health aftercare. Nord J Music Ther. 2023;32(2):121–39.

24. Viega M. Evaluation for arts-based research performance: audience perceptions of rising from the ashes. J Music Ther. 2022;59(1):62–86.
25. Campbell KS. A qualitative exploration of music therapist beliefs, education, and uses of hip hop in clinical practice. Music Ther Perspect. 2023;41(1).
26. McFerran K, Skinner A, Hall T, Thompson G. Structure, agency and community: using online music gatherings to support social inclusion for people with disabilities in Australia during the COVID-19 pandemic. Nord J Music Ther. 2022;31(3):259–72.
27. Metell M, Stige B. Blind spots in music therapy. Toward a critical notion of participation in context of children with visual impairment. Nord J Music Ther. 2016;25(4):300–18.
28. Bailey A. The unlevel knowing field: an engagement with Dotson's third-order epistemic oppression. Soc Epistemol Rev Reply Collect. 2014;3(10):62–8.
29. Tuck E. Suspending damage: a letter to communities. Harv Educ Rev. 2009;79(3):409–28.
30. Thambinathan V, Kinsella EA. Decolonizing methodologies in qualitative research: creating spaces for transformative praxis. Int J Qual Methods. 2021;20:16094069211014766.
31. Rodney R, Hinds M, Bonilla-Damptey J, Boissoneau D, Khan A, Forde A. Anti-oppression as praxis in the research field: implementing emancipatory approaches for researchers and community partners. Qual Res. 2024;24(4):872–93.
32. Hudani SE. African studies keyword: "transformation". Afr Stud Rev. 2024;67(3):652–74.
33. Potts K, Brown L. Becoming an anti-oppressive researcher. In: Brown L, Strega S, editors. Research as resistance. Toronto: Canadian Scholars Press; 2015. p. 255–86.
34. Kara H. Identity and power in co-produced activist research. Qual Res. 2017;17(3):289–301. https://doi.org/10.1177/1468794117696033
35. Pavlicevic M. Reflection: crime, community, and everyday practice: music therapy as social activism. In: Stige B, Ansdell G, Elefant C, Pavlicevic M, editors. Where music helps: community music therapy in action and reflection. Farnham: Routledge; 2017. p. 223–42.
36. Norris MS. A call for radical imagining: exploring anti-blackness in the music therapy profession. Voices. 2020;20(3):6.
37. Seabrook D. Music therapy in the era of climate crisis: evolving to meet current needs. Arts Psychother. 2020;68:101646.
38. Pickard B. Anti-oppressive pedagogy as an opportunity for consciousness raising in the music therapy profession: a critical disability studies perspective. Br J Music Ther. 2022;36(1):5–15.

39. Lindan A. Beyond a socially just profession: perspectives of music therapists in Canada. Can J Music Ther. 2019;25:22–49.
40. Scrine E. The limits of resilience and the need for resistance: articulating the role of music therapy with young people within a shifting trauma paradigm. Front Psychol. 2021;12:600245.
41. Hadley S. Dominant narratives: complicity and the need for vigilance in the creative arts therapies. Arts Psychother. 2013;40(4):373–81. https://doi.org/10.1016/j.aip.2013.05.007
42. Barnes C. What a difference a decade makes: reflections on doing "emancipatory" disability research. Disabil Soc. 2003;18(1):3–17.
43. Baines S, Edwards J. Considering the ways in which anti-oppressive practice principles can inform health research. Arts Psychother. 2015;42:28–34.
44. Treloyn S. Music in culture, music as culture, music interculturally: reflections on the development and challenges of ethnomusicological research in Australia. Voices. 2016;16(2).
45. Hjørnevik K, Waage L, Hansen AL. Musical life stories: coherence through musicking in the prison setting. Crime Media Cult. 2022;19:17416590211059135.
46. Palaganas EC, Sanchez MC, Molintas MVP, Caricativo RD. Reflexivity in qualitative research. Nurs Res. 2017;24(4):35–41.
47. Spivak GC. Can the subaltern speak? In: Nelson C, Grossberg L, editors. Marxism and the interpretation of culture. Urbana: University of Illinois Press; 1988. p. 271–313.
48. Fricker M. Epistemic injustice: power and the ethics of knowing. Oxford: Oxford University Press; 2007.
49. Dotson K. Tracking epistemic violence, tracking practices of silencing. Hypatia. 2011;26(2):236–57.
50. de Sousa SB. Epistemologies of the south: justice against epistemicide. New York: Routledge; 2015.
51. Davis E. On epistemic appropriation. Ethics. 2018;128(4):702–27.
52. Medina J. Misrecognition and epistemic injustice. Fem Philos Q. 2018;4(4).
53. Okoroji C, Mackay T, Robotham D, Beckford D, Pinfold V. Epistemic injustice and mental health research: a pragmatic approach to working with lived experience expertise. Front Psychiatry. 2023;14:1114725.
54. Kluger AN, Mizrahi M. Defining listening: can we get rid of the adjectives? Curr Opin Psychol. 2023;52:101639.
55. Kotsonis A. On the virtue of epistemic justice and the vice of epistemic injustice. Episteme. 2023;20(3):598–610.
56. Kumashiro K. Troubling education: "queer" activism and anti-oppressive pedagogy. New York: Routledge; 2002.
57. Corden A, Sainsbury R. Using verbatim quotations in reporting qualitative social research: researchers' views. York: University of York; 2006. p. 11–4.

58. Guba E, Lincoln Y. Paradigmatic controversies, contradictions, and emerging confluences. In: Denzin N, Lincoln Y, editors. Handbook of qualitative research. 3rd ed. Thousand Oaks: Sage; 2005. p. 191–216.
59. Crimmins G. Speaking with others involves placing ourselves explicitly as authors in the research text. Narrat Inq. 2015;25(2):301–15.
60. Alcoff LM. Visible identities: race, gender, and the self. Oxford: Oxford University Press; 2006.
61. Alcoff LM. The problem of speaking for others. In: Jackson AY, Mazzei LA, editors. Voice in qualitative inquiry: challenging conventional, interpretive, and critical conceptions in qualitative research. New York: Routledge; 2009. p. 117–35.
62. Von Fritschen C, Dos Santos A. Perspectives on music healing by traditional healers and music therapists, vol. 41. Music Ther Perspect; 2023. p. 152–8.
63. Carel H, Kidd IJ. Epistemic injustice in healthcare: a philosophical analysis. Med Health Care Philos. 2014;17(4):529–40.
64. Solli HP, Rolvsjord R. "The opposite of treatment": a qualitative study of how patients diagnosed with psychosis experience music therapy. Nord J Music Ther. 2015;24(1):67–92.
65. McCaffrey T. Evaluating music therapy in adult mental health services: tuning into service user perspectives. Nord J Music Ther. 2018;27(1):28–43.
66. McCaffrey T, Carr CE, Solli HPP, Bent C, Boyle D, Dypvik OB, et al. The alliance for recovery research in music therapy: developing a shared research agenda in mental health. Voices. 2024;24(2).
67. Klinke ME, Fernandez AV. Taking phenomenology beyond the first-person perspective: conceptual grounding in the collection and analysis of observational evidence. Phenomenol Cogn Sci. 2023;22(1):171–91.
68. Bruscia K. A qualitative approach to analysing client improvisations. Music Ther Perspect. 2001;19(1):7–21.
69. Meadows A, Wimpenny K. Core themes in music therapy clinical improvisation: an arts-informed qualitative research synthesis. J Music Ther. 2017;54(2):161–95.
70. Metell M. Dis/abling musicking: reflections on a disability studies perspective in music therapy. Voices. 2014;14(3).
71. Dohmen J. "A little of her language": epistemic injustice and mental disability. Res Philos. 2016;93(4):669–91.
72. Oliver M. Changing the social relations of research production? Disabil Handicap Soc. 1992;7(2):101–14.
73. Charlton JI. Nothing about us without us: disability oppression and empowerment. Berkeley: University of California Press; 1998.
74. Stone E, Priestley M. Parasites, pawns and partners: disability research and the role of non-disabled researchers. Br J Sociol. 1996;47(4):699–716.

75. Sinclair J. Don't mourn for us. In: The autistic self advocacy network, editor. Loud hands: autistic people, speaking. Washington, DC: The Autistic Press; 2012. p. 15–20.
76. Low MY, McFerran KS, Viega M, Carroll-Scott A, McGhee Hassrick E, Bradt J. Exploring the lived experiences of young autistic adults in Nordoff-Robbins music therapy: an interpretative phenomenological analysis. Nord J Music Ther. 2023;1–24.
77. Burroughs MD, Tollefsen D. Learning to listen: epistemic injustice and the child. Episteme. 2016;13(3):359–77.
78. United Nations General Assembly. A world fit for children. UN/A/RES/S-27/2. Geneva: United Nations; 2002.
79. Fleming J, Boeck T, editors. Involving children and young people in health and social care research. London: Routledge; 2012.
80. Iacono G, Elsaesser C, Dominique Courts CL. "My resistance melts away": the role of mindfulness in supporting participatory researchers' efforts to share power with youth co-researchers. Am J Community Psychol. 2024.
81. Bakhtiar A, Lang M, Shelley B, West M. Research with and by children: a systematic literature review. Rev Educ. 2023;11(1).
82. Klyve GP, Rolvsjord R. Moments of fun: narratives of children's experiences of music therapy in mental health care. Nord J Music Ther. 2022;1–21.
83. Krüger V, Stige B. Between rights and realities–music as a structuring resource in child welfare everyday life: a qualitative study. Nord J Music Ther. 2015;24(2):99–122.
84. Fairchild R, Thompson G, McFerran KS. Exploring the meaning of a performance in music therapy for children and their families experiencing homelessness and family violence. Music Ther Perspect. 2017;35(1):36–49.
85. Hakomäki H. Storycomposing as a path to a child's inner world: a collaborative music therapy experiment with a child co-researcher [dissertation]. Jyväskylä: University of Jyväskylä; 2013.
86. Scrine E, McFerran K. The role of a music therapist exploring gender and power with young people: articulating an emerging anti-oppressive practice. Arts Psychother. 2018;59:54–64.
87. Thomas NP. Child-led research, children's rights and childhood studies: a defence. Childhood. 2021;28(2):186–99.
88. Thomas N, Norris MS. "Who you mean 'we?'" Confronting professional notions of "belonging" in music therapy. J Music Ther. 2021;58(1):5–11.
89. dos Santos A. What research questions are we asking in English-language music therapy journals? A descriptive analysis. Nord J Music Ther. 2025. https://doi.org/10.1080/08098131.2025.2525566
90. Roginsky E, Elefant C. Silent sounding: communicability, musicality, and the use of music with nonspeaking individuals with cerebral palsies and multiple disabilities. Nord J Music Ther. 2021;30(1):61–78.

91. Trondalen G. Resource-oriented Bonny Method of Guided Imagery and Music (R-oGIM) as a creative health resource for musicians. Nord J Music Ther. 2016;25(1):5–31.
92. Aitchison KA, McFerran KS. Six adolescents' lived experiences of resource-oriented music therapy assessment in a community-based mental health day program. Arts Psychother. 2023;82:101991.
93. Mössler K, Halstead J, Metell M, Gottschewski K, Schmid W. "The room is a mess": exploring the co-creation of space for attunement dynamics between an autistic child and a non-autistic music therapist. Nord J Music Ther. 2023;1–21.
94. O'Callaghan C, McDermott F. Discourse analysis reframes oncologic music therapy research findings. Arts Psychother. 2007;34(5):398–408.
95. McCaffrey T, Edwards J. Meeting art with art: arts-based methods enhance researcher reflexivity in research with mental health service users. J Music Ther. 2015;52(4):515–32.
96. Rickson DJ. The relevance of disability perspectives in music therapy practice with children and young people who have intellectual disability. Voices. 2014;14(3)
97. Solli HP. Battling illness with wellness: a qualitative case study of a young rapper's experiences with music therapy. Nord J Music Ther. 2015;24(3):204–31.
98. McSorley K. Sexism and cisgenderism in music therapy spaces: an exploration of gender microaggressions experienced by music therapists. Arts Psychother. 2020;71:101707.
99. McFerran KS, Lai HIC, Chang WH, Acquaro D, Chin TC, Stokes H, et al. Music, rhythm and trauma: a critical interpretive synthesis of research literature. Front Psychol. 2020;11:324.
100. Viega M, Druziako V, Millrod J, Hoberman A. Entering the ambient: a performative collaborative autoethnography of music therapists' improvising with digital music technologies. Voices. 2023;23(1).
101. Fairchild R, McFerran KS. "Music is everything": using collaborative group songwriting as an arts-based method with children experiencing homelessness and family violence. Nord J Music Ther. 2019;28(2):88–107.
102. Bolger L, Murphy M. Understanding the impact of international music therapy student placements on music therapy practice and professional identity. Nord J Music Ther. 2023;1–19.
103. Nind M. What is inclusive research? London: Bloomsbury; 2014.
104. Reason P, Bradbury H. Introduction: inquiry and participation in search of a world worthy of human aspiration. In: Reason P, Bradbury H, editors. Handbook of action research. Concise Paperback Edition. Los Angeles: Sage; 2006. p. 1–14.

105. Dege M. Action research and critical psychology an investigation of subjectivity and participation. Cham: Springer; 2023.
106. Rickson D. Researching one's own clinical practice: managing multiple roles in an action research project. Voices. 2009;9(1).
107. Schwantes M, Rivera E. "A team working together to make a big, nice, sound": an action research pilot study in an inclusive college setting. Arts Psychother. 2017;55:1–10.
108. Stuart-Röhm K, Clark I, Baker FA. Development of a person-centered caregiver singing model for formal caregivers of people living with dementia in South Africa. Geriatr Nurs. 2023;53:261–9.
109. Mooney R, Dempsey C, Brown B, Keating F, Joseph D, Bhui K. Using participatory action research methods to address epistemic injustice within mental health research and the mental health system. Front Public Health. 2023;11:1075363. https://doi.org/10.3389/fpubh.2023.1075363
110. Elephant C. Reflection—giving voice: participatory action research with a marginalized group. In: Stige B, Ansdell G, Elephant C, Pavlicevic M, editors. Where music helps: community music therapy in action and reflection. Farnham: Ashgate; 2010. p. 189–99.
111. Devlin K, Meadows A, Johnston M, Johnston C. Ethical considerations in co-authoring research with music therapy stakeholders. Music Ther Perspect. 2024.
112. Rolvsjord R. Resource-oriented music therapy in mental health care. Gilsum, NH: Barcelona Publishers; 2010.
113. Bolger L, McFerran KS, Stige B. Hanging out and buying in: rethinking relationship building to avoid tokenism when striving for collaboration in music therapy. Music Ther Perspect. 2018;36(2):257–66.
114. Mulvihill TM, Swaminathan R. Collaborative qualitative research. New York: Guilford Publications; 2022.
115. Stige B, Aarø LE. Invitation to community music therapy. New York: Routledge; 2012.
116. Cochran PA, Marshall CA, Garcia-Downing C, Kendall E, Cook D, McCubbin L, et al. Indigenous ways of knowing: implications for participatory research and community. Am J Public Health. 2008;98(1):22–7.
117. Gergen MM, Gergen KJ. Playing with purpose: adventures in performative social science. New York: Routledge; 2016.
118. Barone T, Eisner EW. Arts-based research. Thousand Oaks: SAGE; 2012.
119. Foster V. Collaborative arts-based research for social justice. New York: Routledge; 2015.
120. Tumanyan M, Huuki T. Arts in working with youth on sensitive topics: a qualitative systematic review. Int J Educ Art. 2020;16(3):381–97.

121. Hammond C, Gifford W, Thomas R, Rabaa S, Thomas O, Domecq MC. Arts-based research methods with indigenous peoples: an international scoping review. AlterNative. 2018;14(3):260–76.
122. Baines S, Edwards J. A constructivist grounded theory research project studying music therapy as an anti-oppressive practice in long-term and psychiatric residential care. Arts Psychother. 2018;60:1–8.
123. Charmaz K. Constructing grounded theory: a practical guide through qualitative analysis. London: Sage Publications; 2006.
124. O'Callaghan C. Grounded theory in music therapy research. J Music Ther. 2012;49(3):236–77.
125. Schreiber R, Tomm-Bonde L. Ubuntu and constructivist grounded theory: an African methodology package. J Res Nurs. 2015;20(8):655–64. https://doi.org/10.1177/1744987115619207.
126. Spandler H. "What matters to you"—an antidote to "What's wrong" and "What happened". Mad in America: science, psychiatry and social justice [Internet]. 2024 [cited 2024 Mar 21].
127. Bruscia K. Defining music therapy. 3rd ed. Gilsum, NH: Barcelona Publishers; 2014.
128. Rizkallah M. In defence of working with "patients" in music therapy. Approaches. 2024;16(1).
129. Rolvsjord R. The competent client and the complexity of dis-ability. Voices. 2014;14(3).
130. Thompson G. Respect-focused writing: an invitation to reflexivity in the use of terminology. Nord J Music Ther. 2022;31(5):383–6.
131. Carr C. On home-perspectives on homelessness [master's thesis]. St. Davids, PA: Eastern University; 2022.
132. Tsai J, Kelton K, Gluff J, Elbogen E. Terms that refer to homeless populations: national surveys of several stakeholder groups. Psychiatr Serv. 2023;74(4):415–8.
133. Rice C, Cook K, Bailey KA. Difference-attuned witnessing: risks and potentialities of arts-based research. Fem Psychol. 2021;31(3):345–65.
134. Maracle L. Memory serves: oratories. Edmonton: NeWest Press; 2015.
135. Ermine W. The ethical space of engagement. Ind Law J. 2007;6:193–203.
136. Lavallée L. Practical application of an indigenous research framework and indigenous research methods: sharing circles and anishnaabe symbol-based reflection. Int J Qual Methods. 2009;8(1):21–40.
137. Ermine W, Sinclair R, Browne M. Kwayask Itotamowin: indigenous research ethics—report of the Indigenous Peoples' Health Research Centre to the Institute of Aboriginal Peoples' Health and the Canadian Institutes of Health Research [Internet]. Regina: Indigenous Peoples' Health Research Centre; 2005 Mar [cited 2024 Mar 21]. Available from: http://iphrc.ca/assets/Documents/IPHRC_ACADRE_Ethics_Report_final.pdf.

138. Milton DEM. On the ontological status of autism: the 'double empathy problem'. Disabil Soc. 2012;27(6):883–7. https://doi.org/10.1080/09687599.2012.710008
139. Folkes L. Moving beyond 'shopping list' positionality: using kitchen table reflexivity and in/visible tools to develop reflexive qualitative research. Qual Res. 2023;23(5):1301–18.
140. Dwyer SC, Buckle JL. The space between: on being an insider outsider in qualitative research. Int J Qual Methods. 2009;8:54–63.
141. Finefter-Rosenbluh I. Incorporating perspective taking in reflexivity: a method to enhance insider qualitative research processes. Int J Qual Methods. 2017;16(1):1609406917703539.
142. Lindblad K. "No, I guess it's kind of sensitive"—communication patterns in a music listening group with older men. Nord J Music Ther. 2021;30(5):424–39.
143. Skånland MS. Music therapy and social recovery in flexible assertive community treatment. Nord J Music Ther. 2023;32(4):290–306.
144. Leurs K. Feminist data studies: using digital methods for ethical, reflexive and situated socio-cultural research. Fem Rev. 2017;115(1):130–54. https://doi.org/10.1057/s41305-017-0043-1
145. McDonough S, Brandenburg R. Who owns this data? Using dialogic reflection to examine an ethically important moment. Reflective Pract. 2019;20(3):355–66.
146. Anyan F. The influence of power shifts in data collection and analysis stages: a focus on qualitative research interview. Qual Rep. 2013;18(18):1–9.
147. Kvale S. Dominance through interviews and dialogues. Qual Inq. 2006;12(3):480–500.
148. Bashir N. The qualitative researcher: the flip side of the research encounter with vulnerable people. Qual Res. 2020;20(5):667–83.
149. Bishop R. Interviewing as collaborative storying. Educ Res Perspect. 1997;24(1):28–47.
150. Rothe JP, Ozegovic D, Carroll LJ. Innovation in qualitative interviews: "sharing circles" in a First Nations community. Inj Prev. 2009;15(5):334–40.
151. Ortega Y. Charlas y Comidas: humanising focus groups and interviews. Qual Res. 2024;24(4):773–92.
152. Salmon A. Walking the talk: how participatory interview methods can democratize research. Qual Health Res. 2007;17(7):982–93.
153. Thompson G, McFerran KS. "We've got a special connection": qualitative analysis of descriptions of change in the parent-child relationship by mothers of young children with autism spectrum disorder. Nord J Music Ther. 2015;24(1):3–26.
154. Rolling JH Jr. A paradigm analysis of arts-based research and implications for education. Stud Art Educ. 2010;51(2):102–14.

155. dos Santos A, Wagner C. Musical elicitation methods: insights from a study with becoming-adolescents referred to group music therapy for aggression. Int J Qual Methods. 2018;17(1):1609406918797427.
156. Allett N. "As soon as that track starts, I feel...": unravelling attachments to extreme metal music with music elicitation. In: Skinner J, editor. The interview: an ethnographic approach. London: Berg; 2012. p. 107–26.
157. DeNora T. Music and emotion in everyday life. In: Juslin PN, Sloboda JA, editors. Music and emotion: theory and research. Oxford: Oxford University Press; 2006. p. 161–80.
158. Keightley E, Pickering M. For the record: popular music and photography as technologies of memory. Eur J Cult Stud. 2006;9(2):149–65.
159. Chilton G, Leavy P. Arts-based research practice: merging social research and the creative arts. In: Leavy P, editor. The Oxford handbook of qualitative research. Oxford: Oxford University Press; 2014. p. 403–22.
160. Green S, Denov M. Mask-making and drawing as method: arts-based approaches to data collection with war-affected children. Int J Qual Methods. 2019;18:1–13.
161. Flicker S, Danforth JY, Wilson C, Oliver V, Larkin J, Restoule JP, et al. "Because we have really unique art": decolonizing research with Indigenous youth using the arts. Int J Indig Health. 2014;10(1):16–34.
162. Boni A, Walker M. Epistemic justice and the capabilities approach: agency, participation and inclusion. In: Chiappero-Martinetti E, Osmani S, Qizilbash M, editors. The Cambridge handbook of the capability approach. Cambridge: Cambridge University Press; 2020. p. 639–58.
163. Salma J, Ginsburg L, Nguyen M, Mayan M. Arts-based methods as tools for knowledge translation in health research: a systematic review of the literature. Int J Qual Methods. 2023;22:1–13.
164. Walter M. The voice of indigenous data: beyond the markers of disadvantage first things first. Griffith Rev. 2018;60:256–63. Available from: https://griffithreview.com/articles/voice-Indigenousdata-beyond-disadvantage/
165. United Nations Human Rights. Report of the Special Rapporteur on the right to privacy [Internet]. 2018 Oct 17 [cited 2024 Mar 21]. Available from: https://www.ohchr.org/Documents/Issues/Privacy/SR_Privacy/A_73_45712.docx.
166. Sorbie A, Gueddana W, Laurie G, Townend D. Examining the power of the social imaginary through competing narratives of data ownership in health research. J Law Biosci. 2021;8(2).
167. Johnson-Bailey J, Cervero RM. Mentoring in black and white: the intricacies of cross-cultural mentoring. Mentor Tutoring. 2004;12(1):7–21. https://doi.org/10.1080/1361126042000183075

168. Viega M. Science as art: axiology as a central component in methodology and evaluation of arts-based research (ABR). Music Ther Perspect. 2016;34(1):4–13.
169. Gatwiri K, Krupka Z, James S. Mentors and sponsors: making a difference for racially and culturally minoritised academics in Australian universities. Aust J Soc Issues. 2024.
170. Williams MS, Brown Burnett TJ, Carroll TK, Harris CJ. Mentoring, managing, and helping: a critical race analysis of socialization in doctoral education. J Coll Stud Retent. 2018;20(2):253–78.
171. Brunsma DL, Embrick DG, Shin JH. Graduate students of color: race, racism, and mentoring in the white waters of academia. Sociol Race Ethn. 2017;3(1):1–13.
172. Bager-Charleson S, McBeath AG. Containment, compassion and clarity: mixed-methods research into supervision during doctoral research for psychotherapists and counselling psychologists. Couns Psychother Res. 2022;22(3):689–707.
173. Charura D, Lago C. Black identities + White therapies: race respect and diversity. Ross-on-Wye: PCCS Books; 2021.
174. Malan R, Erwee R, van Rensburg H, Danaher P. Cultural diversity: impact on the doctoral candidate-supervisor relationship. Int J Organ Behav. 2012;17(1):1–14.
175. Louw I, Wood L. Reconsidering postgraduate "supervision" from a participatory action learning and action research approach. S Afr J High Educ. 2018;32(4):284–97.
176. Ansdell G. Music therapy as discourse and discipline: a study of 'music therapist's dilemma' [dissertation]. London: City University London; 1999.
177. Lorenzetti L. Research as a social justice tool: an activist's perspective. Affilia. 2013;28(4):451–7.

CHAPTER 8

Relational Reflexivity

Some music therapy research dips its toes into Relational Reflexivity. A small number of studies go swimming. In this chapter, we'll explore examples from both groups. In every other chapter in this book (to greater and lesser degrees), reflexivity has included exploring what we as researchers bring into a study with us: how our pre-existing biases need to be carefully managed and reduced in Sentinel Reflexivity; how our preconceived ideas will shape the study in Lens Reflexivity; how our subjectivity is the place from which we tell our stories in Authorial Reflexivity; how our abilities to empathically attune to another individual are in play in Empathic Reflexivity; and how our commitments to social justice inform our decisions in Restorative Reflexivity. Here—in the territory of Relational Reflexivity—we don't bring a backpack of meaning into the study. Meaning grows in the relational processes of the study itself. We become in the study in relation to those around us, who are also becoming in relation to us [1]. We are co-constructing worlds and Relational Reflexivity invites us to explore how these worlds are being created.

As Katie Beavan [2, p. 102] asked so evocatively,

Deliberately acknowledging and exploring our active participation in creating and shaping knowledge in our study *as interconnected, mutually affecting parts of dynamic assemblages* and being affected by these insights *through emergent processes.*

A. dos Santos, *Reflexive Research in Music Therapy*,
https://doi.org/10.1007/978-3-032-02033-8_8

> What if knowledge isn't made by me or you, an act of imparting to our reader but, rather, is made in our doing together? Together scholar-to-scholar? Together with our readers? A temporal and spatially decentred experience sensing meanings rather than conceiving them from on high?...Textualised bodies, feeling scholarship, letting it seep into our skin and melt into the marrow of our bones, move in our blood, our borders bleeding...Knowledge, a collective endeavour. Intersubjective. Flesh to flesh, emergings in the moments between us.

In this chapter we'll play and think with a range of conceptual tools: intersubjectivity; Indigenous perspectives; and the notion of assemblages. We'll also discuss positioning theory. These cover vast theoretical terrains and approach the idea of how meaning is made between us in different ways. I've included quite a few questions to prompt our explorations of Relational Reflexivity as we go along in this chapter in an attempt to make concepts that can sometimes feel a bit abstract more practical.

Intersubjectivity

Feminist philosopher Kelly Oliver [3] argued that the self/other split is an illusion because all subjectivity arises from a process of witnessing and co-constructing one another through engagement. A researcher's subjectivity takes shape as an intersubjectivity relationship with others. The notion of bracketing then becomes quite redundant [4]. Leeat Granek [5, p. 178] referred to the way that our beings are co-developed within intersubjective exchanges as "the epistemology of the hyphen." As researchers, we occupy and work with the hyphen between self-other: "We do not exist on one side of the divide and the participant on the other. We are on the line. We are the hyphen" [5, p. 180].

In Chap. 1, I described Husserl's [6] views on intersubjectivity as being part of a shared world of meaning-making; as what occurs between minds [7] as we engage in participatory sense-making [8, 9]; and as the space that forms where subjectivities intersect [10]. Intersubjectivity has also been explored through a psychodynamic frame. Both conscious and unconscious forces shape the research process. For example, some authors have explored how transference/countertransference and projective—identification offer tools for examining the unconscious intersubjective aspects of these dynamics [11, 12].

Here are some questions about intersubjectivity that you may wish to explore:

- *What new ways of being, feeling, and relating are coming into being through our interactions in this research study?*
  - How do I feel during and after different research encounters, and how do these emotions shape my role in the study?
  - How do moments of connection, tension, or misunderstanding shape the relationships forming within the study?
  - Are there new patterns of relating (e.g., trust, hesitation, authority, vulnerability) emerging between myself and participants)?
- *How are our individual "selves" taking shape through shared moments in this research process?*
  - Do I notice myself acting, speaking, or responding differently depending on the participant or context?
  - What does this tell me?
  - How do participants describe themselves or their experiences differently in my presence compared to how they describe themselves in other contexts?
  - Are there times when participants shift how they present themselves (e.g., as an expert, as uncertain, as resistant)?
  - What might be prompting this?
  - How does the act of being in this research process affect how I understand myself—not only as a researcher but as a person?
- *How do power relations shift and fluctuate through intersubjective encounters in this study, and what does this mean for the research?*

The Transactional Model of Communication

To think practically about how intersubjectivity emerges, we can draw on understandings of communication. Early linear models depicted communication as a one-way flow from a sender to a passive receiver. In contrast, the transactional model of communication emphasises the dynamic nature of interpersonal interactions. Everyone holds multiple roles in a communicative exchange. In any moment of communication, you may be sending a message (such as speaking or singing) while also interpreting and receiving a message simultaneously as the other person makes eye contact, says "mmm," nods, or crosses their arms [13].

Listening is a dynamic process of creating meaning. It's not just about paying attention and absorbing another person's words or music; it's an intersubjective process [14]. The listening state is a social dance where each partner plays a crucial role, and neither of them can create it alone [15]. The listener brings commitment to be present and the speaker/vocaliser brings vulnerability, with both offerings influencing the other. Listening always anticipates dialogue and shapes future communication [16]. In dialogic listening, both parties are seen as co-constructors of knowledge [14, 17]. Listening reflects how dedicated a person is to jointly explore with the other [15].

Communication evolves over time (even at the start and end of a research interview, people will be communicating differently because they now know each other slightly better). Noise is also always present in interpersonal communication. This may be literal noise or metaphoric noise (like "buzzy" preconceived ideas). Each communicator brings a field of experience, and there are also shared experiences between the communicators. The transactional model also illustrates how communication takes place within systems that influence what is communicated and how meanings are formed. As we reflexively examine how we (researchers and participants) are making meaning through getting to know each other, these aspects of the transactional model of communication give us a model to think with [13].

Indigenous Perspectives

Willie Ermine et al. [18, p. 5] defined Indigenous Peoples as "the tribal peoples in independent countries whose distinctive identity, values, and history distinguishes them from other sections of the national community.

Indigenous Peoples are the descendants of the original or pre-colonial inhabitants of a territory or geographical area." Indigenous knowledge arises through the experiences of communities as they navigate the challenges of everyday life [19–21], and Indigenous Peoples' heritage includes complete knowledge systems, comprising epistemology, philosophy, and validity.

Indigenous knowledge is diverse [22], but falls within Indigenous paradigms that view knowledge as inherently relational and deeply connected to all aspects of creation, including the cosmos, animals, plants, and the earth [23]. Most Indigenous worldviews are grounded in a systems model. Knowledge in this paradigm is communal and found within networks of relationships [23, 24]. As Bagele Chilisa [25, p. 2] wrote, "I am known and communicate in relational terms that connect me to all my relations, living and the non-living." In his book *Ideas to postpone the end of the world*, Ailton Krenak [26, p. 8]—an Indigenous writer and activist in Brazil—wrote, "...For a long time, we were fed the story that we, humanity, stand apart from the great big organism of Earth, and we began to think of ourselves as one thing, and Earth, another: humankind versus Earth. We have to abandon our anthropocentrism." Indigenous research holds responsibility not just to human participants but to all relationships, encompassing the natural and spiritual realms. When research adopts this more holistic perspective, it centres collaboration and ethical interconnectedness, instead of being on a quest for personal advantage [23]. In Marlene Castellano's [24] paper on the Ethics of aboriginal research, she explained that when researchers seek objectivity by distancing themselves from what and whom they're studying, they violate the ethics of reciprocal relationship. We need to uphold relational accountability by establishing and nurturing respectful, mutually beneficial relationships [23].

Many types of methods can be used in this form of research (e.g., oral interviews, or observations [27]). Outside the context of music therapy, Eve Tuck and K. Wayne Yang [28] showed how storytelling in research with communities can reveal the roles of both listener and teller and how a narrative evolves in the connection between everyone involved. Martha Brown and Sherri Lallo [29] discussed the value of Talking Circles as a culturally responsive practice. The circle itself is seen as sacred because it represents the interconnectedness of all things [30]. People are invited to share their thoughts and stories in safe contexts. While Talking Circles and focus groups are similar in some ways, there's often a deeper relational and dialogic dynamic in Circles. The structure is more egalitarian and the purpose explicitly includes relationship building and even healing, not just data generation [29]. Time is more open-ended than it usually is in focus groups and storytelling typically plays a central role [23, 31].

Assemblages

Simon Gilbertson [32, p. 488] argued that the dominant theoretical discourse that underpins our understanding of the use of music in or as therapy

> is reliant, at least to some extent, on the presumption of a person-world separation. By comparison, contemporary research studies into multiple constitutions of human life within and outside health care have focused on the embodied, situated, and inseparable facets of life in which humans and other living and non-living beings and materials, processes, and stories intertwine…These emerging approaches offer an alternative stance through which music therapy as a practice can be considered from a person of the world meta-perspective. Here, intertwining is not preferential, it is an ontological imperative.

In the relational ontology that underpins this chapter, living beings are part of ongoing, dynamic relationships with their environment and objects within it. This is interobjectivity, which I briefly mentioned in Chap. 1. Gary Ansdell [33] argued that it's more helpful to replace the narrower concept of "musical communication" with a broader idea of "musical relationship," which involves following the natural expansion of a phenomenon within its ecosystem and creatively linking musical individuals, objects, and contexts. Every musical event can be viewed as a complex ecology that involves the interaction of musical tone relationships, relationships between people and situational relationships between sounds/tones, individuals, and groups, as well as the physical environment and the social and cultural meanings it carries [34]. Meaning arises through all these relationships. In Michael Viega's [35] *Evaluation for arts-based research performance*, he wrote that he identifies as a music-centred music therapist and that he sees the experiences, relationships, and rituals that take place in music therapy as analogous to human growth. Therefore, knowledge is intrinsically revealed through the aesthetics and experience of performance and in the relationship between himself as the performer and the audience. In *Entering the Ambient*, Viega et al. [36] discussed how technology can also be a co-agent in the therapeutic interaction. Karette Stensæth [37] presented a meta-theoretical framework for collaboratively developing interactive digital musical media with the family of a child with disabilities. She highlighted that non-human entities, such as music technology, possess agency by enabling change and transformation through a sequence of actions. This is particularly evident in generative music technology, which functions as an improviser with its own agency and collaborates with participants as a co-creator. As mentioned in Chaps. 1 and 2, we can explore how artificial intelligence is playing a role in interobjectivity too, how this is and will be shaping our research, and the importance of reflexivity in this regard [22].

Elizabeth St. Pierre [38] argued that if we let go of the idea of a discrete humanist self, we need to reevaluate qualitative methods. Relational Reflexivity invites researchers to engage in "orienting to assembling" [39, p. 377]. Gilles Deleuze and Félix Guattari [40] introduced the idea of "agencement," a French word that encompasses a variety of meanings, such as combining, arranging, ordering, and assembling. A single English translation falls short, but the term is often rendered as "assemblage," which can be understood as both a verb and a noun [41]. However, attempting to define what an assemblage "is" isn't quite appropriate because the concept signifies an ongoing process of becoming [42]. We can't tie it down. We can think about an assemblage as a "web-in-motion" [43]. What is significant is the dynamics that emerge among the parts of an assemblage [44], although each element transforms through its relationships with others, which makes labelling them as "constituent parts" also somewhat illogical [45]. (This is an important distinction between assemblages and systems.) Assemblages represent "a temporary grouping of relations" [46, p. 9] that continuously shift and evolve as an uncertain, unfolding, and tentative process. Research assemblages consist of the bodies, objects, and concepts involved in an inquiry, including the events being studied and the researchers who are taking part [46, 47]. Assemblages produce effects, inviting us to ask: What do these relationships do? What is emerging from this assemblage? Research assemblages generate knowledge. We can also be part of creating new assemblages (ones that are more generative, healthier, and more helpful) [48].

Assemblages consist of various other assemblages, and the processes of connecting and disconnecting define which ones are active at any moment. For example, research questions define what is studied. Interviews elicit accounts relevant to the research question and privilege human interpretations of events. Experiments test affects in a controlled setting and impose limits on the affects that can and can't enter the assemblage. Statistical analysis imposes statistical models onto data; thematic analysis imposes the researcher's categories. Writing up and disseminating research uses the affective flows of the research assemblage to affect audiences. Peer review incorporates the value of the research community into the study assemblage [49].

As we think about our own studies, we could ask ourselves questions such as these:

- How are our research questions themselves products of particular assemblages of knowledge, institutions, and relationships?
- Rather than seeing your data as something separate that you collect and analyse, how do you and your data influence each other?
- How do different research settings (e.g., formal interviews vs. casual conversations, individual vs. group discussions) shape what participants feel able to share?
- Are there ways in which the research process itself (e.g., ethical guidelines, methodologies, power structures) limits or expands what participants and researchers can become in this space?
- Whose perspectives are your research methods good at capturing? Who or what might they be missing?
- Which voices, perspectives, or experiences are becoming more central in this study?
- Are there inconsistencies or contradictions in the data that might point to something being left unsaid or obscured?
- How might the technology you use (like recording equipment, analysis software, or AI tools) be actively shaping what information you gather and how you interpret it?
- Think of a time when your research took an unexpected turn. Instead of seeing this as a problem to fix, how might embracing this uncertainty lead to new insights?
- Beyond your formal research outcomes, what other effects is your research having? On participants? On you? On your institution or community?

In Claire Flower's [50] thesis on music therapy with children and parents, she used anthropologist Ingold's idea of "meshwork," which closely overlaps with the notion of assemblages [51]. Tim Ingold [52] highlighted the dynamic interdependence and mutual influence between human beings and their environments. There are other examples in music therapy studies where—even if the researcher doesn't use the terminology of "assemblage"—we see some similar thinking, at least in parts of the study. For example, in a performative collaborative autoethnography by Viega et al. [36, p. 24], where the authors took part in improvising with digital music technologies, Josh Millrod, one of the authors stated,

> I came to realise that the point of this research was the meeting in the spaces created by these tools. I experienced deep states of togetherness, loss of boundary between myself and others, fear of the non-human, birth and death, swirling chaos and cathartic swells of sound that engulfed the group.

Simon Gilbertson [32] wrote a paper called *In visible hands: The matter and making of music therapy*. Six music therapists were asked to recreate a hand position from their memory of a pivotal therapy moment. In one-on-one research meetings, they discussed their reflections on this moment while Gilbertson created a body cast of their selected hand gesture. He noted how his study emphasised how matter, creativity, and storytelling in music therapy are inseparable and multiple. The data analysis process was adaptive and evolving. Gilbertson referred to Radman [53], who argued that the dynamics of materiality intertwine in a state of interobjectivity where intention and affordance become indistinct. Gilbertson's study explored whether there are other narratives—both visible and invisible, silenced, or yet unheard—about the interconnected ways a music therapist and their environment are intricately linked, as expressed through the body.

There are flows of energy—affects—that occur within assemblages [54, 55]. We can understand "affects" in more than one way. They can be thought of as a kind of sensation or intensity (atmosphere; "vibes"; surges in vitality affects; feeling moved). The term can also describe how we affect and are affected by events [43]. By saying we are affected, we're aware of some kind of change in our state or capacity [56]—psychologically, emotionally, mentally, physically, or socially [57].

Within an assemblage, affects can be free-flowing or trapped. Energy can intensify, heat up, or cool down and dissipate. Jette Kofoed and Jessica Ringrose [58, p. 10] introduced the concept of "sticky affects," which refers to force relations that temporarily fix or attach certain affects to specific bodies. There can become a sticky "point of fixation" and processes that "put people in their place" (e.g., "scratchy" resentment that's hard to shift; or becoming identified as "the resistant participant"). We have the ability to map and analyse affect intensities and how they flow (or get stuck) in assemblages [59].

In relation to a research study, we could explore questions like these:

- What affects are circulating in these research encounters, and how do they move between myself, participants, materials, and spaces? (Is there tension, excitement, or anxiety in the room during interviews? Is there a feeling of hesitation when certain topics come up? Does energy seem to build or diminish around particular discussions?)
- If a participant becomes uncomfortable, do I notice myself mirroring that discomfort?
- When someone shares an emotional story, does that feeling spread to others present? How so? Do I notice myself or participants getting "caught up" emotionally in particular stories or ideas?
- Are there research interactions where participants seem to feel more free to explore, express, or question things? What makes these moments possible?
- Are there times when certain conversations or ways of thinking feel shut down, uncomfortable, or "off-limits"? Why might that be?
- Are there institutional or power dynamics that make certain topics emotionally charged?
- When do participants repeatedly return to certain topics, even when the conversation has moved on?
- What personal experiences might be making these points sticky for participants?
- How do my own emotional responses participate in shaping the research?

Methodological Considerations in Research Assemblages

New researchers are often taught that their designs and methods should follow a clear, logical path, facilitating their reader's ability to locate and confirm validity and rigour. Some researchers might then feel pressured to conform to the "correct" procedures. In tightly controlled research methodologies or settings, being open to surprises and adjusting accordingly would be challenging or even unimaginable. However, in certain situations, neat designs do break down because of unexpected events, urgent decisions that need to be made, or unforeseen interactions. Surprises can bring opportunities to be more flexible and to step out of limiting boxes. Methodology is a journey, particularly when we're using qualitative methods. When we see the process as inherently fluid and complex this can enrich our perspectives (even if it feels a bit scary and less under our control). Instead of depicting a fixed, linear plan, we can visualise our unfolding decisions on a map that shows how we're exploring in various directions. This isn't just a map that we draw to show what we've done, it's a map that we live in action. It develops through our interactions and we can share it with others for feedback along the way. (You can see an example of a map like this in [60] Koro-Ljungberg's book *Reconceptualising qualitative research.*)

In their article on how arts-based reflexivity can offer new knowing about humour in music therapy, Nicky Haire and Raymond MacDonald [61] invited music therapists to share their experiences within focus groups. During the analysis, Haire decided to engage in a group improvisation to play with the data, with others and in the presence of an audience in unpredictable ways so that a polyphony of meanings could open up. When we discussed the process in our interview, Nicky Haire described asking:

> How can I surprise myself? I'd done interview encounters and my own self-reflexivity, but a lot of my own improvisations were really representative. It's really difficult to surprise yourself. And that's what I was looking to do. I felt there was a link between surprise, improvisation and experiences of humour. So, the self-reflection was a bit like being caught in this spiral. I was trying to use music improvising to get myself out, to expand my frame, but I didn't quite make it. But it happened within the group performance, it really happened. I was filled with this sense of awe that people would do this thing. So

> there was this huge warmth. But then there was, there was surprise because…It's a completely unknown arena and in terms of finding out about humour, I learned so much from the audience's reactions to what we were doing and it taught me so much about my own perspective about the things that I thought were important. I was shaken in the improvised performance out of the earnestness I was beginning to feel studying humour. This thinking through the body with others was such a valuable and freeing experience. Sharing it with an audience allowed me to laugh at myself and learn more.

In Haire and MacDonald's [61, p. 10] study they explained how, as well as affording possibilities for surprise by "throwing everything up in the air," this co-operative experience also surfaced new knowing about the performativity of humour and the significance of this in relation to perceptions of a professional music therapy identity, as well as offering an innovative and differently embodied way to share the process and findings.

I asked Simon Gilbertson how working in the more flexible, unpredictable way he described might come at a cost professionally when it pushes against dominant approaches and pressures, especially within academia. He replied:

> There is a cost and the cost unfortunately is a loss. You have to pay through loss first. Can you bear being yourself without the power of the methodology? How many of us have ridden on the back of the fact that something is so widely accepted? Are you able to go somewhere where nobody else has gone before and design the ways to get there? You're being an outsider, you're writing in different tongues. We need to practise making safe spaces for people to tell things differently. For me, that's the reflexivity key. I mean, our students, they go through many, many years before they get to write a project, a proposal for the Masters. How many of those are choosing the method and the topic because they think it's safe?

Connecting to Other Literature

In writing this book, my thinking has taken shape differently within each chapter as I've "plugged into" different bodies of knowledge. Meanings of reflexivity become differently as they entangle in different knowledge assemblages. As we grow our studies out of and in connection with different bodies of literature (and conversations, world events, and life experiences…) this is a dynamic process that generates unique meaning.

If we plug a study into a literature assemblage (as opposed to another, different literature assemblage), what does this do? Let's look at a few examples. In Kaja Enge and Brynjulf Stige's [62] paper on children's use of music therapy when they are refugees, they plug into Community Music Therapy literature, which offers ecological and social perspectives on how music therapy can promote health in everyday life. In a paper on the role and impact of group songwriting with multiple stakeholders in recovery-oriented mental health services, Tríona McCaffrey et al. [63] used literature that critiques the alignment of modern health services with a medical model of practice, showing how this poses a fundamental challenge to embracing recovery. They then referred to research indicating that the key to effective operational transformation in recovery-oriented mental health services lies in building meaningful, respectful, and equitable relationships among various stakeholders, including service users, providers, and caregivers. This philosophy is promoted by the principle of "co-production," which is fundamental to the implementation of recovery-oriented services. Linking this to their music therapy approach, they plug into literature that works to show how songwriting can foster meaningful co-construction of knowledge.

Emerging Questions

Research questions take shape through the interplay of human and non-human forces (e.g., theoretical frameworks, methodologies, institutional pressures, funding structures, researcher positionality, data itself, and ethical constraints). Instead of assuming a fixed hierarchy where theory drives questions, or questions drive data collection, we can consider how different elements co-compose each other. Because assemblages are inherently open-ended and shifting, the initial research question might fragment, morph, or multiply as the study progresses. We can also think about how our research questions themselves are as active participants that call particular kinds of interactions and data into being.

In Viega and colleagues' [34] study *Entering the ambient*, they described how multiple strands converged to produce their research questions, including music therapists' growing experiences of technology during the Covid-19 pandemic; their awareness of how non-human objects like music technology can have agency; how people's relationships with music technologies are entangled in collective and cultural histories relevant to therapeutic rapport; and how ambient listening provides an approach to help therapists become reflexive about the multidimensional use of music technology in music therapy. Through the intermingling of these ideas, their main research question emerged as: What is our collective experience of entering the ambient in group digital improvisation experiences?

You may want to ask:

- What are the various elements (theoretical, practical, institutional, material) that are converging to shape my/our research questions? How are the questions situated within the broader ecology of forces that shaped its emergence? How can I/we map these elements and forces?
- Can I/we identify moments of rupture and reconfiguration (points where the question shifted or became significant in a new way due to interactions within the assemblage)?

An Evolving Design

As mentioned above, the design of studies that embrace research-as-assemblage tend to be more fluid. We don't have many examples from music therapy research that explicitly use this language, although there are a fair number that acknowledge how meaning-making emerges in relational ways. The studies that lean in this direction and those that have explicitly embraced these theoretical tools have often incorporated the arts, which is understandable given how arts-based methods can play with messiness, invite non-linear explorations, evoke interconnections, and resist overly neat and tidy conclusions. When qualitative researchers (using any methods) add creative and artistic exploration into their academic work, they may find themselves more at ease with uncertainty and incomplete thoughts and practices [60].

As mentioned earlier, Viega et al. [36] presented their research as a collaborative autoethnography. Through dialogue they created shared meaning and incorporated diverse voices, ideas, and perspectives. They aimed to question prevalent assumptions about knowledge creation in research, particularly regarding how data are generated, analysed, and shared, using digital music improvisation as their central method. Tríona McCaffrey and Jane Edwards [64] described how arts-based research offers participants and researchers ways to creatively invent new ways to explore research questions and issues in the social world. Narrative research can also embrace how stories emerge through assemblages. Indigenous oral cultures specifically teach us about the entangled relationships between stories, listeners, and tellers [65].

Participants-and-Researchers

Our positions and positioning are always developing relationally. Luk Van Langenhove and Rom Harré's [66] Positioning Theory shifts the focus from an individual self to the practices of the researcher *and* participants as they co-form their identities and relationships. How am I actively positioning myself and being positioned in relation to you and this fluid context, even as you are positioning yourself and being positioned relative to me and this context? How does my positioning (and yours) shape what I (and you) can perceive or understand? As we negotiate interpersonal encounters, we take up positions within them. Social situations are shaped by storylines and the positions people take are linked to these storylines.

As Peta Malins [67, p. 85] noted, "A body's function or potential for meaning becomes completely dependent on the other bodies…it forms an assemblage with." As emotions flow through these connections, we enact our subjectivities [68] as becoming and emerging intra-actions [69]. In a paper I wrote about the usefulness of aggression as explored by becoming-teenagers in group music therapy [70], I described how the context where the study was conducted—an area called Eersterust ("first rest"), which is close to Pretoria in South Africa—is produced in relation to many different dynamic features. Rather than providing a direct, pure, or objective representation of reality, the description of a context also plays a role in shaping that reality. I described how my journey as a becoming-music therapist/researcher evolved through my interactions with the teenagers who were part of this study. The intersectionality of my Whiteness, identification as female, higher socioeconomic status, life in suburban Johannesburg, educational background, and musical identity was intertwined with and took shape in relation to the teenagers' gender identification, lower socioeconomic status, residence in Eersterust, limited opportunities for further education, their musical identities, and their racial identity as "Coloured." (This is a term used in South Africa as an official classification category for people with mixed racial heritage [71]. It's used to self-identify [72], and is "made into a socially relevant category" [73, p., i] in people's lives. The term is fluctuating, complex and contested.)

In Katarina Lindblad's [1] paper on communication patterns in a music listening group with older men, she explained how, as a participant in the group, she was influencing evolution of the group process. Some of the participants knew of her through her previous professional role as a classical music radio presenter and were curious to learn more about music. This shaped the way they constructed her as a music expert, rather than as a therapist. As she answered their questions about music, she also unintentionally reinforced this construction. At the end of the process, the participants highlighted how much they valued developing their knowledge.

We can explore questions such as:

- How do participants respond to me, and what assumptions do they seem to make about my role, authority, or background?
- In what ways do I feel recognised, resisted, or reinterpreted by participants and the research context?
- How do my own expectations about my role (e.g., expert, listener, facilitator, co-learner) align with or differ from how others perceive me?
- How do participants present themselves in relation to me and the research?
- Are there ways in which my reactions—verbal, nonverbal, or emotional—affect what participants choose to share?
- How do participants' expectations of me as a researcher influence what they highlight or downplay?
- Are there moments where participants challenge or reshape the roles expected of them in the research process?
- How does the research context (institutional, cultural, methodological) influence how participants are seen, heard, or expected to act?
- How does the research open up possibilities for participants or researchers to take up different positions?

Data Entanglements

If our quest was to discover some T/truth about a certain topic, we would seek to gather data that contained and revealed the already-existing nature of this topic. Our quest here is different: we want to explore and share unfolding meaning about a topic, knowing that meaning emerges relationally. It's in the interactions between us as researchers, the participants, the space, the music, methods, ideas and so on (and so on…) that knowledge comes into being. To describe this process would entail showing how human and non-human elements intra-act to generate meaning in a particular context.

We see some nods to this in music therapy literature. Laura Beer [74] wrote about including music in arts-based music therapy research, mentioning how revelations came about as she and the participants either listened to or spoke about music together. In their study on humour in music therapy with dementia patients, Haire and MacDonald [61] used video clips to stimulate discussion in a more improvisatory atmosphere. In Anna Helle-Valle and colleagues' [75] study on boys' restlessness they engaged in reflexivity in relation to co-construction of behaviour during music therapy, but also in terms of how processes of observation were co-constructed. During the project, the music therapy students, the primary investigator, the music therapists, the educational leaders, the children, and towards the end, the parents, exchanged perspectives on how the unfolding process could be understood. For Kari Batt-Rawden et al. [76]—in their study on music listening and empowerment in health promotion—the data (gathered through interviews) was seen as the collaborative result of researcher-participant dialogues.

In their study on co-creating space for attunement dynamics between an autistic child and a non-autistic music therapist, Karin Mössler et al. [77] conducted an interview with a music therapist (Iris) who had worked with an autistic boy (Aram) as well as focus groups with parents of autistic children and colleagues related to the field of music therapy, using a video excerpt vignette showing Iris and Aram interacting. In their focus groups, they wanted to create joint meaning-making processes. The authors explained how they sought to understand how ecologies are co-created by interacting partners. Mössler et al. [77, p. 327] described how they aimed "to stay with the data by arranging and re-arranging them in several ways." They moved the data around, drew coloured sketches of a vignette, and created fictional dialogues between the music therapist and the focus group members. They didn't finalise and extract definite codes, but used an embodied "becoming analysis" [78, p. 327] "to form an understanding of the material in a hermeneutic spiral, moving back and forth between details and the whole of data collection." They explained how drawing on multiple role-players' perspectives of the video vignette created "understanding grounded in an acknowledgement of the partiality and positionality of all knowing" [78, p. 327].

It can be valuable to reconsider our relationship with data, imagining what possibilities could emerge if we loosened some control. What does the data want? What does it want to become? How do data interact with us? How does our role as researcher-knower restrict and bind us, the data and the analysis? What potential transformations could occur if we redirect our attention from manipulating or analysing data to understanding how data emerges through all the relational entanglements of the study and influences us? [60]

In your own research, you could (re)consider approaching your data with curiosity instead of certainty by exploring the following:

- Think of a moment when something unexpected emerged during your research. What constellation of elements (people, materials, ideas, spaces) came together to make this possible?
- If your data could speak directly to you, what might it be trying to tell you that you haven't heard yet?
- What non-human elements (instruments, room arrangements, weather, etc.) have played significant roles in shaping your research encounters?
- How do your recording methods (audio, video, notes) not just capture but actively shape what emerges as data?
- When did timing and rhythm (of sessions, of research phases, of conversations) create particular possibilities for what could emerge?
- In what ways have institutional contexts and constraints (time limits, ethical frameworks, expectations) participated in determining what could happen?

(*continued*)

(**continued**)

- Think about a moment when your understanding of your research topic shifted significantly. What relationships or interactions were happening at that moment?
- How has your relationship with participants evolved throughout the research process? How has this changing relationship affected what data emerged?
- How have moments of resonance or dissonance between you and participants created particular kinds of knowledge?
- What happens when you imagine your data as having its own agency or desires? What might it want to become?
- When have you felt resistance from your data? What might this resistance be telling you about your assumptions or approach?
- How do different pieces of your data interact with each other when you bring them into conversation? What new meanings emerge from these interactions?
- When have you felt most deeply connected to or moved by your data? What was happening in that moment of connection?
- How have you changed or been transformed through your interactions with the data? What aspects of yourself have been revealed or developed?

Engaging in supervision, mentorship and teaching is also part of the meaning-making assemblage. In my interview with Simon Gilbertson, we explored how he creates and uses spaces and materials for students to think in/with/through. His supervision room contains diverse objects—furniture, tools, art materials—that "introduce difference just by way of being there." He repurposed a large canteen table where students can spread out their texts and materials, inviting them into a space inhabited differently with different things and objects. In his improvisation classes, Gilbertson invites his students to build a full-scale mock music therapy room using coloured masking tape on the floor and relevant furniture pieces. The process spans several weeks and evokes critical discussions about spatial design considerations. (What chairs should be at the piano? Do we need four walls?) Problem-solving scenarios are navigated, like enlarging doorways to accommodate pianos. This also leads to deeper conversations about inclusion, such as providing space for wheelchairs or additional chairs for parents/carers and considering their appropriate positioning within the therapeutic space. Gilbertson also introduces recording equipment progressively, from single microphones to multi-camera systems, encouraging students to examine what different recording methods reveal or conceal. Who do we see and hear, and who do we not?

Trustworthiness in a Study Employing Relational Reflexivity

If we were on a research quest to identify an external truth or stable reality we may use triangulation, for example. We might employ different methods in the hope that if they lead to the same conclusion, then this finding is more likely to be true. In our current quest where we see reality as multiple and fluid, we need different tools. Donna Haraway [79] and Karen Barad [80] proposed diffraction as an alternative to triangulation. The term comes from physics, where diffraction occurs when waves (like light or water) encounter an obstacle and bend around it, creating patterns of interference. In research, using the idea of diffraction means that we look for how knowledge emerges from the interaction of different perspectives. We embrace differences rather than trying to resolve them into a single truth. In this kind of research, we also need to explore how we're remaining open and accountable to the ongoing, unfinished nature of the assemblage beyond the formal end of the study.

In a study using Relational Reflexivity, we can think about trustworthiness in terms of how the research responsively attends to and tracks that ways that meaning comes about through relational processes. Are we showing how we've remained open to shifts, contradictions, and emergent ideas and practices? Also, instead of seeking stability (an accurate, valid, reliable final answer), trustworthy research in an assemblage could be judged by its generativity. Does it provoke new questions? Does it welcome multiple interpretations and acknowledge its own incompleteness? What new questions, connections, or possibilities does the research generate? Trustworthiness here is not just about what we've personally accomplished as a researcher. We need to be alert to all sorts of entanglements. Who or what is shaping the research? Whose voices are amplified or marginalised, and how does power operate in these networks? How are we attending to the ethical implications of the entanglements within this research? How is meaning-making ongoing…?

An Accessible Summary

Relational Reflexivity views meaning as something that emerges through the dynamic relationships and interactions that occur during the research process itself. Rather than carrying a "backpack of meaning" into a study, researchers using this approach understand that they become who they are through their relationships with participants, who are simultaneously becoming who they are through these same interactions.

A range of relational perspectives from Indigenous and Western contexts can inform this way of working. The concept of assemblages provides a helpful framework for understanding how research operates relationally. Rather than viewing studies as linear processes controlled by researchers, assemblages recognise research as involving dynamic networks of human and non-human elements, including participants, research questions, spaces, technologies, musical instruments, and institutional pressures. These elements transform each other continuously.

This approach gladly embraces methodological uncertainty and flexibility. For example, researchers might find that their initial questions fragment or change as the study progresses. This is not a problem; it's an opportunity for new insights. Data is also understood as emerging through the entanglements and relationships within the study. Researchers might ask what the data wants to become or how it interacts with them. Analysis involves ongoing meaning-making processes rather than extraction of predetermined truths. Arts-based methods work well here because they can accommodate messiness, non-linear explorations, and they resist overly neat conclusions.

Trustworthiness in this approach shifts away from traditional concepts like triangulation towards ideas like diffraction, which embraces differences between perspectives rather than trying to resolve them into a single truth. The quality of research is judged by its generative capacity to provoke new questions, welcome multiple interpretations, and acknowledge its own incompleteness. This type of reflexivity invites researchers to stay open to changes, contradictions, and new possibilities as their work unfolds. Meaning-making even continues beyond the formal end of the study.

References

1. Lindblad K. "No, I Guess it's kind of Sensitive"—Communication patterns in a music listening group with older men. Nord J Music Ther. 2021;30(5):424–39.
2. Beavan K. Breaking with the masculine reckoning: an open letter to the Critical Management Studies Academy. In: Pullen A, Helin J, Harding N, editors. Writing Differently (Dialogues in Critical Management Studies, vol 4). Bingley: Emerald Publishing Limited; 2020. p. 91–112.
3. Oliver K. Witnessing: beyond recognition. Minneapolis, MN: University of Minnesota Press; 2001.
4. Groven K, Engelsrud G. Allowing one's own bodily experience to "count": elaborating on inter-subjectivity and subjectivity in phenomenological studies. J Educ Res. 2013;3(1):24–40.
5. Granek L. Putting ourselves on the line: the epistemology of the hyphen, intersubjectivity and social responsibility in qualitative research. Int J Qual Stud Educ. 2013;26(2):178–97.
6. Husserl E. Ideas pertaining to a pure phenomenology and to a phenomenological philosophy, second book: studies in the phenomenology of constitution. Rojcewicz R, Schuwer A, translators. Dordrecht: Kluwer; 1989.
7. Beebe B, Rustin J, Sorter D, Knoblauch S. An Expanded View of Intersubjectivity in Infancy and its Application to Psychoanalysis. Psychoanal Dialogues. 2003;13(6):805–41.
8. Zlatev J. The co-evolution of intersubjectivity and bodily mimesis. In: Zlatev J, Racine TP, Sinha C, Itkonen E, editors. The shared mind: perspectives on intersubjectivity. Amsterdam: John Benjamins Publishing Company; 2008. p. 215–44.
9. De Jaegher H, Di Paolo E. Participatory sense-making: an enactive approach to social cognition. Phenomenol Cogn Sci. 2007;6:485–507.
10. Buirski P, Haglund P. Making sense together. Northvale, NJ: Jason Aronson; 2001.
11. Clarke S, Hoggett P, editors. Researching beneath the surface. London: Karnac; 2009.
12. Hunt J. Psychoanalytic aspects of fieldwork. London: Sage; 1989.
13. Wood J. Interpersonal communication. Boston: Cengage; 2016.
14. Shotter J. Listening in a way that recognizes/realizes the world of 'the other'. Int J Listen. 2009;23(1):21–43.
15. Kluger AN, Mizrahi M. Defining listening: can we get rid of the adjectives? Curr Opin Psychol. 2023;52:101639.
16. Bakhtin MM. Speech genres and other late essays. McGee VW, translator. Emerson C, Holquist M, editors. Austin: University of Texas Press; 1986.
17. Helin J. Dialogic listening: toward an embodied understanding of how to "go on" during fieldwork. Qual Res Organ Manag. 2013;8(3):224–41.

18. Ermine W, Sinclair R, Browne M. Kwayask Itotamowin: Indigenous Research Ethics—Report of the Indigenous Peoples' Health Research Centre to the Institute of Aboriginal Peoples' Health and the Canadian Institutes of Health Research [Internet]. Regina: Indigenous Peoples' Health Research Centre; 2005 Mar [cited 2024 Mar 21]. Available from: http://iphrc.ca/assets/Documents/IPHRC_ACADRE_Ethics_Report_final.pdf.
19. Matsika C. Traditional African education: its significance to current education practices with special reference to Zimbabwe. Gweru: Mambo Press; 2012.
20. Warren MD, Slikkerveer LJ, Brokensha D, editors. The cultural dimension of development: indigenous knowledge systems. London: Intermediate Technology Publications; 1995.
21. Khumalo NB, Baloyi C. African Indigenous knowledge: an underutilised and neglected resource for development. Libr Philos Pract [Internet]. 2017 [cited 2024 Mar 21];1663;1–15. Available from: https://digitalcommons.unl.edu/libphilprac/1663/.
22. Battiste M, Youngblood HJ. Protecting indigenous knowledge and heritage: a global challenge. Saskatoon, SK: Purich Publishing Ltd; 2000.
23. Wilson S. Research is ceremony: indigenous research methods. Halifax: Fernwood Publishing; 2008.
24. Brant CM. Ethics of aboriginal research. J Aborig Health. 2004;1(1):98–114.
25. Chilisa B. Indigenous research methodologies. 2nd ed. Thousand Oaks: Sage Publications; 2020.
26. Krenak A. Ideas to postpone the end of the world. Toronto: Anansi International; 2020.
27. Lebaka MEK. Ethnographic Research of the use of Music in Healing as a Cultural Phenomenon in Greater Sekhukhune District Municipality, Limpopo Province in South Africa. Dialogo. 2020;7(2):60–6.
28. Tuck E, Yang KW. Applying Indigenous research methods: storying with peoples and communities. In: Windchief S, San Pedro T, editors. Indigenous Research Methods. New York: Routledge; 2019.
29. Brown MA, Lallo SD. Talking circles: a culturally responsive evaluation practice. Am J Eval. 2020;20(10):1–17. https://doi.org/10.1177/1098214019899164
30. Running Wolf P, Rickard JA. Talking circles: a Native American approach to experiential learning. J Multicult Couns Dev. 2003;31(1):39–43.
31. Pranis K, Stuart B, Wedge M. Peacemaking circles: from conflict to community. St. Paul, MN: Living Justice Press; 2003.
32. Gilbertson S. In visible hands: the matter and making of music therapy. J Music Ther. 2015;52(4):487–514.
33. Ansdell G. How music helps in music therapy and everyday life. Farnham: Ashgate; 2014.

34. Ansdell A. Yes, but, No, but: a contrarian response to Cross. Psychol Music. 2014;42(6):820–5.
35. Viega M. Evaluation for arts-based research performance: audience perceptions of rising from the ashes. J Music Ther. 2022;59(1):62–86.
36. Viega M, Druziako V, Millrod J, Hoberman A. Entering the ambient: a performative collaborative autoethnography of music therapists' improvising with digital music technologies. Voices. 2023;23(1).
37. Stensæth K. Music therapy and interactive musical media in the future: reflections on the subject-object interaction. Nord J Music Ther. 2018;27(4):312–27.
38. St. Pierre EA. Post qualitative research: the critique and the coming after. In: Denzin NK, Lincoln YS, editors. The SAGE handbook of qualitative inquiry. 4th ed. Los Angeles, CA: Sage; 2011. p. 611–35.
39. McLeod K. Orientating to assembling: qualitative inquiry for more-than-human worlds. Int J Qual Methods. 2014;13(1):377–94.
40. Deleuze G, Guattari F. A thousand plateaus: capitalism and schizophrenia. London: Athlone; 1987.
41. Law J. After method: mess in social science research. London: Routledge; 2004.
42. Lancione M. Homeless people and the city of abstract machines: assemblage thinking and the performative approach to homelessness. Area. 2013;45(3):358–64.
43. Dos Santos A. Empathy Pathways. Cham: Palgrave Macmillan; 2022.
44. Deleuze G, Parnet C. Dialogues. London: Athlone; 1987.
45. McPhie J. Mental health and wellbeing in the Anthropocene: a posthuman inquiry. Cham: Palgrave Macmillan; 2019.
46. Coleman R, Ringrose J. Introduction: deleuze and research methodologies. In: Coleman R, Ringrose J, editors. Deleuze and Research Methodologies. Edinburgh: Edinburgh University Press; 2013. p. 1–22.
47. Fox NJ, Alldred P. The sexuality-assemblage: desire, affect, anti-humanism. Sociol Rev. 2013;61(4):769–89.
48. Russell B, Pusey A, Chatterton P. What can an assemblage do? Seven propositions for a more strategic and politicized assemblage thinking. City. 2011;15(5):577–83.
49. Fox NJ, Alldred P. New materialist social inquiry: designs, methods and the research-assemblage. Int J Soc Res Methodol. 2015;18(4):399–414.
50. Flower C. Music therapy with children and parents: toward an ecological attitude [dissertation]. London: Goldsmiths, University of London; 2019.
51. Rival L. The materiality of life: revisiting the anthropology of nature in Amazonia. In: Harvey G, editor. The handbook of contemporary animism. Oxon: Routledge; 2014. p. 92–100.
52. Ingold T. The textility of making. Camb J Econ. 2010;34(1):91–102.

53. Radman Z. On displacement of agency: the mind handmade. In: Radman Z, editor. The hand, an organ of the mind: what the manual tells the mental. London: MIT Press; 2013. p. 369–98.
54. Dewsbury JD. Performative, non-representational, and affect-based research: seven injunctions. In: DeLyser D, Herbert S, Aitken S, Crang M, McDowell L, editors. The SAGE Handbook of Qualitative Geography. Los Angeles, CA: Sage; 2010. p. 321–44.
55. Merchant S. The body and the senses: visual methods, videography and the submarine sensorium. Body Soc. 2011;17(1):53–72.
56. Martin AD. Affective reverberations: the methodological excesses of a research assemblage. In: Taylor CA, Ulmer J, editors. Decentering the researcher in intimate scholarship. Bingley: Emerald Publishing Limited; 2018. p. 9–23.
57. Fox NJ, Alldred P. New materialist social inquiry: designs, methods and the research-assemblage. Int J Soc Res Methodol. 2014;18(4):399–414.
58. Kofoed J, Ringrose J. Travelling and sticky affects: exploring teens and sexualized cyberbullying through a Butlerian-Deleuzian-Guattarian lens. Discourse. 2012;33(1):5–20.
59. Ringrose J, Renold E. "F**k rape!" Exploring affective intensities in a feminist research assemblage. Qual Inq. 2014;20(6):772–80.
60. Koro-Ljungberg M. Reconceptualizing Qualitative Research: methodologies without Methodology. Thousand Oaks, CA: Sage; 2016.
61. Haire N, MacDonald R. Thinking through improvisation: how arts-based reflexivity can offer new knowing about music therapists' experiences of humour in music therapy. Voices. 2021;21(2).
62. Enge KEA, Stige B. Musical pathways to the peer community: a collective case study of refugee children's use of music therapy. Nord J Music Ther. 2022;31(1):7–24.
63. McCaffrey T, Higgins P, Monahan C, Moloney S, Nelligan S, Clancy A, et al. Exploring the role and impact of group songwriting with multiple stakeholders in recovery-oriented mental health services. Nord J Music Ther. 2021;30(1):41–60.
64. McCaffrey T, Edwards J. Meeting art with art: arts-based methods enhance researcher reflexivity in research with mental health service users. J Music Ther. 2015;52(4):515–32.
65. Rice C, Cook K, Bailey KA. Difference-attuned witnessing: risks and potentialities of arts-based research. Fem Psychol. 2021;31(3):345–65.
66. van Langenhove L, Harré R. Introducing Positioning Theory. In: Harré R, van Langenhove L, editors. Positioning theory: moral contexts of intentional action. Oxford: Blackwell Publishers; 1999. p. 14–31.
67. Malins P. Machinic assemblages: deleuze, Guattari and an ethico-aesthetics of drug use. Janus Head. 2004;7(1):84–104.

68. Renold E, Mellor D. Deleuze and Guattari in the nursery: towards an ethnographic multi-sensory mapping of gendered bodies and becomings. In: Coleman R, Ringrose J, editors. Deleuze and research methodologies. Edinburgh: Edinburgh University Press; 2013. p. 23–41.
69. Mazzei L, Jackson A. Voice in the agentic assemblage. Educ Philos Theory. 2017;49(11):1090–8.
70. Dos Santos A. Empathy and aggression in group music therapy with teenagers: a descriptive phenomenological study. Music Ther Perspect. 2019;37(1):14–27.
71. Adhikari M. Not white enough, not black enough: racial identity in the South African coloured community. Athens, OH: Ohio University Press; 2005.
72. Tewolde AI. Self-identification in post-apartheid South Africa: the case of coloured people in Johannesburg, South Africa. Soc Sci Humanit Open. 2024;9:100866.
73. Nilsson S. Coloured by race: a study about the making of coloured identities in South Africa [thesis]. Uppsala: Uppsala University; 2016.
74. Beer LE. From embedded to embodied: including music in arts-based music therapy research. Music Ther Perspect. 2016;34(1):33–40.
75. Helle-Valle A, Binder PE, Anderssen N, Stige B. Is restlessness best understood as a process? Reflecting on four boys' restlessness during music therapy in kindergarten. Int J Qual Stud Health Well-being. 2017;12(sup1):1298266.
76. Batt-Rawden KB, DeNora T, Ruud E. Music listening and empowerment in health promotion: a study of the role and significance of music in everyday life of the long-term ill. Nord J Music Ther. 2005;14(2):120–36.
77. Mössler K, Halstead J, Metell M, Gottschewski K, Schmid W. "The room is a mess": exploring the co-creation of space for attunement dynamics between an autistic child and a non-autistic music therapist. Nord J Music Ther. 2023;1–21.
78. Ellingson LL. Embodiment in qualitative research. New York: Routledge; 2017.
79. Haraway D. Otherworldly conversations; terran topics; local terms. Sci Cult. 1992;3(1):64–98.
80. Barad K. Meeting the universe halfway: quantum physics and the entanglement of matter and meaning. Durham, NC: Duke University Press; 2007.

CHAPTER 9

Mixing and Clashing

What is reflexivity for? We can use Sentinel Reflexivity to show that our findings are close to the T/truth of what we're studying, which matters as we continue to seek to understand what music therapy accomplishes and how it can be most effective, as we continue to advocate for our profession, and seek funding opportunities. We can use Lens Reflexivity to show that we've been intellectually honest and made wise decisions, or Authorial Reflexivity to demonstrate humility, which matters as we acknowledge that our story is only one of many stories. We could engage in Empathic Reflexivity to care for and honour our participants and their experiences, or we can employ Restorative Reflexivity to advocate for and participate in advancing social justice. We become part of Relational Reflexivity as we decentre humans, embrace ecological thinking, and celebrate multiple, ever-evolving meanings. These are all worthy goals and they all have their place. Our task is to select our approach with purpose, thoughtfulness, and fine-tuned understanding so that we can accomplish these important goals well.

Most of the music therapy studies I reviewed for this book drew on more than one form of reflexivity. As I mentioned in Chap. 2, sometimes this was fruitful; sometimes, it was jarring; and sometimes, it birthed questions and opened up possibilities. Certain combinations create substantial friction. For example, if we try to use both Sentinel Reflexivity and Authorial Reflexivity, we'd be attempting to balance a claim that there's an

A. dos Santos, *Reflexive Research in Music Therapy*,
https://doi.org/10.1007/978-3-032-02033-8_9

objective reality that we can present to our readers *and* that we can only ever share our personal, subjective perspective. If we use Sentinel Reflexivity and Relational Reflexivity, we'd be trying to argue both for an objective, external reality that we can report on *and* that meaning always emerges through relationships. When trying to combine Authorial Reflexivity and Relational Reflexivity it would be hard to argue coherently that we only see through our own individual stories *and* that all meaning is generated relationally. Let's look at some examples of approaches that can be blended well.

Lens Reflexivity + Restorative Reflexivity

If we acknowledge that our own lenses cloud what we see and we work to become more aware of this and manage the implications of this well (Lens Reflexivity), we could pair this approach with reflexivity that serves a social justice agenda (Restorative Reflexivity). For example, researchers have acknowledged how their experiences and perspectives shape their research decisions while using a design that creates space for social critique and inclusion [1]. They have carefully reflected on the impact of their theoretical frame and preunderstandings while critiquing the production of knowledge and the power dimensions of meaning-making [2]. Researchers have created journal memos throughout a study to reflexively process their emerging themes, paying cautious attention to their presumptions, while critiquing the topic they're exploring and the language that has been previously used to describe the phenomenon and the problematic effects thereof [3]. Some have been transparent about how their previous experiences and knowledge impacted their findings and the steps they took to think through this, while emphasising participants' right to be heard and to be agents in the research process [4–6].

Some researchers have shown careful awareness of relationships between personal engagement, data processing and interpretation while explaining the decision to use a resource-oriented perspective [7] and purposefully describing participants in a non-pathologising manner [8]. Researchers have emphasised how they speak from their own positionality while highlighting the importance of using a critical lens grounded in healing justice and decolonial theory [9]. Authors have examined their positionality, lived experiences, feelings, motives and reactions and the impact of these, and, through this, showed how they became more aware of their privilege, working to avoid cultural appropriation and embrace cultural humility

[10]. Some worked on revisiting and questioning existing theories they used in previous studies, engaging in crystallisation to look through different theoretical lenses, and examining the influence of their clinical experience, while acknowledging how their choices support or destabilise the status quo [11].

Lens Reflexivity + Empathic Reflexivity

As we seek to empathically attune to participants, we need to be aware of our own emotions and perspectives so that we can be alert to potential projections or emotional contagion. Blending tools from Lens Reflexivity and Empathic Reflexivity can serve us well as we do this. Some researchers showed how their goal was to lean into their participants' lived experiences while recognising that other researchers may have viewed the data differently because their subjectivity and background shaped the design and outcomes [12]. Others highlighted how arts-based research can afford rich and versatile ways to access participants' experiences but that meaning-making will always be influenced by the researcher's own past experiences and preunderstandings [13]. Some researchers explained how their research interests and questions emerged from their clinical work, and how dialogue with participants in the study led to understanding their experiences better [14]. Others showed how their positioning informed their research choices and meaning-making, and how the participants could connect with the authors due to similar positioning, thereby leading to more open sharing [15].

Restorative Reflexivity + Empathic Reflexivity

In Restorative Reflexivity, we deliberately acknowledge and explore how we are active participants in the creation/shaping of knowledge in our study as we seek to promote greater social justice and respond to these insights by continuously critiquing power relations and acting in the best service of others. Empathy can be helpful in this regard if used carefully and with critical thinking so as not to reinforce problematic power relations ("I am the empathiser and you are the one receiving my generous service") or assume sameness where there is in fact valuable, and glorious difference. Researchers have critiqued the lack of first-hand accounts of service users in the literature—and the silencing that this perpetuates. This has prompted decisions to focus on service users' views and more socially just orientations in the context of a study where the researcher is also the music therapist, lowering the stress levels of participants, and enabling a deeper understanding of their experiences and context, for example using interpretive phenomenological analysis to lean into the participant's psychological world [16]. Other researchers have used collaborative studies to engage in participant-centred processes, seeing participants as co-researchers and including arts-based processes that afford creative expression to afford deeper understanding [17].

Lens Reflexivity + Restorative Reflexivity + Empathic Reflexivity

We can acknowledge, reflect on and work with the impact of our own preconceived ideas, use this to better empathise with others, while serving an overarching goal of researching in a more socially just way. Examples of this integration of three approaches can be found in studies where the researcher explains how a dual role can be helpful in gaining empathic understanding of participants, while critiquing pathologising approaches and working collaboratively, and critically reflecting on their interpretations and how meaning is shaped through the application of theoretical perspectives [18]. Some researchers used musicking in interviews to enhance empathic understanding and for the interviews to offer a sense of support and safety. They also explained how reflexive thematic analysis required examination of their own lenses and stance while they respected the participants as experts of their own experience [19]. Researchers have described their positioning and acknowledged how they played an active role in the entire study as the researcher. At the same time, they were involved in musicking with participants and engaged in interviews with a quality of mutuality, humour and warmth, which enabled rich sharing, participants feeling heard and valued, and room for voices that tend to be silenced [20].

Restorative Reflexivity + Relational Reflexivity

As we seek to work in socially just ways, more research needs to loosen the shackles of Western prescriptions of what counts as valuable research. Embracing relational perspectives offer (and have offered for centuries) ways of doing just that. One can critique pathologising perspectives on human experiences and behaviours, and look at how that concept can be relationally entangled in other perspectives to create new knowledge, also exploring intersections between encounters with participants and researchers, as well as other role players, and the meanings that emerge [21]. Some researchers have explored the circumstances through which certain dynamics and meanings emerge and how ecologies of human and other-than-human elements are co-constituted, how an analysis process can form new understandings, and the purpose of this can be to trouble existing potentially unjust pathologising perspectives [22]. A study can view participants as co-researchers, seeing how meaning is co-constructed as part of deconstructing more expert-driven models, while also valuing emergent and embodied knowledge that is generated in specific contexts [23].

Now That We See the Map More Clearly...

The broad definition of reflexivity that I worked with in this book was that it entails researchers deliberately acknowledging and exploring how they are (or have the potential to be) active role players in the creation/shaping of knowledge in their studies—and beyond—and how they might respond or be shaped in return. I mentioned in Chap. 2 that I included the words "and beyond" because I noticed in the conversations I had with researchers that these matters extend beyond the bounds of a singular study, or even beyond the bounds of research. Reflexive processes are shaped by where we come from and where we're going, the aspects of the world that trouble us and our hopes for the future. Reflexivity is about how we move through the world as people in relationships with others. I would argue that one of the most important skills for people to possess in the current world that we live in is reflexivity. Can we think about our thinking? Can we become more aware of our biases? Can we admit when we're wrong? Can we see how we and others are active role players in meaning-making—for good and for harm? Can we empathise well and think critically about how we are doing so? Can we see ourselves as part of ecologies of meaning, where humans can be decentred and the planet may be nurtured back to health? These are the fundamental questions of our time. As we grow as reflexive music therapy researchers, we are also growing as human beings who can contribute to a better world.

References

1. Schwantes M, Rivera E. "A team working together to make a big, nice, sound": an action research pilot study in an inclusive college setting. Arts Psychother. 2017;55:1–10.
2. Metell M, Stige B. Blind spots in music therapy. Toward a critical notion of participation in context of children with visual impairment. Nord. J Music Ther. 2016;25(4):300–18.
3. Roginsky E, Elefant C. Silent sounding: communicability, musicality, and the use of music with nonspeaking individuals with cerebral palsies and multiple disabilities. Nord J Music Ther. 2021;30(1):61–78.
4. Fairchild R, Thompson G, McFerran KS. Exploring the meaning of a performance in music therapy for children and their families experiencing homelessness and family violence. Music Ther Perspect. 2017;35(1):36–49.
5. McCaffrey T. Evaluating music therapy in adult mental health services: tuning into service user perspectives. Nord J Music Ther. 2018;27(1):28–43.
6. Rickson DJ. The relevance of disability perspectives in music therapy practice with children and young people who have intellectual disability. Voices: World Forum Music Ther. 2014;14(3).
7. Trondalen G. Resource-oriented Bonny Method of Guided Imagery and Music (R-oGIM) as a creative health resource for musicians. Nord J Music Ther. 2016;25(1):5–31.
8. Aitchison KA, McFerran KS. Six adolescents' lived experiences of resource-oriented music therapy assessment in a community-based mental health day program. Arts Psychother. 2023;82:101991.
9. Thomas N, Blanc V. Break it then build again: an arts based duoethnographic pilot reconstructing music therapy and dance/movement therapy histories. Arts Psychother. 2021;73:101765.
10. Campbell KS. A qualitative exploration of music therapist beliefs, education, and uses of hip hop in clinical practice. Music Ther Perspect. 2023;41(1).
11. Oosthuizen H. Unleashing the potential of chaos: how music therapists and young people can engage chaos as a resource in short-term music therapy groups. Nord J Music Ther. 2023;1–18.
12. Ørjasæter KB, Ness O. Acting Out: enabling meaningful participation among people with long-term mental health problems in a music and theater workshop. Qual Health Res. 2017;27(11):1600–13.
13. Krøier JK, Stige B, Ridder HM. Non-Verbal Interactions Between Music Therapists and Persons with Dementia. A Qualitative Phenomenological and Arts-Based Inquiry. Music Ther Perspect. 2021;39(2):162–71.
14. Arnason C. Music therapists' listening perspectives in improvisational music therapy: a qualitative interview study. Nord J Music Ther. 2003;12(2):124–38.

15. Lindo D. Examining the accessibility of MA Music Therapy training in the United Kingdom for ethnic minority communities. Br J Music Ther. 2023;37(1):5–16.
16. Solli HP, Rolvsjord R. "The Opposite of Treatment": a qualitative study of how patients diagnosed with psychosis experience music therapy. Nord J Music Ther. 2015;24(1):67–92.
17. Fairchild R, McFerran KS. "Music is everything": using collaborative group songwriting as an arts-based method with children experiencing homelessness and family violence. Nord J Music Ther. 2019;28(2):88–107.
18. Solli HP. Battling illness with wellness: a qualitative case study of a young rapper's experiences with music therapy. Nord J Music Ther. 2015;24(3):204–31.
19. Skånland MS. Music therapy and social recovery in flexible assertive community treatment. Nord J Music Ther. 2023;32(4):290–306.
20. Tuastad L, Stige B. The revenge of Me and THE BAND'its: a narrative inquiry of identity constructions in a rock band of ex-inmates. Nord J Music Ther. 2015;24(3):252–75.
21. Helle-Valle A, Binder PE, Anderssen N, Stige B. Is restlessness best understood as a process? Reflecting on four boys' restlessness during music therapy in kindergarten. Int J Qual Stud Health Well-being. 2017;12(supl):1298266.
22. Mössler K, Halstead J, Metell M, Gottschewski K, Schmid W. "The room is a mess": exploring the co-creation of space for attunement dynamics between an autistic child and a non-autistic music therapist. Nord J Music Ther. 2023;1–21.
23. McFerran K, Skinner A, Hall T, Thompson G. Structure, agency and community: using online music gatherings to support social inclusion for people with disabilities in Australia during the COVID-19 pandemic. Nord J Music Ther. 2022;31(3):259–72.

Appendix: Biases

CONTEXT	
Our research interests can be shaped by multiple forces	
Academic bias	We may allow our beliefs (e.g., personal/religious/political/cultural etc.) to shape our research interests and our scientific communities
Funding bias	We may tailor our research projects to support the interests of sponsors
Intergroup bias	We may want to produce results through a research study that affirms the power and benefits of music therapy because we are part of this field, and these results also then help us feel good about ourselves as individuals
Social comparison bias	As researchers, we may assess our worth based on how we see ourselves compared to others
Our sense of how we will manage our research project can be influenced by biases	
Hyperbolic discounting (Present bias)	We may choose topics and design studies that will bear smaller, immediate rewards rather than ones that will offer larger rewards at a later date
Planning fallacy	We could underestimate how long it will take to complete a study or a section of the study
Bias could play a role as we develop projects in research teams	
Illusion of transparency	In a research team we may assume that other people have access to our mental state without us needing to "overexplain"

(*continued*)

A. dos Santos, *Reflexive Research in Music Therapy*,
https://doi.org/10.1007/978-3-032-02033-8

(continued)

SELECTING A TOPIC AND DEVELOPING A RESEARCH QUESTION	
We may be more likely to select certain topics to explore because we can more easily access those ideas in our mind	
Availability bias	We might rely on information that comes to mind most quickly and easily as we decide on our topic of exploration and the methodology we wish to use
Attentional bias	We could selectively attend to certain information and exclude other information from our attention
Mere exposure effect	We may find ourselves liking or being drawn to a topic or methodology because we are more familiar with it
The Baader-Meinhof phenomenon (the frequency illusion)	After learning about something, we may then tend to notice it everywhere/frequently
Certain topics may feel more comfortable to explore	
Confirmation bias	As we decide what we want to study, we may have a tendency to notice, search for, favour, and remember information that supports our pre-existing beliefs and values
Ostrich effect	We may avoid unpleasant, dangerous, or inconvenient information by closing ourselves off from it
Subjective validation (personal validation effect)	We could consider a piece of information as correct if it is personally meaningful or significant
Status quo bias	As we decide what to study and how to study it, we may prefer to maintain our current beliefs, approaches, and the present state of affairs (rather than offering critique, novel ideas, and "rocking the boat")
Bandwagon effect	We could be jumping on the bandwagon to study a popular topic
Certain topics may feel more exciting to explore	
Appeal to novelty	We may assume that a topic is more worthy of exploration because it is novel
We project our current assumptions onto our studies	
Self-consistency bias (commitment bias)	We may assume that our beliefs remain relatively consistent
Certain topics or groups may appear to us as more worthy of study and/or as having more favourable attributes than others	
Halo effect	An initial positive impressions could then shape our favourable impression of the phenomenon or person in general
Horn effect	A negative first impression can lead us to perceive and treat someone or something less favourably in general
Reactive devaluation	We may disregard or disparage suggestions made by others (e.g., a research supervisor or colleague) especially if that person is viewed as antagonistic or negative

(*continued*)

(continued)

Implicit bias; implicit prejudice	We may hold a negative, unconscious attitude against a certain social group (ageism, sexist, racism, ableism, lookism, sizeism, classism) and this could shape our decisions of what to study and how to study it
We may focus on an angle of investigation because it appears to make most sense to frame it in a certain way	
Framing	We may be relying on a schema of interpretation (e.g., from the media, a politician, an academic discourse) as we decide on a valuable topic to explore
Pro-innovation bias	We could believe optimistically that innovation should be widely adopted (without fully considering drawbacks and limitations)
Out-group homogeneity bias	We might assume that members of an out-group are all similar to each other
We can get stuck in a certain perspective on a topic	
Choice-supportive bias (post-purchase rationalisation)	Once a decision has been made, we may tend to view that decision positively and downplay its potential faults, while amplifying perceived faults of other potential options
Continued influence effect	Misinformation can continue to influence our thinking even after it has been debunked or corrected
We act when we are confident that we can make an impact, when we feel that what we're doing is important, and when we feel safe and supported	
Optimism bias	We may be overestimating the likelihood of positive events occurring and downplaying the likelihood of negative events happening
Risk compensation	We might be adjusting our behaviour in relation to perceived levels of risk
READING THE LITERATURE	
When looking for literature, some studies, authors, or perspectives may come to mind more easily	
Availability bias	We may rely on literature and authors that come to mind most quickly and easily
Anchoring	We may rely on the first piece of information we encounter to ground our subsequent interpretations
Confirmation bias	We can have a tendency to notice, search for, favour, remember, and draw on studies that support our pre-existing beliefs and values
The Baader-Meinhof phenomenon (the frequency illusion)	After learning about something, we then tend to notice it everywhere/frequently
We can access certain information more easily	
Full text on net bias	Scholars may cite open access articles more frequently than ones behind a paywall
We use particular lenses to interpret and work with what we read	

(continued)

(continued)

Framing	We may be relying on a schema of interpretation (e.g., from the media, a politician, an academic discourse) when looking for and reading literature
Status quo bias	As we draw on certain literature, theories and bodies of thought, we may prefer to maintain our current beliefs, approaches and the present state of affairs (rather than offering critique, novel ideas, and "rocking the boat")
Implicit bias; implicit prejudice	We may hold a negative, unconscious attitude against a certain social group (ageism, sexist, racism, ableism, lookism, sizeism, classism) and this could shape what we read and how we interpret and use the text
Belief bias	We could judge the strength of an argument based on how plausible the conclusion seems, rather than how strongly it is justified
DESIGNING THE STUDY AND SELECTING A METHODOLOGY	
Our existing beliefs can guide how we design a study in light of what we hope to find	
Status quo bias	As we design a study, we may prefer to maintain our current beliefs, approaches, and the present state of affairs (rather than offering critique, novel ideas, and "rocking the boat")
Implicit bias; implicit prejudice	We may hold a negative, unconscious attitude against a certain social group (ageism, sexist, racism, ableism, lookism, sizeism, classism) and this can shape how we design our study
Our biases can guide our practical methodological decisions	
Availability bias	As we select which methodology to use, we may rely on designs and strategies that come to mind most quickly and easily
Illusion of control	We could overestimate our ability to control events in the research
PERCEIVING, DESCRIBING, SELECTING, RECRUITING, AND RELATING TO PARTICIPANTS	
Bias can inform who we select to participate	
Selection bias	Due to non-random sampling, some members of the population may be more likely to be selected for the sample than others
Attentional bias	We may be selectively attending to certain information about participants and excluding other information from our attention
Mere exposure effect	We may like or feel drawn to someone because we are more familiar with them and this could influence who we invite to participate
Our biases can shape how we perceive participants and the groups we see them as belonging to	
Implicit bias; implicit prejudice	We may hold a negative, unconscious attitude against a certain social group (ageism, sexist, racism, ableism, lookism, sizeism, classism) and this can inform how we select and engage with participants

(*continued*)

(continued)

Out-group homogeneity bias	We could assume that members of an out-group are all similar to each other
Framing	We may rely on a schema of interpretation (e.g., from the media, a politician, an academic discourse) as we invite, perceive, and relate to participants
Confirmation bias	As we invite and work with participants, we may have a tendency to notice, search for, favour, and remember information that supports our pre-existing beliefs and values
Mere exposure effect	We may like or feel drawn to someone because we are more familiar with them and this could influence how we engage with participants in the study
Halo effect	An initial positive impression could then shape our favourable impression of the phenomenon or person in general
Horn effect	A negative first impression can lead us to perceive and treat someone or something less favourably in general
GATHERING DATA	
We may gather data to affirm our pre-existing assumptions	
Confirmation bias	As we gather data, we may have a tendency to notice, search for, favour, and remember information that supports one's pre-existing beliefs and values Observer bias: We may see what we want or expect to see
Status quo bias	As we gather data, we may prefer to maintain our current beliefs, approaches, and the current state of affairs (rather than offering critique, novel ideas, and "rocking the boat")
Interviewer bias	The interviewer's opinions and expectations lead/shape the interviewee's responses
Implicit bias; implicit prejudice	We may hold a negative, unconscious attitude against a certain social group (ageism, sexist, racism, ableism, lookism, sizeism, classism) and this can inform what data we gather and how we gather data
We can think we know what other people are thinking	
Observer's illusion of transparency	We may have a tendency to overestimate how well we understand others' mental states
Illusion of asymmetric insight	As a researcher we may assume that our knowledge of and insight into another person (e.g., the participant) is greater than that person's knowledge of and insight into themselves
Some data may seem more interesting to collect	
Appeal to novelty	We may assume that particular data is more important to gather because it is novel
Bias can influence our practical data collection choices	
Time-saving bias	We might assume that increasing the speed with which we do a task will decrease the time required for the project

(*continued*)

(continued)

Information bias	We may believe that more (and more) information should be acquired to reach a conclusion, even if that extra information will actually be irrelevant or unnecessary
ANALYSING DATA	
We may reach conclusions because of cognitive shortcuts	
Anchoring	We may rely on the first piece of information we encounter to ground our subsequent interpretations
Halo effect	An initial positive impression could then shape our favourable impression of the phenomenon or person in general and this could inform our analysis
Horn effect	A negative first impression can lead us to perceive and treat someone or something less favourably in general and this could inform our analysis
We may be more likely to notice and highlight certain themes because we can more easily access those ideas in our mind	
Availability bias	We might relying on insights and interpretations that come to mind most quickly and easily when analysing data
Attentional bias	We may selectively attend to certain information and exclude other information from our attention when analysing the data
Mere exposure effect	We may like or feel drawn to something because we are more familiar with it and this could shape our analysis and interpretation
The Baader-Meinhof phenomenon (the frequency illusion)	After noticing something in the data, we may then tend to notice it everywhere
Our pre-existing convictions shape our interpretations	
Confirmation bias	As we analyse our data, we may have a tendency to notice, search for, favour, and remember information that supports our pre-existing beliefs and values
Framing	We may rely on a schema of interpretation (e.g., from the media, a politician, an academic discourse) as we interpret the data
Status quo bias	As we analyse the data and draw conclusions, we may prefer to maintain our current beliefs, approaches, and the current state of affairs (rather than offering critique, novel ideas, and "rocking the boat")
Naïve realism	As we interpret the data and reach conclusions, we may have a tendency to believe that our perception of the phenomenon we're studying reflects it exactly as it is
We can interpret the actions of others differently from how we interpret our own	
Attribution bias	We might interpret others' actions as being a result of internal factors (whilst we tend to interpret our own actions as being a result of external factors)
Bias blind spot	We may find it easier to spot other people's biases and their impact than our own

(*continued*)

(continued)

We find stories and patterns where there may be none	
Apophenia	We could be perceiving meaningful patterns within random data
Illusory correlation	We could be perceiving a relationship between variables when no relationship exists
Clustering illusion	We could be underpredicting the variability that is likely to appear in a small sample of random or pseudorandom data
Anecdotal fallacy	We may be drawing on limited personal experience to reach a sweeping conclusion
We make meaning in context	
Context effect	We make sense of a stimulus or piece of information in relation to the context around it (even if this is not necessarily relevant and without having the necessary awareness that we are doing this)
We fill in characteristics from stereotypes, prior histories, and generalities (general theories)	
Stereotyping	We may hold a generalised belief about a particular group of people and this could be informing our interpretations and conclusions
Essentialism bias	We may be conceptualising a social group as essentially and naturally, distinct, leading us to overestimate the extent to which a person becomes defined by the group that they belong or are seen as belonging to
Functional fixedness	We might tend to use an object (or a research strategy) only in the way it is traditionally used, which limits our creativity and problem-solving
Authority bias	We may hold overly high confidence in the correctness of information verified by a person who holds formal authority. We may be more influenced by the opinions of people we see as being in authority
Bandwagon effect	We may be jumping on the bandwagon to interpret data in a manner that is aligned with current, popular opinion
We project onto the past	
Hindsight bias	We may perceive past events and outcomes as being more predictable than they actually were, which can also make us overconfident about predicting outcomes of future events
We favour simplicity over complexity and ambiguity	
Occam's razor	We could prefer the simpler option when we are presented with two competing explanations
Conjunction fallacy	We might mistakenly believe that two (or more) events happening together is more likely than one of those events happening in isolation
We might not make the most of supervision or peer-consultation meetings	
Bike-shedding effect	We can have a tendency to spend more time discussing trivial matters rather than focusing on the important issues
Ambiguity bias	We tend to avoid options we consider to be ambiguous
We discard specifics to form generalities; we reduce events and lists to their key elements	

(*continued*)

(continued)

Negativity bias	We tend to highlight aspects that are more negative or unpleasant and these can have a greater effect on us
Implicit bias; implicit prejudice	We may hold a negative, unconscious attitude against a certain social group (ageism, sexist, racism, ableism, lookism, sizeism, classism) and this may inform how we interpret data
Serial position effect	We may have a tendency to remember information at the start or end of a series, rather than information in the middle
Recency effect	We tend to recall more recent information more accurately
Primacy effect	We tend to better remember the first piece of information we encounter rather than information we received later on
Sharpening and leveling	*Sharpening* refers to how we remember small, vivid details when retelling experienced stories *Leveling* refers to how we exclude or alter aspects of stories in their retelling
Peak-end rule	When reflecting back on an experience, our recollections are strongly shaped by what happened during the event's peak intensity as well as at the end
Bias can shape how we manage our time during analysis	
Time-saving bias	We may assume that increasing the speed with which a task is done will decrease the time required for the project
PRESENTING FINDINGS	
Self-serving bias	Our actions (e.g., highlighting what "worked" and minimising what did not) can be prompted by our need to maintain self-esteem
Reporting bias	The results of a research study can be skewed due to the way we reported them
Post-purchase rationalisation	We may feel we need to justify the value of our results because we "bought into" this project and expended lots of energy on it
Overconfidence effect	Our confidence in our judgement (e.g., that our findings are correct) can be greater than the objective accuracy of our judgement
RESPONDING TO REVIEWERS' FEEDBACK	
We may wish to push back against critical feedback we don't like	
Social comparison bias	We may assess our worth based on how we see themselves compared to others
Ostrich effect	We may avoid unpleasant, dangerous, or inconvenient information by closing ourselves off from it
Subjective validation (personal validation effect)	We could consider a piece of information as correct if it is personally meaningful or significant
Halo effect	Initial positive impressions then shape our favourable impression of the phenomenon or person in general
Horn effect	A negative first impression can lead us to perceive and treat someone or something less favourable in general

(*continued*)

(continued)

Reactive devaluation	We may disregard or disparage suggestions made by others (e.g., a research supervisor or colleague) especially if that person is viewed as antagonistic or negative
Choice-supportive bias (post-purchase rationalisation)	Once a decision has been made, we tend to view that decision positively and downplay its potential faults, while amplifying perceived faults of other potential options
Post-purchase rationalisation	We may feel we need to justify the value of our results because we "bought into" this project and expended lots of energy on it
Overconfidence effect	As a researcher receiving feedback, our confidence in our judgement can be greater than the objective accuracy of our judgement
We may struggle to engage with feedback that does not seem immediately self-evident	
Ambiguity bias	We tend to avoid options we consider to be ambiguous
GUIDING, SUPERVISING, AND REVIEWING OTHER RESEARCHERS' STUDIES	
We may push a certain research agenda for our own interests	
Academic bias	When scholars allow their beliefs (e.g., personal/religious/political/cultural etc.) to shape their research their scientific communities
Mere exposure effect	Liking or being drawn to something because one is more familiar with it
Confirmation bias	As we assess others' studies, we may have a tendency to notice, search for, favour, and remember information that supports our pre-existing beliefs and values
Subjective validation (personal validation effect)	Considering a piece of information as correct if it is personally meaningful or significant to oneself
Status quo bias	As we assess or guide another study, we may prefer to maintain our current beliefs, approaches, and the current state of affairs (rather than offering critique, novel ideas, and "rocking the boat")
Overconfidence effect	As a reviewer/supervisor giving feedback, our confidence in our judgement can be greater than the objective accuracy of our judgement
We may push certain perspectives because it's easier	
Availability bias	We may rely on perspectives, theories, and other findings that come to mind most quickly and easily as we assess this study
Attentional bias	We may selectively attend to certain information and exclude other information from our attention when assessing a study
The Baader-Meinhof phenomenon (the frequency illusion)	After learning about something, we then tend to notice it everywhere/frequently
Ostrich effect	We may avoid unpleasant, dangerous, or inconvenient information by closing ourselves off from it

(*continued*)

(continued)

Anecdotal fallacy	We may use limited personal experience to make a sweeping conclusion
Ambiguity bias	We tend to avoid options we consider to be ambiguous
We may push certain perspectives because it's more interesting	
Appeal to novelty	One may assume that a topic is more worthy of exploration because it is novel
We may rigidly prefer certain interpretive frames and strategies	
Framing	We may rely on a schema of interpretation (e.g., from the media, a politician, an academic discourse) when reviewing another researcher's study
Halo effect	Initial positive impressions then shape our favourable impression of the study in general
Horn effect	A negative first impression can lead us to perceive and treat a study as less favourable in general
Implicit bias; implicit prejudice	We may hold a negative, unconscious attitude against a certain social group (ageism, sexist, racism, ableism, lookism, sizeism, classism) and this may inform how we assess a study and what we notice and do not notice
Naïve realism	We have a tendency to believe that our perception of the world reflects it exactly as it is
Functional fixedness	We tend to think that a methodology should be used in the way it is traditionally used, which can limit creativity and problem-solving
Bandwagon effect	We may be jumping on the bandwagon to assess a study in a manner that is aligned with current, popular opinion

Index

A. dos Santos, *Reflexive Research in Music Therapy*,
https://doi.org/10.1007/978-3-032-02033-8

FSC
www.fsc.org
MIX
Papier | Fördert
gute Waldnutzung
FSC® C083411

Kolibri 360 GmbH
Ferdinand-Jühlke-Straße 7
99095 Erfurt, Deutschland
produktsicherheit@kolibri360.de